Los Dos Mundos

Rural Mexican Americans, Another America

Photo by Richard Baker

Ninety-three-year-old Jesuscita Salazar enjoying a Cinco de Mayo celebration.

Los Dos Mundos

Rural Mexican Americans, Another America

Richard Baker

UTAH STATE UNIVERSITY PRESS
Logan, Utah
1995

To Estella Zamora, a quintessential grass roots leader who works tirelessly on behalf of the Mexican American community. Her commitment and dedication redefined the concept of citizenship for me.

Utah State University Press
Logan, Utah 84322-7800

10 9 8 7 6 5 4 3 2   97 98 99 00

Library of Congress Cataloging-in-Publication Data

Baker, Richard, 1941 Nov. 27–
    Los dos mundos : rural Mexican Americans, another America / by Richard Baker.
    p.   cm.
    Includes bibliographical references and index.
    ISBN 0-87421-184-0
    1. Mexican Americans–Idaho–Social conditions. 2. Idaho–Social conditions. I. Title.
F755.M5B34   1994
305.868720796–dc20   94-28073
                                               CIP

CONTENTS

Photo courtesy Boise State University News Service

A folk dance as performed by Maria Elena Pantoja.

PREFACE

In *Small Town in Mass Society* (1968), Vidich and Bensman advanced the thesis that industrialism had progressed to the point where beliefs and ways of life in the United States are becoming homogeneous regardless of region or size of community. Therefore, since racial attitudes may be quite similar in Middlewest, Boise, and elsewhere in America, it is my view that this community study may be able to inform the reader about the state of race relations in America. The small-town setting of this study allows the reader to listen, as it were, to how Anglos talk about a racial minority. Most Americans publicly censor and monitor their thoughts on racial minorities, but Anglos in Middlewest expressed openly what many Anglo Americans think. Anglo administrators did not conceal their thoughts or hide behind the cloak of "client confidentiality," but instead they candidly shared their views and allowed me to examine and observe how the local social institutions functioned. This study, then, allows for a comprehensive examination of how institutionalized racism operates in American society.

The essence of my discipline was revealed as I observed Anglos invariably explain that they were not prejudiced; to them it was just a plain and simple fact that Mexican Americans were consistently abusing the welfare system and represented the criminal element in their community. Through their social interaction with one another and through the functioning of their social institutions, the Anglos had created and were sustaining a social system that implied that Mexican Americans are inferior to Anglos. This belief system had become a self-fulfilling prophecy that relegated and maintained Mexican Americans in a subordinate position in the community.

The Anglos of the study, for the most part, did not believe that their community had a race problem. They blamed the Mexican

Americans as being the source of the community's problems and they had an amazing facility for denying the social injustices inflicted upon Mexican Americans in their community. Reading this book will enable the reader to better understand why the race problem in America does not disappear.

In becoming acquainted with the town I have called "Middlewest," the reader will learn about a sociological method that adheres to J. Lopreato's (Gans 1982) perspective on our discipline. He states: "Sociology is a moral discipline. Its fundamental assumption is that society and culture constitute an apparatus devised by man, partly conscious and partly unconscious, to cope with the physical and human habitats. This means that at the highest levels of theorizing the discipline cannot avoid passing judgements—science if you will—but inevitably moral in their significance—about the functioning of social institutions and social arrangements.... [and how] well they serve man and his groups."

This book could not have been published without the support of many people. My participation in a National Endowment for the Humanities program, "Writing Across the Curriculum," instructed by Richard Leahy and Roy Fox of the Department of English at Boise State University, was of great benefit in teaching me as well as my students how to improve our writing.

Writing articles of publishable quality is a difficult skill to master. My colleague Michael Blain shared with me the searing letters of rejection he received from editors of sociological journals who ruthlessly critiqued the articles he had submitted for publication. His strong desire to publish and his perseverance and eventual success encouraged me to return to conducting field research and to writing professional articles after a long hiatus following the devastating criticisms made by journal editors regarding articles I had submitted.

Several administrators at Boise State University assisted and supported the writing of this book. Martin Scheffer, friend and chair of the Department of Sociology at Boise State University, provided both encouragement and support for conducting the field research. The Boise State University Office of Research and its assistant director, Larry Irvin, also provided resources for the writing of this book. Boise State University awarded me a sabbatical to conduct the field research. My thanks are extended to Boise State University and to all my colleagues and staff who supported my efforts.

I owe a great debt of gratitude to many Mexican Americans in Idaho who assisted with my field research and who served as key informants. Mexican American leaders interceded on my behalf, enabling me to attend meetings and cultural events from which I might otherwise have been barred. I will always appreciate the assistance of Rudy Peña, Maria Salazar, Humberto Fuentes, Maria Nava, Héctor DeLeón, Emma Pantoja, Baldimar Elizondo, Gracie Rivera, Sam Byrd, Chris Rivera, Rudy Rodriguez, Danny Ozuna, Francie Peña Katsilometes, Don Peña, Jesús DeLeón, Ernesto Sánchez, Ricco Barrera, Marta Torres, Father Commacho, and Father Covarrubias.

Special thanks are extended to Jean Terra, who handled with great skill the difficult task of editing the book. Jim Aho, a professor of Sociology at Idaho State University, provided me with an invaluable sociological critique that assisted in clarifying the theoretical analysis of this book. I also cannot fail to thank my two student research assistants, Christine Muller and Kathleen Baggs, for the many hours they devoted to the project.

Listed last, but without whose support this book could not have been written, are Alecia and Nicolas, who throughout the research and writing were always there supporting, encouraging, and listening to me. They did my household chores, sacrificed vacations, and graciously changed their lives to fit my schedule.

Not all Mexican American males act out the machismo stereotype.

Juan Grazia recalls his father who fought in the Mexican Revolution.

Chapter 1

OVERVIEW OF FIELD RESEARCH AND THEORETICAL MODELS

One night my eye was caught by a familiar-looking word on the spine of a book. The title was 450 Years of Chicano History in Pictures. *On the cover were black-and-Anglo photos: Padre Hidalgo exhorting Mexican peasants to revolt against the Spanish dictators; Anglo vigilantes hanging two Mexicans from a tree; a young Mexican woman with rifle and ammunition belts criss-crossing her breast; Cesar Chavez and field workers marching for fair wages; Chicano railroad workers laying creosote ties; Chicanas laboring at machines in textile factories; Chicanas picketing and hoisting boycott signs.... I showed the book to friends. All of us were amazed; this book told us we were alive. We, too, had defended ourselves with our fists against hostile Anglos, gasping for breath in fights with the policemen who outnumbered us. The book reflected back to us our struggle in a way that made us proud.*

–Jimmy Santiago Baca

Introduction

I undertook this research project because Mexican Americans are the largest minority in the state of Idaho, yet no major studies of Mexican Americans in Idaho exist. Also, a number of racial conflicts developed in 1989 and 1991, heightening the need for such a study.

The Boise newspaper, *The Idaho Statesman*, and the Idaho Commission on Mexican American Affairs reported on racial incidents which occurred in several Idaho communities. The most publicized conflict occurred when the U.S. Attorney for Idaho reported the involvement of a "Mexican American Mafia" in drug trafficking in Idaho. Idaho Mexican American leaders sharply rebuked this view and, while not denying some Mexican American culpability, contended that Mexican Americans should not be singled-out as the primary culprits. The Idaho media reported in 1990 that Marsing, Idaho, a community of fewer than 2,000 people, had several incidents where Anglo parents attending local football games used racial epithets against the Mexican American players on the team.

The community of Idaho Falls in eastern Idaho faced a situation where a group of Mexican American youths, calling themselves "Mexican Americans with an Attitude," and Anglo youths, calling themselves "The Posse," had a series of encounters. The school administration expelled the Mexican American youths, and the police depicted them as "a gang." However, the school did not expel the Anglo youths, and the police viewed them as "a social club."

In 1991 the Glenns Ferry school received a five-year federal grant to develop a bilingual education program in its elementary school. The kindergarten class participated in an immersion bilingual class. Half the day the class spoke Spanish and half the day English. The bilingual program became controversial and this caused the school board to cancel the program.

In the spring of 1991 a racial incident occurred in Dubois, Idaho, where a monolingual Mexican American worker was arrested for allegedly stealing a roll of toilet paper from his place of employment. The authorities incarcerated the man for several days. The man not only was fired from his job but also was not able to seek other work while languishing in jail.

The Mexican American leaders of Idaho view each of these incidents as having racist implications. The Anglo authorities involved in these episodes deny that the conflicts indicate racial bias. One cannot properly evaluate these opposing views without the aid of thorough field research. Are these racial conflicts incidental or are they symptoms of an underlying racism?

I chose the name "Middlewest" for the community in which I conducted the study. Robert and Helen Lynd conducted the first and now classic community studies, *Middletown: A Study in Contemporary American Culture* (1929) and *Middletown in*

Transition: A Study in Cultural Conflicts (1937). They named their community "Middletown" because they thought the community to be representative of life in America. I believe this study will provide insights into race relations in American society. Chapter Eight of the book examines institutionalized racism through the use of interviews and observations of the community's social institutions. I believe the insights concerning race relations in rural Middlewest will be helpful in assisting the reader to understand race relations in the urban areas of the United States.

Research Expansion

The original research plan focused on interviewing Mexican Americans in Middlewest. However, after interviewing twenty-five Mexican American families in the community, I learned that most of them had arrived in Middlewest via the migrant trial. Consequently, I expanded the study to include Mexican American migrant workers. I also decided to interview Anglo farmers to try to understand their views of their work force. This in turn led me to interview Anglos in Middlewest to gain an appreciation of how they viewed the Mexican Americans. The result is that unintentionally I ended with a rural community/area study; however, the focus still remained the analysis of race relations in this rural community.

The study is strengthened by its examination of the entire community and its social institutions along with its assessment of community values and daily life. The reader can gain an appreciation of the fact that a community has many dimensions; few individuals devote much of their energy or thought to race relations in their community. People of all races are earning a living, caring for their families, and enjoying their leisure time. The average person in Middlewest likes his/her community and sees his/her efforts and those of others as improving the quality of life in the community. There is some concern, as is the case in many rural communities, regarding the economic viability of their community. (Community life will be reviewed in Chapters Two and Three.)

Population Data

The 1990 U. S. Census data, made available in 1992 through the Idaho Department of Commerce, reports that there were 52,927 Mexican Americans in Idaho in 1990. The Mexican American population accounts for 5.26 percent of Idaho's official population. However, Mexican American leaders believe the Mexican American population to be significantly higher, since the census undercounts lower-class minority groups.

Middlewest has the highest proportion of Mexican Americans of any town in Idaho with a population of 5,000 or more. Middlewest is the seat of a county I have named "Farm County." Farm County has the most Mexican Americans, both permanent resident and migrant, of any county in Idaho. Additionally, Farm County has the highest total output of agricultural products of any county in the state.

The population of Middlewest is approximately 18,000 according to the Idaho Department of Commerce (1992). The 1990 census reported that almost 4,000 Mexican Americans reside in this community. This means that approximately 20 percent of the permanent population is Mexican American.

Qualitative social research allows for the modification of the research design while conducting the field research. To interview Mexican American leaders and Mexican American farm workers I traveled to the labor camps and small towns of Farm County. This county had a population of 92,661 as reported by the Idaho Department of Commerce (1992). Approximately 13 percent of the county's population is Mexican American. The Migrant Health Program of the U.S. Department of Health and Human Services reports that in 1990 some 7,691 migrant farm workers came to Farm County (Idaho Department of Employment 1991b). This means that during the farm season approximately 17 percent of the population of the county is Mexican American, not counting the undocumented workers in the county. Some Mexican nationals who have green cards that allow them to legally work the farm season in the U.S. work in Farm County.

The Idaho Migrant Council (1990) estimates that 99 percent of the field workers in Farm County are Mexican American. While conducting the field research for this study, I never saw an Anglo field worker.

Farm County ranks as the thirty-fifth largest agricultural producer in the United States. Farming developed in Farm County because of the availability of irrigation water and a satisfactory growing season. Farmers there produce over 90 percent of the seed corn for the United States. The largest crop is sugar beets, but Farm County also produces onions, mints, hops, potatoes, apples, and additional seed crops.

Farm County consistently has one of the highest unemployment rates in the state. During the period of the field research, the county's rate of unemployment for Mexican Americans was more than twice as high as that for Anglos. The Idaho Department of Commerce (1992) reports that 12 percent of the non-Mexican American population of Farm County lives below the poverty level. The poverty rate for Farm County Mexican Americans is 33 percent. Furthermore, most Farm County Mexican Americans work in low-income positions: agricultural worker, laborer, production worker, and service worker. The per capita income of Farm County is among the lowest in the state. Twenty-five percent of the county is economically disadvantaged, one of the highest ratios in the state. The report *Hispanics in Idaho* (Mabbutt 1990) is relevant here because Richard Mabbutt, the author of the report, found that the statistics vary from one source to another. However, regardless of which set of statistics one uses, the data reveals that high numbers of Mexican Americans live in poverty and earn low incomes.

Qualitative Methodology

This study required fourteen months of field research, from August 1990 to October 1991. Even after this period, I attended meetings, conducted interviews, and maintained contact with key informants.

The primary research methodology was the conducting of in-depth interviews. I conducted 335 interviews; two research assistants completed forty additional interviews. I attended seventy-five meetings of local civic groups. I observed thirty community social events, including the Christmas parade. As I came to know Middlewest, I was able to map the social institutions and significant social groups in the community. I then arranged interviews with Mexican Americans and Anglos from a cross-section of the community. The methodology consists of a processual activity: as I learned more about the community, I also learned who were the most important groups and individuals in Middlewest, according to the community. In a short time, I obtained a thorough sense of race relations within the research area.

When conducting interviews, I taped the dialogue and took extensive notes. The tapes were valuable for two reasons: they allowed me to find exact quotes of pertinent comments by the subjects, and, when necessary, they provided a check to clarify my notes.

After completing three interviews, I would review my notes and record the interesting aspects of the interviews in a notebook. In this notebook I created a set of working hypotheses. I kept another journal of notes on community observations, which included notes from meetings that I attended. I also discussed my sociological interpretations with the key informants in order to obtain their reaction to my assessments of their community.

I may perhaps claim to know Middlewest better than any of its residents, because in many ways the Mexican Americans and Anglos, though living in the same town, have separate communities. I came to know both communities.

I did not realize, until writing the book, how many sources of data regarding the community I possessed. I developed a significant set of key informants who were in strategic places to observe their community. They shared with me their views of Middlewest. To enhance my knowledge of Middlewest, I subscribed to the local daily paper. I found the coverage to be significant and this led to a six-months content analysis of the paper, which I have named the *Daily News*.

Since much theory in minority studies focuses on the role of the economic structure in race relations, I arranged tours with most of the businesses having twenty-five or more employees. Most of the owners or managers of these businesses became interview subjects and I received considerable cooperation from them. They frequently arranged, on company time, for me to interview some of their employees. Government agencies allowed access to their records and employees. Most of the businesses and government entities provided me with relevant documents and reports generated by their organizations.

Studying a small rural town has some advantages. I found my subjects, both Anglo and Mexican American, to be open and accessible. Almost everyone I approached agreed to be interviewed. This receptivity allowed for as many as fifteen interviews in a week. The interviews varied in length from thirty minutes to four hours. The average interview lasted two hours.

Human social attitudes and presentations of self are based on a complex web of thoughts. Anglo subjects in Middlewest wanted to influence me regarding what to think both about their community and about themselves. At the same time, small-town life makes them less sophisticated in this process. The Anglo subjects did not seem to realize or recognize that their comments concerning Mexican Americans revealed prejudicial attitudes. Anglo subjects generally avoid talking about or recognizing the existence of Mexican Americans, but their discourse has racist content when they do. Overall, I felt like the cultural anthropologist who has the good fortune to be the first to study a culture.

Emile Durkheim, a French sociologist, in his classic work, *The Elementary Forms of the Religious Life* (1965), states that sociology should study the simpler forms of social life to gain an understanding of more complex societies. This research project unintentionally benefitted from studying race relations in a simpler social environment. Studying race relations in a small community allows for an examination of all of the complex dimensions of the problem. Though this study examines rural race relations, the examination of social institutions and the institutionalized racism manifested therein should enhance readers' ability to understand racism in urban America.

The reader may find it surprising that the Anglo subjects expressed on tape such harsh views toward the Mexican Americans in the community. The subjects may have been disarmed by the fact that the researcher informed them that he was conducting a community study. The topic of Mexican Americans in the community did not arise during the first hour of most interviews. If the research project had been limited to questions of race relations or if the person conducting the research had been of a minority ethnic group, the subjects might have been less forthright in their comments regarding the Mexican American population.

Theory

An analysis of social life is meaningless without sociological theory. Theory attempts to accurately explain the data and observations of the research. However, sociological theories tend to overgeneralize and oversimplify the complexity of race relations. A descriptive account of social life is valuable in itself. This report attempts to provide a healthy dose of both descriptive analysis and sociological theory.

An initial question posited in my research attempted to determine the appropriate term for the Hispanic people of Idaho. The subjects responded with a variety of answers. Older people and those recently from Mexico prefer to be called "Mexicanos" or "Mexicans." Those preferring the term "Hispanic" are younger or have resided longer in Middlewest. The third choice of identification was "Mexican American." Many subjects dislike the term "Chicano," which they associate with troublemakers. The majority of the subjects preferred to be called Hispanic. This is perhaps unique to Idaho, because Hispanic originated as a bureaucratic term to refer to all people who live in the U.S. whose native tongue is Spanish. I will use the term Mexican American to refer to this population.

Social life is complex. Sociology looks for social patterns and then attempts to explain what social variables create and sustain those patterns. Social behavior generally has several causal variables that to different degrees account for a particular social phenomenon. The intent of the following section is to simplify and clarify the theories that relate to the sociological analysis of minority groups.

An important first step in understanding race relations in America involves an appreciation of the general character and values of Americans. One recent book to examine the American national character is *Habits of the Heart* (1985). In this important work, Robert Bellah and his associates interviewed 200 Americans in an attempt to determine the key attributes of the American people. The researchers concluded that Americans have lost what they call the "habits of the heart," and the researchers believed this situation has disturbing consequences for our country. Tocqueville in *Democracy in America* found that Americans had three fundamental sets of values: individuality, spirituality, and democracy. However, Bellah (1985) found that today these values have been reduced to one—individuality. He noted, as Tocqueville predicted, a loss of social responsibility. Bellah found that many Americans, with their abandonment of a spiritual explanation for life, have lost their sense of a meaning of life. Additionally, the loss of democratic values means that the idea of a "common good" has become an obsolete factor in American politics.

The importance of Bellah's work is reflected in the Middlewest Anglo community's indifference toward the problems facing the Mexican American community. For example, Anglo school administrators and civic leaders boasted of having the best schools in the state, seeming to ignore the Mexican American dropout problem.

Most sociologists define Mexican Americans as an ethnic group, a group of people with a distinctive way of life that is separate from that of the dominant culture (Schaefer 1991; Marger 1985). Some sociologists (Moore and Pachón 1985; Feagin 1991), however, define Mexican Americans as a race because of their predominantly Indian heritage. Tom Berry's recent book (1992) on modern Mexico indicates that most Mexican Americans come from the predominantly indigenous Indian heritage of Mexico. Regardless of the difference of opinion as to whether Mexican Americans constitute a race or an ethnic group, most sociologists agree that race is less a biological difference than a matter of social definition. Without a doubt, the majority of Anglos in Middlewest and Farm County perceive Mexican Americans as being members of a race.

Omi and Winant (1986) have comprehensively explored the issue of race as it applies to the United States. They contend that race is a central feature in American history. To them, race is the fundamental axis of social organization in America. They agree with Feagin (1989) that few academics consider the concept of race to have a legitimate biological foundation, but they maintain that the social definitions of race continue to play a major role in social relationships in this country.

These authors do not believe that race can be reduced to an element of ethnicity. They reject the whole ethnicity approach to racial minorities because they consider the underlying premise of the ethnicity school to be invalid when it is applied to racial groups. The ethnicity school contends that economic success and acceptance depends on a group's willingness and ability to accept the norms and values of the majority. Omi and Winant assert that the evidence is overwhelming that racial groups remain outside the mainstream regardless of their acceptance of the values of the dominant society. They view the notion of race as operating through a set of "interpretative codes" which operate in daily life. They believe that notions of race pervade the social life of American society, including people's identities, social institutions, and daily social practices.

The concept of race then can be viewed as an ideological vehicle to define racial minorities as subordinate. The Anglos in this study held a host of negative perceptions about Mexican Americans; these will be reviewed in Chapter Two. Many of the Mexican American subjects in this study claimed that darker-skinned Mexican Americans faced more discrimination than those with lighter skins. The idea that race is a significant factor in understanding the circumstances of Mexican Americans is a perspective included in the exploitive model that will be reviewed later in this chapter.

Much has been written in sociology concerning which theoretical approach would best capture the immigrant, ethnic, and racial experiences of America's numerous minorities. Each theory has abundant research supporting its perspective. My field research leads me to support an eclectic approach that draws from many aspects of various exploitive models to explain the circumstances of rural Mexican Americans in Idaho. Therefore it is necessary to briefly review the theories and research pertaining to Mexican Americans.

The theoretical frameworks concerning Mexican Americans can be depicted as occurring on a continuum. They are: exploitive theory—pluralistic theory—assimilation theory. The last, assimilation theory, views the ethnic experience as one of gradual integration and adaptation into American society. These theorists hold that it generally requires three generations for racial and ethnic groups to integrate into the host society. Simultaneously, as the minority becomes more incorporated, the dominant society gradually reduces the level of discrimination. However, these circumstances do not result in the total loss of ethnicity. The fusion of groups occurs in the secondary institutions, so that American ethnic groups have nearly equal participation in the economic and political institutions of society. The critical variables involve the ability and opportunities that immigrants and ethnic minorities have to acquire the skills to compete economically in American society.

The current researchers following the assimilationist perspective (Stolzenberg 1990; Borjas and Tienda 1985; Portes and Truelove 1987; DeFreitas 1991; Reimers 1985) recognize that poverty rates and unemployment rates are far higher for Mexican Americans than they are for Anglos. Sociologists agree that the median income of Mexican American families is approximately 70 percent of that of Anglo families. How to explain this inequality is the critical question. The latest assimilationist theorists analyze census data using the concept of "human capital." When these researchers compare African Americans and Mexican Americans with Anglos, they find that the low status and low paying jobs of minorities are consequences of their own deficiencies in education, recency of migration, lack of language proficiency, and inadequate occupational skills. In other words, Mexican Americans and other minorities face severe economic inequality as a result of having not learned to speak English fluently, having not acquired job skills, and having not obtained an adequate formal education—all of which are seen as individual deficiencies.

On the surface this may seem quite plausible, but such an approach is limited. In the first place, quantitative census data leaves much to be desired. Yes, Stolzenberg and Tienda find correlations between education and income that can explain the difference between the economic positions of Mexican Americans and of Anglo Americans, but they know little about the social relationships between Mexican Americans and Anglos. They also provide no information as to how Mexican Americans fare when they enter the dominant social institutions. As a qualitative sociologist with field research experience, I find this a strange way to analyze race relations. It seems to me that without interviews and observations of both Anglos and Mexican Americans crucial questions would remain unanswered. An examination of the census data alone cannot explain the economic exploitation, discrimination, and institutionalized racism experienced by Mexican Americans.

The methodology employed becomes a key factor in the type of "facts" the researcher discovers. From my own twenty-five years of studying sociology I would conclude that, generally speaking, quantitative sociological research is the methodology of choice for structural-functionalists, assimilationists, and those sociological researchers whose theories and research lack a critique of the economic and political establishment.

What is even more interesting is that this research is often compatible with the views expressed by the Anglo leaders I interviewed. The "human capital" approach implies the need for Mexican Americans to accept conformity with Anglo society in order to become successful. The Anglo subjects of this study insisted that it is necessary for the Mexican Americans in their community to become "Americanized." These Anglos also believe that in America everyone has an equal chance to become economically successful. Thus, both assimilationist theorists and the Anglo subjects of this research agree that inequality in America is the consequence of individual deficiencies. Discrimination and racism are discounted by both groups as salient factors in explaining the poverty of Mexican Americans. This community/area study will provide detailed empirical research to the contrary.

Keefe and Padilla's book, *Chicano Ethnicity* (1987), is the best current work using a pluralistic model. Their research on Chicanos in three California communities reveals many insights into contemporary race relations between Mexican Americans and Anglos. They found that each generation of Mexican Americans lost some of its "cultural awareness," that is, knowledge of its culture. However, they also found that one's generation was not significant when it came to "ethnic loyalty," that is, the survival of Chicano ethnicity. These authors found that because of strong family and kinship relationships in the Chicano community and the fact that most live in separate or semi-separate ethnic enclaves, the Chicanos were able to maintain a strong and viable ethnic community.

Keefe and Padilla reject both the assimilation and exploitive models, stressing the ethnic resilience of their subjects. However, they do stress the modest economic advancement of latter generations of Chicanos and they inexplicably downplay the extensive discrimination reported by their subjects.

Within the general theoretical continuum previously presented there are numerous theoretical variations, themes, and concepts. Some theorists interpret the pluralistic model to be a synthesis or middle position that can best explain the complicated nature of race and ethnic relations in the United States. They believe that ethnic groups and racial groups have an unequal socioeconomic position both because of their limited education, occupational skills, and English language deficiencies (especially for Mexican Americans) and because these groups face some minor discrimination and exploitation (Aponte 1991; Connor 1985; Marden, Meyer, and Engel 1992).

A critical point to be aware of in examining the pluralistic model and its variants is that the Mexican American literature is replete with authors such as Achor (1982), Barrera (1979), Blea (1980), Horowitz (1986), and Moore and Pachón (1985), whose research reveals that Mexican Americans are not disorganized, as Wilson (1987) depicts the black inner city community to be, because Mexican Americans have a strong and viable ethnic community.

I believe the exploitive models best account for the poverty, inequality, and racism that exemplify the social relationships between Mexican Americans and Anglos in the present study. I use the exploitive model as a generic term for the studies of those sociologists who essentially work from a critical perspective. The essence of this model is the idea that the majority of members of racial minorities, including Mexican Americans, live in an exploited condition as a consequence of the structure of the American economy. Many of my colleagues will believe that I include too many distinct perspectives under the exploitive model, but I do this because each critiques the predominant assimilationist perspective and each recognizes the importance of the economic system as the key to understanding racial inequality.

I would like to present a progression from the more moderate to the more radical exploitive approaches, recognizing that this analysis has no time sequence. First, we have the structuralists and those who write about institutionalized racism (Schaefer 1991; Marden, Meyer, and Engel 1992; Moore and Pachón 1985; Portes and Bach 1987; Portes and Rumbaut 1990); they contend in standard sociological analyses that America's racial minorities, including Mexican Americans, face a social environment that severely limits their opportunities. The establishment social institutions inhibit and deny full participation of minority groups in educational and political institutions. The criminal justice system is depicted as discriminating against these groups at each level of the administration of justice.

The ghetto, barrio, or reservation creates poverty conditions that result in a myriad of social problems. Generally, residents of these enclaves are denied full access to health care, city services, and the general mix of social services. To a considerable extent, the structuralists and institutionalized racism writers contend that much of the inequality and hardship faced by racial minorities is due to the way Anglo America has organized its social institutions. This approach is moderate because it downplays the intentions of the actors in those institutions. It also denies that these institutions and their managers operate for personal benefit, maintaining that they are merely carrying out their own cultural imperatives. The advantage of this approach over the assimilationist approach is that it at least challenges the idea that an individual member of a minority group is responsible for his/her own victimization.

The Mexican American ethnographers are the next group of sociological writers I include under the exploitive heading. They include Achor (1982); Blea (1980); Horowitz (1986); and Foley (1990). Achor, Blea, and Horowitz carried out ethnographic field research in, respectively, Texas, Colorado, and Illinois. Each author found those studied to be living in rich and vibrant ethnic communities. These communities were neither disorganized nor plagued with deviance and the subjects were members of hard-working families. Crimes and gangs did exist but not to the extent perceived by the Anglo community. These writers found, as did the structuralists and institutionalized racism sociologists, that their Mexican American subjects faced systematic racism and discrimination. They had little political power and their children had exceedingly high dropout rates from school. A great problem was the relegation of Mexican American workers to the secondary job market. The excessive poverty was the consequence not of Mexican American culture but of unemployment and underemployment.

Horowitz (1986), like some of the structuralists, examines the conflicts between the two cultures. Her perspective somewhat downplays the exploitive nature of the relationship between the Mexican American and Anglo communities she studied because to her mind Mexican Americans have some cultural characteristics that inhibit their economic success.

Foley (1990), however, has a different focus and his work more nearly matches my own. He conducted ethnographic field research in a small Texas town for nearly ten years. He found the Anglo community more intentional in its attempts to maintain political power even though it represented a minority of the population. His primary focus was on the public schools. There he found a system of education that replicated the class structure of the community. The school personnel were involved in shaping social reality and even the self-perceptions of students as well as in providing formal educational instruction. The result was that Mexican American students "learned their place," economically and politically, in the community. Essentially they were instructed to remain in the same social class position as their parents. Foley has no doubts that the failure of Mexican American students is not due to individual deficiencies but rather to an educational system that labels them as failures. Mexican Americans are viewed by the Anglo community and schoolteachers as outsiders who are dumb, lazy, and incapable of learning English. This extremely negative stereotyping of Mexican Americans leads to a type of self-fulfilling prophecy where Mexican American males join gangs to gain self-esteem, which only further alienates them from the school.

Blauner (1972) developed the basic model of colonialism, in which he extrapolated ideas from the experience of European colonialism to examine the circumstances of black Americans. The essence of colonialism is that it provides an economic advantage to the dominant members of the society. Such a system establishes a relationship of domination and subordination. Blauner recognized many similarities between the conditions of blacks in the United States and those of colonized peoples during the period of European imperialism. These similarities include the fact that the entry of blacks into this country was not voluntary, that there was a consistent effort to destroy the African cultures, that blacks exist as a segregated work force, that they face institutional and governmental controls that maintain them in a subordinate position, and that they face systematic racism that justifies to the dominant society the legitimacy of their subordination as a people.

This approach has many critics (Feagin 1991; Moore 1970) who contend that the situations of colonized majorities are very distinct from those of internal minorities in the United States. For example, the geographic areas the latter occupy are not separate, the internal minorities do not have resources to exploit, the arrangements are not formalized, and there are no indigenous elites benefiting from the exploitation. Murguia (1975) has the most insightful critique of the colonial model. He compares the assimilation model to the colonial model and finds five crucial variables that affect the relationship between the host and immigrant groups. These include the mode of entry, the size of the minority, the distribution of the minority, the ethnic or racial characteristics of the minority, and the degree of difference between the majority and minority cultures. Murguia contends that Mexican Americans fall between assimilation and colonialism. But he rejects the colonial model because Mexican Americans do not have separate social institutions and because many have become assimilated. He also believes that the level of economic opportunity for Mexican Americans is such that it would be incorrect to view them as being in a colonial status.

Marxists (Barrera 1979; Bonacich 1989; Reich 1981; Li 1988; Szymanski 1978) also critique the colonial model for not taking more into account social class and class relationships. For these neo-Marxists, understanding the role of economic production is crucial to understanding race relations because of the economic basis of racial exploitation. They maintain that race problems are essentially labor problems, not a result of cultural misunderstanding.

These authors recognize the importance of racism as a deliberate ideology designed to justify the treatment and exploitation of ethnic and racial minorities. Still, the critical element is the need for cheap labor in a capitalist economy. Therefore, any means that can be used to legitimate paying people less and to enable capitalists to increase profits is standard procedure. This practice is maintained for the economic benefit it provides the dominant group, although there is some disagreement about whether the economic inequality benefits all Anglos or just the elite. The capitalist class is able to control the working class by dividing the working class along ethnic, race, and gender categories. The keys to power for the capitalist class are its ownership of the means of production and its ability to influence the political sector of society. All workers are exploited; it is just that minorities are exploited to a greater degree and in greater numbers.

Barrera (1979) presents an excellent synthesis of the Marxist and the colonial models. He believes that the Marxist position is deficient because it does not take race into account as a separate factor influencing majority-minority relationships. He also recognizes that Mexican Americans achieve solidarity across class lines because they are all victims of racism and because of the strength of their ethnic community. Barerra also contends that the economic role of Mexican Americans relegates them to the worst jobs or to the reserve army of the unemployed. They experience labor repression, severe wage differentials, and intense occupational stratification. To Barerra, the key factors in the exploitation of the Mexican American population are racism and social class position.

Bonacich (1972) provides a variation on the Marxist model by developing the concept of the segmented or split labor market, where racial minorities are relegated to the worst jobs. Minorities are likely to be exploited because they lack familiarity with the economic and social structure and because of their social separation from other workers. Bonacich (1989) examines the distribution of income in the United States and concludes that racism in American society is linked to capitalism. In summary, she writes: "Stripped of all its fancy rationalizations and complexities, the capitalist system depends upon the exploitation of the poor by the rich."

A logical conclusion of those sociologists using the exploitive model is presented in the work of Mirande (1985) and Blea (1988). They both present strong critiques of the assimilationist model and of "establishment" sociology for thinking that the inequality faced by Mexican Americans is the result of deficiencies in Mexican culture. They both think that Barrera has moved the furthest in developing a Chicano social science. For them, the key factors in the oppression of Chicanos are economic exploitation, political oppression, restriction of educational opportunities, historical oppression, negative ideology, negative images in the mass media, a biased criminal justice system, and segregated housing.

Mirande and Blea both emphasize that Chicanos have both adapted and created a culture, and they believe Chicanos have actively resisted oppression. I agree with their view that "scientific research" that involves surveys and census data analysis leads to a blaming of the victim. They contend that Chicano culture has many positive features and that social scientists should participate in social activism to assist Chicanos to achieve social justice.

My field research on rural Mexican Americans in Idaho led me to concur with those sociologists using the exploitive model. I believe that the work of Barrera and Mirande most accurately confirms the findings of my field research.

The reader will find that this book combines several elements from the general exploitive model to explain the subordinate position of the Mexican Americans of this study. The field research findings support many of the views expounded by Barrera and Mirande. One of the significant contributions of this research project is the interviews with Anglos in the community studied and their observations from within Anglo-dominated social institutions. I have coined the term "ideological colonialism" to signify the set of negative ideas about Mexican Americans the Anglo community has created, which has then enabled it to establish a social reality that accepts as fact the idea that in America everyone has an equal opportunity to succeed and that economic failure is the consequence of individual and cultural deficiencies of the members of the Mexican American community.

The work of Omi and Winant (1986) is relevant here because of their use of the term "ideological racism" to refer to the situation where race becomes a pervasive aspect of American social life. Race is seen as the indicator of social inferiority in society. The term "ideological colonialism" is somewhat more broad and inclusive than ideological racism. Ideological colonialism also denotes the hidden and softer nature of colonialism faced by the Mexican American subjects of this research project. This ideology enables its believers to see oppressive race relations as normal. This is accomplished, in part, by ignoring the existence of the Mexican American population. The confidence and ardent belief in the correctness of the "American" Anglo way of life in Middlewest leave little room for concern about the well-being of the Mexican Americans in the community. The ideology of Anglo Middlewest leads to what I consider indifference by Anglos toward the poverty faced by the Mexican American community. Few Anglos question the systematic relegation of Mexican Americans in Middlewest to subordinate positions.

This research (as was the case with the Mirande and Blea studies) found strength and vitality in the Mexican American ethnic community. A chapter is devoted to examining the active resistance to oppression mounted by the Mexican American leaders of southwestern Idaho. Central to the book are Chapters Eight and Nine, which explore the intensive institutionalized racism faced by Mexican Americans in Middlewest. The educational system, political institutions, criminal justice system, and mass media are all seen to sustain the subordinate position of the Mexican American community.

In the Marxist tradition, the economic position of the Mexican American community is viewed by this researcher as most crucial. The social position of the majority of Mexican Americans in Middlewest and Farm County is lower class. Farm County employs the most Mexican American migrant workers in the state of Idaho, all of whom have an income approximately one-half the official poverty level. Migrant workers are among the most exploited workers in America (Cockcroft 1986). Chapter Seven of this book will reveal details of the numerous inequitable working situations faced by Idaho's Mexican American migrant workers.

Several sections of the book examine how Mexican Americans who work as seasonal farm workers and at low paying jobs in the local factories describe the segmented nature of their work and illustrate their lack of participation in local government and Anglo society. These sections also document the unwillingness of some Anglo businessmen to employ Mexican Americans.

Ideological colonialism operates to synchronize the exploitive circumstances of the Mexican Americans in Middlewest and Farm County. The consequence is that most Anglos and some Mexican Americans accept without question the systematic subordination of the Mexican American population.

Summary Comments

Some university students in this country have a difficult time understanding and appreciating exploitive theories of race relations. Many have grown up with little experience or understanding of the validity of critiques of our society. From my teaching experience in Idaho, I have found that most Idaho students have been sheltered from any serious analysis of the social problems facing American society. This is in part because of the conservative climate of the state and the jingoistic view that America is the "greatest country on the planet"; consequently, we could not have a serious race problem in this country. This view appears to have a considerable number of adherents throughout our society today. One aim of this book is to help demonstrate to students and citizens that rural Mexican Americans in Idaho are victimized by serious social injustices; my hope is that this field research might assist Americans in understanding that, as a nation, we have yet to solve or even recognize all of our race problems.

All sociological theory attempts to explain human social behavior. Sociology is an inexact science, in part because many variables are unaccounted for in any one research project. Sociology has a limited ability to influence social policy because of the complexity and inexactness of human social behavior. The recommendations of sociologists can differ significantly from the public perception of a race problem. There is a dispute between many citizens and sociologists over how well racial minorities succeed in our society. Public surveys (Schaefer 1991) consistently reveal that the majority of Anglos do not believe that racism is a serious problem in America.

Most social scientists report their findings in appropriate journals, which few people read. Some social scientists believe that their research should be made public and used to influence social policy. I hope that this book will assist in educating the citizens and politicians of Idaho; social justice demands a set of social policies to assist the Mexican Americans of Idaho.

Sociological field research attempts to maintain the confidentiality of its subjects. The names of the community, the county, and the subjects described and quoted in this research have all been changed. However, Idaho is a rural state with a sparse population, and many people in Idaho will be able to identify the community of this study. To protect and respect the subjects' privacy, in some cases I have changed not only the name but also the profession or occupation of the subject.

Chapter 2

THE ANGLO COMMUNITY OF MIDDLEWEST

Just as a people who oppress another cannot be free, so a culture that is mistaken about another must be mistaken about itself.

–Jean Baudrillard

Introduction

Middlewest has two distinct communities, one Mexican American and one Anglo. The two communities share considerable social interaction but everyone recognizes their fundamental separation. The social interaction between the two communities has negative as well as positive connotations. The reason for researching the Anglo community is that, as the dominant group, its behavior is more likely to influence the behavior of the Mexican American minority.

Anglo pioneers settled Middlewest shortly after the Civil War. However, the town did not begin to flower until about 1900. Most of the Anglos interviewed have local family histories going back only two or three generations; however, a few families have a long history in Middlewest. The Hobson print shop has been operated by four generations of one family; a fifth generation member has begun his apprenticeship.

Geography of Middlewest

My initial impressions of Middlewest were derived from my entering local businesses to request interviews with the owner or manager. I had the sensation of being "time-warped" to the

1950s. Only the bank buildings have modern facades. Many other downtown business buildings appear old and run-down. The local radio station building, located on a corner lot, is shaped like a triangle. The windows are elongated and the roof rises toward the tip of the triangle where a rotating globe displays in neon the call letters of the station. The building is vintage 1950s.

With its absence of traffic and of parking meters, Middlewest has the distinctive physical appearance of a small town. Many downtown businesses have closed. The boarded windows and lack of activity had for me a discomforting feeling. The emptiness of Sears and two other large department stores adds to the sense of a town whose prosperity and vitality have disappeared. The gift shop, a flower shop, and a pawn shop all occupy buildings greatly in need of renovation. A few antique and craft businesses appear out of place because they are located in buildings designed for much larger enterprises. The local five-and-ten variety store does a brisk business, but it too needs remodeling. The disagreeability of the downtown increased for me with each visit until I became familiar with it.

The interiors and exteriors of many of the downtown buildings need paint. Much of the office equipment and furnishings appear obsolete. Yet after this first impression of a drab and seedy business district that totally lacks a contemporary business atmosphere, a visitor who becomes more familiar with the community tends to be become less judgmental, sensing a local adherence to and manifestation of a simpler time when frugality came more naturally.

Helen Schmidt, the assistant manager of the local variety store, informed me that the owner, who has worked beyond retirement age, has no intention of modernizing the store. She said that purchasing, record keeping, and accounting require much of her time because of the antiquated technology. A new businessman whose establishment is located out on the "boulevard" east of town commented: "The old businesses downtown are not competitive. They conduct business just as their fathers did. On most items in their stores you can go to the mall and buy the same item for half the price." Another boulevard businessman stated: "The local businesses just do not want to change the way they do business. They want someone to fix it so they can make money again. They want business to somehow return to the downtown."

Downtown restaurants project a small-town, folksy image. One local market has a luncheonette that caters to a retired clientele and rarely has the opportunity to serve an out-of-towner. One never sees a suit and tie in this establishment, but you can order the special of the day, with a drink, for around $2.50. Another restaurant serves three meals a day and local businessmen frequently use the banquet room. The entrees served are somewhat bland, and the owner has yet to acknowledge the legal requirement to provide non-smoking areas. The Oriental Cafe has the most steady customers though it is located adjacent to boarded-up businesses. Everyone appears to know each other. During the crowded lunch hour, patrons have their meal interrupted by the greetings of those arriving and departing. Rumors are confirmed or refuted as locals dine on an American version of Chinese food. The decor in all three establishments would challenge the average interior decorator. On the main freeway exit are located a pizza parlor, a drive-in hamburger stand, and a corner convenience-and-gas store. None could be called attractive.

In a recent study of Middlewest undertaken to assist community development, RUDAT (Regional Urban Design Assistance Team), an arm of the American Institute of Architects, made several observations and recommendations regarding the community's appearance. It criticized the run-down appearance and the lack of attention paid to the maintenance of the public domain, and it recommended that the town impose effective planning and zoning standards. RUDAT also recommended preserving and refurbishing the town's many historical buildings. The study suggested planting trees and shrubs to soften the stark and barren appearance of the community's major thoroughfares.

While businesses are sparse in the downtown section of Middlewest, this is not the case on the boulevard, where a three-mile strip of businesses has emerged as the result of unplanned and unfettered free enterprise. On both sides of the boulevard, establishments loom uninvitingly. One can go to dinner, buy groceries, purchase shoes or a new car, and go to the movies without ever leaving the strip. Few city ordinances seem to exist to control signs, design, or structural appearance. The boulevard landscape lacks bushes, shrubs and trees. It even lacks curbs and gutters. What it doesn't lack is traffic.

On the west end of town lies the industrial section of Middlewest—dominated by a trailer factory, a seed company, and a giant potato-processing plant that employs 1200 people. These plants seem strikingly large for such a small community. Built of steel, wood, and cinder block, they do nothing to improve the town's appearance. The processing plant produces a "what's that smell" reaction in out-of-town visitors.

An interstate freeway, which bisects the town instead of skirting it, features extensive cement shoulders to control erosion. Cement and traffic dividing a small rural town produce a discordant visual effect.

Railroad tracks also run through the town. Abandoned grain elevators stand here and there near the tracks. The proverbial "other-side-of-the-tracks" is where the Mexican American population resides. The houses are small and in need of paint and repair. House trailers squeeze between the frame houses. The Mexican American section of town appears cluttered because of a lack of landscaping and the presence of old vehicles on the streets. A few small businesses service this rural barrio: a neighborhood grocery store, a laundromat, a gas station, a television-repair shop, and two small Mexican restaurants.

One section of town enjoys large trees and spacious homes. Here also is a small private college with its bricks and ivy. Here, one can envision the Middlewest of the past, a town confident and self-assured. South of town are new subdivisions, resembling those of any community, where the newly affluent and the urban commuters reside.

Emblematic of the economic decline of the downtown was the burning down of the Springs Hotel and Restaurant, the last commercial reminder of the town's affluent days. Its architecture had a grandeur reflecting the early twentieth century, and its restaurant once catered to state and national celebrities. The historical museum has photographs showing trolleys traveling by the hotel on their way to the state capital of Boise. Many old-timers saw the burning down of the Springs as a sign of the end of Middlewest as a thriving, independent community. The post-fire cleanup took months, as though the community did not want to relinquish its past.

Middlewest has a nine-hole public golf course within the city limits. With its few golfers—mostly retirees—puttering along its fairways, it mirrors the unhurried atmosphere of Middlewest. The town also has a lovely and spacious park with numerous large trees providing a shaded canopy for the many family pic-nickers. The park's baseball fields and swimming pool stay busy throughout the summer.

Another prominent image in Middlewest is of its many steep-led churches. Presbyterian, Mormon, Methodist, First Christian, First Baptist, and Catholic churches have the largest member-ships, but many others also flourish here; they include the Evangelical, Nazarene, Seventh-Day Adventist, and Baptist de-nominations. The Chamber of Commerce's visitor information packet boasts that Middlewest has forty churches. Many of the larger churches are located on prominent corners. The Mexican Americans have converted houses in the barrio into churches. The Assembly of God, Pentecostal, and Jehovah's Witness re-ligious groups have Mexican American congregations ranging from 15 to 100 people.

Most of the Anglo middle class of Middlewest attend church regularly, while only about 50 percent of the working class do so. Most Mexican American families in Middlewest are working class or lower class. They attend church more regularly than do the Anglo working class people. The young adults of both races have less of a religious commitment. The churches rely on women to perform most of their organizational activities.

Local Businesses

Middlewest prides itself on three businesses with long his-tories in the community. Hobson Printers employs more than 100 workers. The shop has a regional reputation for publishing books by western authors. The local dairy employs approximately 125 workers. The dairy's manager proudly proclaims that the plant's production of cheese rivals that of the largest dairies in the western United States.

Another company with a long history in Middlewest is the Harvest Seed Company, which employs over 150 workers. This company operates as a family-owned business. The son and grandson now running the seed company refused to be interviewed; they told me to mail them my questions because they had been misquoted in the press. From my difficult interaction with these two men, I can see why a journalist might be hard-pressed to treat them fairly. In all three of these companies, the management gained its business experience on the job.

Middlewest has some farm-related businesses that employ from fifteen to fifty workers; most are family-owned. I interviewed twenty-two businessmen who had inherited family enterprises; these included a machine company, a funeral business, a monument company, a car dealership, a seed company, a food-distributing company, and the Hobson Print Shop. Three brothers manage the downtown drug store following their father's retirement. The downtown office-supply store is jointly operated by a father and son team.

A significant number of young professionals, including doctors and lawyers, return to Middlewest to practice with their fathers when they complete their education. Farmers have a tradition of passing the family farm down to the next generation.

The overall impression of Middlewest is of a declining rural community, with a few historical buildings and parks that remind one of its better days. The town appears squeezed and disjointed because of its ugly boulevards, freeways, and factories.

As the county seat, Middlewest remained the commercial center of the area until the mid-1960s when a neighboring community began to usurp the commercial trade of the county. I was told a legendary story about the decline of the downtown area. It all began twenty-five years ago when the city leaders had the opportunity to have a shopping mall built in Middlewest. The city leaders rejected change because they wanted to retain the status quo. Middlewest was the economic center of the area until the mall was built in an adjoining town. The community leaders were unwilling to apply for federal grants to improve the infrastructure of Middlewest that is necessary for growth. Following the loss of the mall, a series of internal conflicts developed among the city's elected officials. These leaders bickered for years. The citizens once recalled three of them. The community even elected a write-in candidate for mayor who was only twenty years old. He had no experience in business or politics. The conflicts were front-page news for the local newspaper for years. The decline escalated as the downtown businesses closed one by one. The chamber of commerce lost most of its membership.

Anglos in Middlewest display bitterness and uneasiness in talking about the decline of the downtown and the subsequent internecine dissension. Many people eventually withdrew from community affairs. Members of the community remain jealous and bitter when acknowledging that Middlewest has deteriorated economically compared to a nearby town. Civic and businesses leaders acknowledge that the decline of small towns has become a trend in America, but one can still sense their discomfort.

Middlewest people are "straight shooters" and they do not modify their rhetoric to please others. Most of the local businessmen and civic leaders are natives of Middlewest. Many have not attended college. Most of the managers of largest local factories started their careers at the lower levels of the companies. When interviewing them, I found them open and trustful. None blocked my access to the company floor or its employees; instead, several businessmen went through their list of employees to see which ones best fit my criteria. They then gave me employee phone numbers, which would be considered a breech of confidentiality by more sophisticated managers.

Community Renaissance

Middlewest community leaders currently are attempting to revitalize the community by developing new community events.

In order to create community pride, business and civic leaders insist that Middlewest has the "best schools" in the state. The schools have won national awards and local school bonds pass with large majorities. The small private college that nearly closed in the 1980s now has a healthy endowment and several new buildings. The community has reaffirmed its affection for the college; community leaders praise the college's fine arts program, which features regularly scheduled cultural events open to the community.

Most residents of Middlewest contend that the greatest community spirit derives from the sports programs of the high school and college. The college has traditionally had winning basketball teams. Attendance at athletic contests represents a cross-section of the Anglo community, and a sure way to start a conversation in Middlewest is to ask how the local athletic teams are doing.

Middlewest's annual rodeo has a long and successful tradition. This week-long commercial event enables many local service clubs to raise money; the rodeo is the largest fund raiser for most clubs. Local rodeo fans are knowledgeable about the sport and enthusiastically cheer the local favorites. During rodeo week most people in Middlewest wear cowboy boots and hats. The Kiwanis Club sponsors an annual chuck wagon breakfast and a steak dinner that are especially popular.

The Kiwanis, Lion's, Rotary, Optimist, and Exchange clubs are well established in Middlewest. Several of these clubs conduct membership drives; in many of them most of the current membership is over forty years old and many are retired. Club members take pride in their charitable activities, which provide resources and labor for many youth programs. The Kiwanis Club recently purchased and planted trees for the new elementary school. Middlewest also has several social clubs with large memberships. The Elks is the largest with over 1,000 members. Its board of directors consists primarily of retired men, and its socials include frequent dinner dances. It also sponsors an annual father and son fishing contest. Shriners are also numerous. They sponsor an annual caravan that collects large quantities of donated food, which is then transported, with police escort, to the regional rehabilitation center.

Middlewest recently received a grant to refurbish and preserve its railway depot, which stands near a decaying section of downtown. The RUDAT committee praised the effort to save this building.

Middlewest prides itself on having two public golf courses. These courses have low greens fees and an inexpensive season pass allows one to play both courses. The newest course, built on donated land from a local farmer, is situated several miles from town. This beautiful and spacious course equals any in the state. In the front lobby of the clubhouse is a plaque of appreciation to all those in the community who contributed to the new course. It contains the names of most of the upper class members of the community. The Mexican American members of this golf course account for less than one percent of the total membership.

Many Anglos proudly assert that their town rejects class formalities, and say no one "puts on airs" in Middlewest. They claim that anyone in the community can play golf with anybody else, and they insist that foursomes frequently include members of both the working and business classes. However, I did not see any Mexican Americans playing golf, nor did I see any Anglo working class golfers dining with the middle class members of the golf club.

People of great wealth in southwestern Idaho have ties to Middlewest. Their donations to the private college and to public facilities in the community reached nearly $100 million dollars over the last twenty-five years. But few of these donations assist the Mexican American community. Nearly 50 percent of the giant food processor's employees are Mexican American. The company moved its management to Boise because most of the managers did not want to live in Middlewest.

Efforts to revitalize Middlewest have involved the establishment of a Christmas parade. In its third year the parade drew approximately 1500 spectators, and the community leaders feel that the Christmas parade is an unqualified success. The parade's major feature consists of a procession of antique vehicles carrying local dignitaries. Oddly, there are no bands and floats, but that does not dampen the community's enthusiasm for the event. The Mexican American community turn out in roughly proportional numbers to watch this event, but they do not have any active participation in the parade itself.

During a recent Christmas season, the mayor announced that some local businessmen had donated $100 each to purchase Christmas lights for the evergreens on the golf course. The chamber of commerce endorsed the plan. The tree-lighting ceremony featured school choirs and a speech by the mayor.

Another new community project, called "Clean Up Middlewest," originated with the chamber of commerce. Approximately 500 people gathered in a bank parking lot on a summery Saturday morning. The event began with coffee and donuts donated by local businesses. The city donated its vehicles to the project and a few dignitaries spoke with gusto about the increased community spirit. The volunteers received assignments in specific areas of town and then dispersed to pick up trash, cut weeds, trim shrubs, and plant grass. Families and friends worked together; some church groups participated. With smiles on their faces, businessmen, city leaders, teachers, and blue-collar workers went about their assignments with a sense of purpose. However, the Mexican American community did not participate in this event. The absence of Mexican Americans in these community events reenforces the theory that Middlewest has two separate communities.

The Middlewest city council recently consisted of a mailman, a small businessman, the manager of a local furniture store, and two businessmen associated with larger local enterprises. The mayor, who operates his father's mortuary, recently appointed a Mexican American businessman to the council. The council members carry out their community duties with little fanfare. At a typical council meeting, a consensus is developed prior to voting. These votes generally involve housekeeping chores to keep city departments operating. Few citizens attend these short meetings.

Economic Development

Nothing appears to match the devotion of Middlewest leaders to "economic growth"; that is, to making money. At least one, Mr. Bailey, whose agribusiness career is linked to Middlewest, has made a fortune. Serious entrepreneurs respectfully utter his name. Two business partners who have recently moved to Middlewest own a thriving farm store. Local businessmen reverently refer to them as "movers and shakers." Soon after their arrival, one was elected to the city council and the other chairs the city's economic development committee. One prominent businessmen who owns a small print shop and fervently supports economic growth proclaimed, "The best political candidate is the one with the most yard signs. The best candidate is the one who can raise the most money because that means the right people in the community are supporting his candidacy."

Most of the community businessmen/civic leaders appear to have a considerable amount of free time which they use to meet with one another to create strategies to encourage business growth. They do not believe that new business growth will fully solve the downtown problem but they fear the town will decline further without new businesses and new jobs. To this end they have recently created several organizations whose purpose is to stimulate the local economy. Only a few individuals question the potential success of these endeavors. The city council funded the Middlewest Economic Development Program. To express the seriousness of their commitment, council members contributed $200,000 of the city's money to the program. They hired a full-time consultant to develop and carry out an ambitious plan for attracting new businesses to Middlewest. As of the summer of 1991, two new businesses had opened their doors in Middlewest.

Another group of community businessmen created an organization called Middlewest Unlimited, whose purpose is to foster economic growth. The group has invested in land on the outskirts of Middlewest in hopes of securing industrial development. In existence for over ten years, it has met with little success.

The Middlewest Chamber of Commerce has also committed itself to the revitalization of the town. The chamber's energetic new CEO has helped double its membership and has attracted a committed group of board members. The chamber has established noon and evening socials where the business and civic leaders can meet and develop solidarity. It also has created a leadership-training conference in an attempt to stimulate younger businessmen and professionals to participate in community affairs. The chamber's executive director states that their ultimate goal is for Middlewest to have a positive self-image.

The concern for economic growth thus has led to the creation of four separate organizations (the committee established by the city council, the committee established by the chamber of commerce, the local businessmen's group, and the Unlimited group) to pursue this goal. This led to the establishment of Team Middlewest, which meets periodically to resolve any potential conflicts among the various economic-development organizations. The RUDAT experts recommended that these organizations merge into a single organization.

Town leaders initiated the application for a RUDAT study, raising $20,000 to have the Regional Urban Design Assistance Team conduct a study for the revitalization of Middlewest. Community leaders wanted to know how to encourage economic growth and to resolve the differences of opinion as to which local group had developed the best economic strategy. RUDAT provided a detailed document following their one-week study of the town. The town leaders may have received more than they anticipated since the RUDAT report examined many other aspects of the community, including race relations and poverty.

Some difference in opinion inevitably has developed concerning how to revitalize Middlewest. Some groups want to attract new industrial growth, while others want to focus on the expansion of small businesses. The anti-industrial group believe that the town does not need any more five dollar-an-hour jobs. The difference of opinions has led to some squabbling and personality conflicts. To an outside observer, the real issue seems to be who will get the credit for any success of these endeavors and, if no success results, who will be blamed? It can seem that the major accomplishment to date of the attempt to stop the economic decline of Middlewest has been bruised egos. Intrigue flourishes as factions jockey for position and advantage. To an outsider, little movement can be seen as accusations and counter-accusations fill the air. Two of the chairs have been accused of having autocratic tendencies. Threats of resignation are heard; some occur.

Through interviews with Anglo leaders, I ascertained the existence of additional business groups. These groups illustrate the conviviality of small-town life. The twenty members of the Key Club refer to themselves as executives although most only have a few employees. This group meets weekly for breakfast in order to share business tips. Each member reports on a new business activity that might generate business for another of their members.

Another group, the Middlewest Coffee Club, consists mostly of retired men who meet daily at a local brokerage firm. They have no agenda and spend their time discussing community affairs. The mayor is a member of this club, and the membership also includes a retired sheriff and a former mayor. Local lore has it that these men are important political brokers who must be consulted by anyone desirous of launching a local political career.

The real purpose of these two groups seems to be camaraderie. The meetings provide a vehicle for sustaining friendships. Both have a gaming ritual similar to a lottery–the loser has to donate money for the coffee fund.

Community and Identity

David Hummon's book *Commonplaces* (1990) examines the nature of community ideologies, which he defines as the ways people depict their group-living arrangements. He is interested in understanding how these ideologies affect and sustain peoples' identities. He contends that a relationship exists between their self-identity and how people perceive their community. Community social interaction operates to create and sustain ideologies and identities. Hummon examines four types of communities: country, small town, city, and suburban. The community of Middlewest provides strong support for Hummon's model of small-town people. Most Anglos of Middlewest agree on their description of the town. Anglos like living in Middlewest, but active adolescents find it boring.

The residents of Middlewest agree that family values and family life are important; their town is a wonderful place to raise children; the town maintains traditional values; their town has fewer social problems than do cities; their community has friendly and neighborly people; the people in their town are not as status conscious or as money oriented as urban people; the people of Middlewest value honesty; and the people of Middlewest do not attempt to deceive one another.

People like the fact that the community has a slower pace than the capital, Boise, only 25 miles to the east. They like the peace and quiet. Many commented they would never live in a city. A businessman who commutes to Middlewest from Boise said, "It takes twice as long to conduct a business deal in Middlewest than Boise; you have to shift to a lower gear in Middlewest, but once you get used to it, it's great." People in Middlewest hate the traffic and pollution in Boise; they feel Boise to be more dangerous and impersonal. They believe that people in Boise have lost respect for the simple ways of life.

Many leisure activities of Middlewesterners involve the outdoors. They enjoy picnics, golf, and fishing in the summer. In the winter, they hunt, ski, and attend sporting events. For many Anglos, being close to nature plays a key role in their lifestyle; their leisure activities often involve the whole family.

One of the alleged attributes of Middlewest, according to its citizens, is the high quality of the public schools. The superintendent enjoys an important leadership role in the community; the athletic programs receive the lion's share of community attention. One indication of community values can be ascertained by noting who is selected as the high school commencement speaker. During the period of the field research, the college basketball coach received this honor.

Small Town Life

A good case for provincialism could be built if a report were limited to the quaint aspects of life in Middlewest. For example, the chamber of commerce continued the local fund-raising tradition of raffling a turkey each day of the holiday season. At one meeting, the chamber board debated whether to support an anti-drug program for elementary children. The board unanimously approved a program that involved urine testing of children. The library held an ice cream social to raise money, and the local dairy donated the ice cream. The women's auxiliary of the library baked cakes. The head librarian declared the event a success, though it raised less than $300.

Most of the managers of the large factories started working for their companies as blue-collar workers. These men do not have MBA degrees or polished communication skills. For example, at a meeting at the Bailey Corporation the personnel director, Tim Sanders, in jeans and hard hat, led a meeting of invited community leaders in a brainstorming session concerning the organization of the fiftieth anniversary celebration of the company. After twenty minutes Sanders abruptly ended the meeting although the group had made no decisions. Sanders scheduled no additional meetings. The shocked and amused participants departed. No hard feelings developed because Sanders is considered a "good guy."

Middlewest cannot avoid its small-town nature. Community bickering recurred sporadically during the time of my field research. One controversy landed the mayor on the front page of the local newspaper when he gave old city playground equipment to a local businessman. Many writers of letters to the editor saw this action as a sure sign of "corruption." The mayor's detractors castigated him for his lack of frugality.

A second squabble was heated. A section of the community has a farm-type irrigation system for watering lawns. The city leaders conducted a survey of voters and the majority supported building a pressurized-pipe system of irrigation. Opposition mounted and letters to the editor began to appear. City council meetings became agitated. Vitriolic denouncements increased, but the city leaders remained steadfast. Retired residents organized backyard meetings. Small-town politics is a cozy affair. A group of senior citizens organized a demonstration in front of city hall. The frustrated city leaders retreated.

Naturally, the local newspaper interviewed all of the participants. The paper reported the debate in agonizing detail. Community leaders groaned. There were rumors that some city council members might resign. Democracy allows people to have political influence, but this battle left many scars. The new city council wants to avoid the image of amateurish politics in Middlewest, but such affairs may be inevitable.

Another community issue arose over selecting a name for the new elementary school. The school administration held a contest among the grade-school children but the school board made the final decision. They selected the name "Sacagawea." The decision soon became controversial. Letters to the editor, both for and against, soon reached the newspaper. The opposition to this name perhaps reflects the underlying orthodoxy of the town, as some questioned honoring a female Native American.

Few women hold leadership positions in Middlewest. The businesswomen have separate service clubs. Even fewer women occupy managerial positions. Women leaders believe their ideas go unappreciated by male leaders. Women feel they must speak less and be less assertive to avoid the label of "bitch." Male leaders deny being sexist; but a female leader comments, "The men expect us to do the work and for them to take the glory."

Middlewest held a debate on sex education in the schools prior to the research project. The outcome was the initiation of a sex-education course in the high school. The course material does not include discussion of sexual intercourse. The only method of birth control discussed is abstinence. The course instructor shared his frustrations with these limitations; he said he may be the only teacher who teaches sex education "without the sex."

Newcomers to Middlewest

Qualitative field work frequently generates serendipitous findings. I did not intend to interview families who had recently moved to Middlewest. However, I found that these people have an important perspective to offer because they can compare their former communities to Middlewest. Sally Benson began her observations by commenting, "I thought all the polyester had been used up years ago, but now I know they shipped it all to Middlewest."

Spike Benson, who works in an electrical repair shop, discussed the anti-Californian attitude in the community. He claimed that it took a long time for his fellow workers to accept him. He explained that his fellow workers and the owner resist doing anything different despite the merits. The Bensons think the people in Middlewest use incorrect grammar and humorous colloquialisms. They found the pay scale to be low. Sally Benson commutes to Boise to work.

The Bensons expressed amazement and delight at the low rate of taxation. They feel the community has outmoded attitudes about social issues. Sally could only laugh at the Christmas parade, because it lacked class; she remarked that if the community is that cheap, it should not bother with a parade. Sally's mother has a part-time job at a local drugstore. Because of the shortage of customers, she found her daily routine to be boring, for it consists of repeatedly dusting the same bottles.

The Bensons have always belonged to the Republican party, but in Middlewest they feel their political views coincide more with those of the Democrats. They said they could not believe people could be as right-wing as are the people in Middlewest. They laughed as they said their friends in California would see some of the people of Middlewest as being old-fashioned.

The Bensons said they "hated" Middlewest the first year, but now they love the town and cannot imagine moving back to California. They like the lack of traffic and the slow pace of life. They feel people in Middlewest are more congenial. For example, Spike's co-workers visited him in the hospital. They have neighbors, who without request, volunteer their assistance.

The Bensons said they felt a certain amount of "culture shock" their first year in Middlewest. They could not believe that store clerks would invariably strike up conversations with them and that these same clerks remembered them the next time they went to that store. The Bensons discussed the sexism and racism in Middlewest. Sally said, "God, they expect you to stay at home and that something is wrong with you if you want to work. There are no professional jobs for women in Middlewest." Spike commented, "In California we have always had a large number of Mexicans, so they are accepted; but here they make derogatory remarks about them." Sally agreed. "At the stores, the clerks will wait on me first, even though a Mexican American person is ahead of me. They also follow them around the store like they were all shoplifters. It's embarrassing."

Stan Hoffman, who owns a local hardware store, is another newcomer. The degree of local conservatism shocks him. Stan, a Republican from Minnesota, expressed exasperation with the anti-tax philosophy of the community. He said that the predominant political view resembles a "convention of neo-Nazis." He also expressed the view that because of the low taxes the town has inadequate services. He commented, "The local businessmen are stuck in the mud; they just won't take the actions necessary for economic growth."

Another recent arrival, Jane Dagher, a businesswoman, belongs to several business organizations in town. She observed, "Most of the local businessmen took over their father's business, so they run it the same way he did. The result is the ho-hum status quo. They want economic growth but they want someone else to do it for them. They want growth but for the community to stay the same; it's impossible."

Johnny Kline, another new businessman, operates a successful store in Middlewest. He commented: "These guys lack any business sense and they are unwilling to compete for business. If you do some comparison shopping you will find that the local businessmen charge at least 25 percent more for items than at the shopping center. You just can't do business that way."

Many people informed me that Anglos in Middlewest and Farm County transfer their children to other schools to prevent them from having contact with Mexican Americans. Some Anglos believe that the quality of education diminishes if a classroom has too many Mexican American students. Quinten Johnson, a newcomer to the community, said, "When we got to Middlewest people told us to send our kids to Meadow View so they wouldn't have to associate with Mexican kids."

Middlewest must be doing something right, because every newcomer said he/she prefers living in Middlewest to their former community.

The Local Newspaper

Sociologists can learn much about a community by reading its newspaper. I conducted a six-months content analysis of the local daily newspaper. The *Daily News* carries articles and features of a small-town nature. The activities of children, clubs, and organizations; news of weddings, funerals, religious activities, retirements, and anniversaries; and agricultural news capture more of the paper's space as compared to an urban paper. The *Daily News* reports many human-interest stories that recount the everyday events of local citizens. For example, on April 15, 1991, the *Daily News* carried a front-page picture of a woman with a baby kitten in her hands. The article reported that the woman had brought the kitten back to life with mouth-to-mouth resuscitation. Another example comes from the May 30, 1991, issue, in which a picture of the new fire truck made the front page. Another major story covered the presentation of good citizenship awards from Middlewest Daughters of the American Revolution to local students. The paper's detailed coverage of a "God and Country" rally reflected the local values.

An appreciation of the conservatism of Middlewest can be acquired by reading the editorials. The *Daily News* opposes the women's movement, environmentalism, big government, teachers' unions, and gun control. The paper supports the privatization of government services, the right-to-work law, getting tough on prison sentences, the right to home schooling, and the free-enterprise system. The quality of writing is generally well below that found in the Boise newspaper. The editorials exhibit a tendency to use slang phases. For example, the paper depicts its opponents as "asinine nuts, who write slop and should wake up and get a life."

The *Daily News* features weekly columns by the town busybody, Philip Martin. Martin is a founder of a libertarian organization that promotes, with biblical fervor, the glories of the free-enterprise system. As the self-appointed emissary of capitalism, he attends most public meetings in Middlewest. He thrives on his own political rhetoric. Martin has one theme in his column: though the spin varies, he fears a socialist take-over of America. His columns strive for economy; most can be read in a few seconds. He receives accolades from the Anglo business/civic leaders of Middlewest, many of whom consider him to be their philosophical spokesman.

Phil Martin owns a large billboard at the edge of town; consequently, upon entering the town one is almost forced to read about his staunch support for capitalism. The popularity of Martin is no aberration. Middlewest and Farm County have a reputation for electing conservatives. Rarely does a Democrat win an election. Farm County prides itself on being the home of one of the most conservative U.S. senators.

Most Mexican Americans believe that the *Daily News* presents a biased and negative view of the Mexican American community. They believe the paper predominantly reports about the drug abuse, violence, gangs, and crimes of the Mexican American community. However, newspapers thrive on the uncommon and sensational behavior of people, and the *Daily News* is no exception. The paper extensively reports the crimes of both Anglos and Mexican Americans. Yet a content analysis does reveal a distorted coverage: a disproportional coverage of Mexican American crime occurs because of the absence of positive coverage of Mexican Americans.

The *Daily News* does present some positive articles on the Mexican American community. A lengthy article detailing the success of a local Mexican American businessman appeared in the March 31, 1991, issue. On May 5, 1991, the newspaper also carried a picture of Mexican American children dancing at the

Cinco de Mayo celebration. It was accompanied by a lengthy story on the fiesta.

Mexican Americans receive the fairest reporting in the sports section of the paper. If a Mexican American quarterback throws a touchdown pass, the sports writer does not overlook the accomplishment. Mexican American adolescents generally are underrepresented in community and school sports programs; however, the sports program is the school activity in which they most participate and in which they receive the least abrasive treatment.

Still, all three of these positive reports on Mexican Americans are connected with their assimilation. The businessmen can be seen as the token Mexican American in local civic organizations; the Cinco de Mayo celebration corresponds to the Anglo view of Mexican Americans; and nothing could be more American than participating in sports. A picture on the front page of the *Daily News* could well symbolize how the paper and the community regard Mexican Americans. The picture contains a close-up of a Mexican American worker with an apple orchard in the background. The article with the picture examines the fall harvest; the paper fails to identify the Mexican American.

Conservative Values

The majority of citizens in Middlewest adhere to a basic set of conservative values that include a vigorous rejection of most expansion of government programs, an ongoing demand for a reduction in taxes, and extensive efforts to protect the free-enterprise system. The Anglo community recognizes these values as being supported by four groups: farmers, businessmen, retired people, and "Christians."

The favorite topic of discussion concerns the evils of high taxation. Local politicians inevitably describe themselves as frugal and hard-working. The worst political "crime" is taxes being raised by a Democrat. In the eyes of Anglo conservatives, the most pernicious enemies of the people are governmental regulatory agencies. Especially frowned upon are the Occupational

Safety and Health Administration (OSHA) and the Environmental Protection Agency (EPA). These entities, they believe, unnecessarily hinder the free-enterprise system. If only the government would "get off the backs of farmers and businessmen," they lament, America would achieve incredible economic prosperity. The Anglo leaders of Middlewest consider unions anathema. They believe that such organizations curtail individual freedom and the spirit of free enterprise. The local dairy has a public-relations brochure which praises itself for having an "uninterrupted work force." The manager informed me that the dairy had defeated a union strike by hiring new workers. The second-largest employer in town has made it clear to its workers that the owner will close the business before recognizing a union.

The service clubs illustrate the intensity of the conservative climate of Middlewest. The guest speakers at their luncheon meetings for the most part are fellow businessmen. Club rituals include opening and closing the meetings with patriotic songs such as "America, the Beautiful." Club members recite the Pledge of Allegiance with reverence; ministers bless the meetings with prayer. Inevitably an informal bond develops among notions of God, the nation, conservative values, and business activity.

One extreme result of these political attitudes could be the creation of an enemy embodying evil—such as the Mexican American community, who could thus become the antithesis of the sacred in the minds of the "true believers."

Cuzzort (1989) explores the use of Durkheimian theory to understand contemporary events. His analysis can assist in explaining how Mexican Americans could become the "enemy." Each society creates sacred symbols, thoughts, and values that represent the collective. These shared tokens hold a special place because they represent the collective consciousness. A disturbing feature of this social development is that it can become necessary to then delineate ideas and groups who represent the antithesis of the sacred values. Cuzzort believes that society will always create its deviants in order to sustain its sacred values. In this case, Mexican Americans easily come to represent those violating the sacred values.

The ideology involves an interesting contradiction. Individual achievement is a key ingredient in the ideology, yet most local businessmen inherited the family business, and most farmers acquired their father's farm. Yet both groups assert that everyone has an equal chance to succeed in America. These findings support a basic sociological premise: social realities do not need to be grounded in facts.

Anglo Leaders of Middlewest

Most Anglo leaders own or manage businesses in the community, and all of them participate extensively in community affairs. Dale Douglas, the owner of the local radio station, has a long history of community leadership. He remains affable and enthusiastic after years of service. Over the years, Douglas has directed more community projects than any other local leader. His latest accomplishment was spearheading the drive to pass the bond for the new elementary school. He has the respect of his fellow leaders, and his reputation derives from him being a cheerleader for the community. His optimism is contagious and his humility prevents petty jealousies.

In our interview, Douglas boosterism rang as genuine. His work ethic in relation to his business would likely withstand the judgment of the Puritans, as would his religious commitment. He started working as an announcer and now owns two radio stations. He did not brag about his accomplishments; neither did it appear that wealth was his objective. Robert Bellah et al. (1985) believe America has lost its moral direction because the country has so few people like Dale Douglas. But Douglas, the model citizen, has little recognition of or sensitivity concerning the Mexican American community; he lacks the ability to reach across the chasm of racial and cultural differences.

Small towns present many opportunities for those seeking to participate in social life. Many community leaders said they like Middlewest because it is small enough to allow them to play leadership roles. They believe their actions can make a difference in community affairs. Sam Huff, a veterinarian and president of the Rotary Club, thinks that the Rotary Club has the most prestige among the service clubs. He proudly reviewed the many community projects completed by his club. Sam's views on community service are commendable: "The way I was taught is you have to give back to your community."

Anglo community leaders affectionately recall the contributions of three senior citizens to the community. Several people told me that if I wanted to know Middlewest I would have to interview Betsy Griffin.

Betsy Griffin's community involvement and attitudes towards Mexican Americans were representative of those of these elderly citizens. She is the unofficial town historian and has collected community photos all her life. She started by displaying the pictures of people, buildings, and social events on the walls of the family business. Soon others began to donate their family photos to her collection. For the Middlewest centennial Betsy published a photographic history of early Middlewest. She also produced a centennial calendar as a fund-raising item, and the centennial committee sold more than 1,000 calendars. Each date featured an account of a special event in the history of Middlewest. As a member of the centennial commission, Betsy worked for months to organize the summer celebrations, and she reported that large crowds came out to enjoy the parade and picnic.

Betsy Griffin has developed six different slide shows on the history of Middlewest, and local elementary schools request her slide presentations. She loves Middlewest. My interview with Betsy was pleasant and lasted some four hours as she showed and explained to me the community photographs.

Betsy's pleasure halted when she expressed her concern with the decline of the community. She surmised that the decline coincided with the arrival of Mexican Americans, who she stereotyped as "prone to crime." Betsy's history of Middlewest does not include the Mexican Americans. She commented: "What's happening to Middlewest is Little Mexico. There is a lot of consternation in Middlewest, these brown people, this is the way the town is going. This goes hand-in-hand with the crime going up, there are some nice ones, but they cause the crime. . . . The high school is tying itself in knots, gun-carrying

Mexican gangs, not a product of our local society. In my book, my opinion, Middlewest used to be a very nice, clean, law-abiding town until this Mexican thing; they're a bad element.... My daughter came to visit last summer, she left her purse in the car, you have to lock up your house these days.... The park is a nice city park, but everything is going downhill—this is the Mexicans."

Jack Smith owns a prosperous business on the boulevard and is a member of several economic development committees. Jack remains optimistic about the possibility of Middlewest regaining its economic vitality. He believes that economic development has to be the "top priority" of the community, because without such "progress" the community will further decline. For Jack, "low morale and negative self-image" are the biggest problems for the community. He believes that the community leaders get unnecessarily involved in petty bickering. Jack had the following comments on the Mexican American community.

> They [Mexican Americans] are the negative element in town. They are always in the newspaper and TV for committing some crime. You soon develop a negative impression. There are different strata: the ones that live here year-around, then you have the migrant class. The migrants are the worst, they run a drug pipeline.... The Mexican American community is very inactive. They are outside the town's decision-making. This fuels the discriminating thinking because all you see is negative, negative. They have no involvement in the town, so we have no interaction with them. This creates a lot of barriers. There is always a negative undercurrent. In the store everyone knows the shoplifters are Mexicans. Whenever there is a crime in Middlewest the first thought is that it is a Mexican.

Bill Johnson has lived in Middlewest for six years. His successful business enables him to take a leadership role. He belongs to the Rotary Club, Middlewest Unlimited, and the city council. Johnson likes Middlewest because of its friendly people and quality schools. His children attend the local college.

However, Johnson's family has less enthusiasm for Middlewest's lack of shopping opportunities and lack of entertainment. He made the following observations: "Yeah, an interesting Mexican American situation, you got the migrants and those who own property here. From my perspective on the city council it appears to be a fact—the drug problem and the crime problem is tied to the Mexican American community. We had to close down some of the Mexican bars. Yes, Middlewest has a serious crime problem. The migrants bring drugs over the border, so we have drug trafficking here. We also have a shoplifting ring. They sell the merchandise at fifty percent of the sticker price. They have a girls club; you have to shoplift to become a member."

I asked Bill Johnson about the positive aspects of having Mexican Americans living in Middlewest; his response was typical of the Anglo community's attitude. "Well, they are citizens, I guess. This is interesting, they are difficult to bring into the mainstream. It's an embarrassing question you ask; [I] have to struggle to come up with an answer. They contribute basically as workers. We have nothing from that community at this point. I don't know if they have any leaders; the Mexican Americans don't attend the city council meetings.... A couple of years ago there was a Mexican American dance. The entire police force was called out, had to put people in jail. They were throwing stuff around; it was really a mess."

Ted Beck, a bank manager, enjoys living in a small town. He likes Middlewest as a place to raise his children; however, he is not optimistic about the economic future of Middlewest. Beck believes that the town lacks a substantial middle class that can build the community. For him, the economic problems of the town exist because of the Simplex Corporation and the other local large companies. This is because the big companies only pay five or six dollars an hour to their employees. Ted serves on the United Way board, the Chamber of Commerce board, and leads a boy scout troop. He expressed the following about the local Mexican Americans:

> I get frustrated with the crime problem; people will not acknowledge the problem originates in the Mexican

American community. Everyone knows it; sounds racist, [but] I am not a racist. We act like the Mexican Americans aren't here; there is little interaction between the two communities. Middlewest has been tolerant of crime because the victim and the perpetrator are Mexican American. To live by Mexican Americans is frustrating. My son is in junior high; I really have to work with him. He has developed a prejudiced view, but you can't blame him. The Mexican Americans have different values. The gang issue is a big problem in the schools. They do not value education. You go to a school parent meeting and there are hundreds of parents there but only two Mexican Americans. It is fair to say they do not value education. They are also a discipline problem in the schools. They are not inferior, but their values are inferior. I have problems with Mexican Americans in this town.

Daniel Hobson is the owner of the large printing shop named after his great-grandfather. He said:

Downtown will always be a problem until we clean up the minority group and the crime they produce for Middlewest. We will never be able to do anything until we take care of crime; no one will ever want to come here and start a business, that's my feeling.... The Mexican Americans play a very detrimental role in Middlewest; they are the bad element. Sure, I know some good ones, but they are so outnumbered by ones that do nothing except fights, break-ins, and do damage to the town. I don't have much use for them.... Yes, we have more poverty in Middlewest because of the Mexican Americans. They don't want to work, they prefer to be on welfare. We pay workers $5.50 an hour to start—a good-paying job. We never have had a Mexican apply for work here.

The opinions of the Anglo leaders profiled are representative of the community's views concerning the Mexican Americans of Middlewest. Pleasant men and women can be racially intolerant. These Anglo leaders care about their community and donate much of their time to improve the quality of life in Middlewest. Still, they avoid and deny responsibility for the Mexican American community. The harsh image of Mexican Americans held throughout the Anglo community reinforces the leaders' biases.

Kelly Moffit, the chair of a business association, became my most important Anglo informant because of her continuous interaction with the Anglo business and civic leaders of Middlewest. She made the following comments on the town's business climate:

> The businessmen want a magic wand to fix up the downtown. They have a learned helplessness. They just had the business handed to them. They have never really had to go to work. They want the chamber to fix it. My God, they charge twice as much for their merchandise as the shopping center. They have no drive, they don't want any changes in Middlewest.... The economic development effort is lost in shooting each other down; everyone has a hidden agenda. They are constantly involved in petty infighting, trying to sabotage one another. The positive thing is we're getting some new people involved who have a lot of energy. These younger business people could turn things around.

Kelly Moffit made the following remarks on sexism in Middlewest. "Oh God, you would ask about the women's issue; it's a nightmare. They pat you on the head; they pay no attention to the women leaders, but they want us to do the work. If we talk too much they call us bitches.... I am a Republican, but people on the chamber think I am a liberal."

In reference to how Anglo leaders view Mexican Americans, Kelly said:

> The leaders and the community ignore and deny the existence, as much as they can, of the Mexican Americans.

The poverty is terrible and there are no social services, no counseling for the Mexican American families with problems. We were thinking of having some of the Mexican American leaders involved in our leadership training program, to present the Mexican American view. People told us to invite the police to talk about the Mexican Americans. Can you believe it? I hear the businessmen talking about the Mexican Americans all the time: it's always the fault of the Mexican Americans. They don't want them in town; they want them to stay in the labor camps. They have absolutely no cultural sensitivity. . . . The school administrators say everything is fine [concerning Mexican Americans]; they have their heads in the sand. All the superintendent does is play a great game of public relations.

I interviewed some younger Anglo professionals and businessmen who operate in a modern fashion and who compete against their counterparts in Boise. These individuals appear preoccupied with becoming successful. They generally did not have prejudicial views about Mexican Americans but they had little knowledge of or interest in Mexican American issues. These men had little interest in becoming community leaders.

The sociologist can never completely capture the diversity of social life in a community. Many Anglos in Middlewest live their lives without exhibiting prejudice. Most of these seem to give little thought to the existence of the Mexican Americans in their community. Some Anglos are sensitive to the problems facing Mexican Americans. Vern Gossett has a small auto repair shop. Though inarticulate on the race issue, he is sympathetic and attempts to assist Mexican Americans. He has two Mexican Americans working in his garage and he does not mind that they speak Spanish.

Kelly Moffitt informed me that there exists a small group of local progressives that includes a teacher, a businesswoman, a school administrator, and a lawyer who recognize the problems facing Mexican Americans. This group, though they maintain a low profile, attempts to assist and support the Mexican American community. For example, they assisted in organizing the community's Cinco de Mayo celebration. However, during the period of my field research, their actions were infrequent and lacking in significance.

Using Sociological Thought

The view that people create a set of ideas about the nature of human behavior and then proceed to interpret the behavior of people in their community as proof of their explanation of social reality is common in many sociological theories. The idea of ideological colonialism is connected to the classical theory of Durkheim (1938), who analyzed how value consensus is necessary in order for a society to function; that is, in order to function, people must agree on what is appropriate behavior. Durkheim recognized that groups operating outside that value consensus are rejected and held to be criminal.

Contemporary symbolic interactionists (Berger and Luckmann 1967) take Durkheim a step further by holding that social reality is constructed by people in social interaction with one another. They also appreciate the arbitrary nature of the social reality that people construct. If we apply this set of concepts to the Anglos of Middlewest, we can appreciate its applicability. The Anglos of Middlewest have developed a set of values and behavior for which there is a high degree of consensus. They consider their way of life to be "sacred" in the Durkheimian sense. Mexican Americans are viewed as outsiders even though, as we will see in the next chapter, they have similar values and live much like their Anglo neighbors. Some of the behavior of the Mexican American community is different, and this difference is magnified to the point that the Anglos, through social interaction with one another, create the belief that Mexican Americans have many negative behavioral characteristics. The Anglo community has very selectively taken small portions of Mexican American life and made them the central features of their perception of Mexican American life. The results of this distorted view are very disturbing. As we will see in the following chapters, Anglo ideas about the Mexican American community lead to the unequal and unjust treatment of Mexican Americans in Middlewest.

As we have seen, the Anglo community of Middlewest has a basic pattern of conformity fostered by the nature of small-town life. The shared public discourse produces a single-mindedness in the Anglo community. Most Anglos had a standard set of stories about important events in Middlewest. The relative absence of diverse values and attitudes inhibits the Anglo community from experiencing much self-doubt about its values. This means that few question the treatment and view of the Mexican American community.

A contributing factor to the general conformity is that most Anglo citizens and leaders have little experience outside their community. The Anglos of Middlewest have a difficult time accepting Anglo outsiders; they have even more difficulty accepting people of a different color and culture.

Anglos make both positive and negative comments concerning the Mexican American population of Middlewest. They frequently ended a series of prejudicial remarks with a positive comment about Mexican Americans. Such statements seem to be an attempt to offset their racist comments. "Mexican Americans commit 80 percent of the crime in Middlewest, but I know some good Mexican Americans."

A critical insight from my field research was the recognition that many people have no cognizance that their views are in fact racist. A corollary finding suggests that the more racist the person is, the less that person perceives racism in Middlewest. For example, Anglos would present a litany of prejudicial comments about Mexican Americans and then proceed to deny that the remarks suggest any racism on their part.

Summary

Obviously all Anglos in Middlewest are not racist. Many live their lives with little involvement with Mexican Americans; these people often remain neutral toward Mexican American issues. Since they and their friends seldom discuss the race situation in their community, they assume little racism exists there. One of the keys to improving race relations in Middlewest would be for these people and the progressive group of Anglos who are concerned about the problems facing the Mexican American community to take a more vocal and active role in developing programs to improve race relations. This group should solicit the assistance of those young professionals who are not involved in community affairs. To date the progressive group has been overly concerned about avoiding community conflict.

I did interview a few business/civic leaders who appreciate the serious degree of racism in Middlewest. Yet most of these Anglos responded in a paternalistic manner toward Mexican Americans. For example, Beth Smith, the city administrator, viewed herself as a liberal, sympathetic toward Mexican Americans. However, in public meetings with Mexican American leaders her comments contained a plethora of insensitive racial presumptions. Her remarks revealed her sense that Mexican Americans need the benevolence of Anglos because of their limited abilities.

Beth Smith did not consider Middlewest to have a serious race problem. She remained unaware of the racism in city government: she did not think that any discrimination existed in spite of the fact that only two of the city's 125 employees are Mexican American. Beth did not realize that the Mexican American deputy clerk in her office complex faced racial problems. The deputy clerk reported: "The administrators bypass me and they don't send me the memos that everyone else gets. I don't get any recognition or respect; it's because I am Mexican American. The former city clerk could not stand my being Mexican American. She would not talk to me. She was always trying to get me fired. . . . The racism in the city departments is unbelievable. When there is a job opening, they always hire Anglos."

In the spring of 1991 the mayor of Middlewest established a committee of Mexican Americans and Anglos to promote a celebration of community unity. The "Pursuit of Unity" group decided to hold a Cinco de Mayo celebration that would include the participation of the Anglo community. The group spent several months planning this celebration, which commenced with a walk from city hall to the park. *Charros*, or Mexican trick riders, led the march. Mexican American contestants for Miss Cinco de Mayo rode in convertibles as part of the mini-parade.

A warm and sunny spring day coincided with the celebration. Mexican food and craft booths attracted a crowd. A fiesta atmosphere developed because of the enthusiastic entertainers performing in brightly colored attire. The singing and dancing were infectious—the crowd displayed broad smiles and a tendency to greet and meet other people. The mayor, the director of the chamber of commerce, and Mexican American leaders addressed those attending the celebration with remarks suitable to the occasion. Lorenzo Ocho, a young Mexican American leader, doubled as the master of ceremony and as a performer. The organizers and participants declared the fiesta a success; however, 90 percent of the entertainment and 90 percent of the people attending came from the Mexican American community, indicating that the pursuit of unity could be generally limited to the Mexican Americans of Middlewest.

Photo courtesty Boise State University News Service

José and Marizela Elizalde performing a traditional folk dance.

Photo by Richard Baker

A family photography session following the traditional wedding of
Rosário Saldivar and Ricardo Navarrete.

Chapter 3

MEXICAN AMERICAN CULTURE AND DAILY LIFE

I am Joaquin,
lost in a world of confusion,
caught up in the whirl of a gringo society,
confused by the rules,
scorned by attitudes,
suppressed by manipulation,
and destroyed by modern society.
                                    –Rodolfo Gonzáles

Introduction

The Mexican Americans of Middlewest and Farm County have a rich and multifaceted culture. A few unpublished reports have examined certain aspects of their role in the early settlement of the state, but there is no written history of Mexican Americans in Idaho.

In the nineteenth century, a few Mexican Americans worked in Idaho as miners, cowboys, and as railroad workers. However, Laurie Mercier and Carole Simon-Smolinski (1990) estimate that at the beginning of the twentieth century fewer than 100 Mexican Americans lived in Idaho. They consider the arrival of Mexican Americans to be associated with the development of agriculture in Idaho starting in the early 1900s. Sugar-beet farmers at that time actively recruited Mexican American workers from South Texas and Mexico. According to Mercier and Simon-Smolenski, in the 1920s approximately 1,000 Mexican

Americans lived in Idaho. Much of the history (as yet to be told) of Mexican Americans in Idaho is connected to their role as migrant agricultural workers.

Most of the Mexican Americans interviewed for this study had at one time been migrant field workers. Pat Ourada (1979) and Erasmo Gamboa (1990), historians who have partially documented the evolution of migrant Mexican Americans in Idaho, agree that the Bracero program from 1942 to 1964, an established agreement between the governments of Mexico and the United States, assisted Idaho farmers to obtain Mexican workers during and after World War II. The Bracero program initiated a movement that continues to this day. People of Mexican American heritage remain the primary group of Idaho farm workers.

Today, most Mexican American field workers in southwestern Idaho come from south Texas and Mexico. Ourada and Gamboa agree that during the Bracero program the Mexican American migrant workers suffered low wages, miserable housing conditions, and racial discrimination. The Mexican American migrant workers participated in periodic protests and strikes to attempt to remedy these inequities. Gamboa, whose work is more comprehensive, has examined the Bracero program in Idaho, Washington, and Oregon.

Gamboa documents the fact that Mexican migrant workers in Idaho received harsher treatment than did those in Oregon and Washington. The Mexican consul in Portland went so far as to cancel the Bracero program for two years in Idaho because of the mistreatment of the Mexican farm workers. The abuse of Mexican Americans in Middlewest could be seen to continue this practice today. Among the Mexican Americans interviewed were some older men who migrated from Texas in the late 1950s and early 1960s. They vividly recall seeing signs in the windows of business establishments warning, "No Mexicans or Dogs Allowed," and they claim that public facilities also displayed these signs.

Population Data and Field Research Techniques

In 1955 the U.S. Public Health Service reported that 21,000 Mexican American migrants came annually to Idaho. However, even in 1960, only 3,341 Mexican Americans resided permanently in Idaho. Today, most Idaho Mexican Americans still work as farm workers and laborers, their average income being two-thirds that of Anglos in Idaho. Many Mexican Americans still work for a minimum wage. It was estimated in 1990 that 33 percent of Mexican Americans live in poverty in Idaho. In my field research, I interviewed some Mexican American businessmen and professionals; but, as the above statistics indicate, most Mexican Americans are still at or near the bottom of the economic ladder.

Because of the high number of Mexican Americans in the poverty category, where they are less likely to be counted, demographers have a difficult time estimating the number of Mexican Americans in Idaho. The statistics also are complicated by the significant number of migrants who come into the state regularly. Another problem in obtaining an accurate count of Mexican Americans occurs because of the many undocumented Mexican migrant farm workers in Idaho. It has been estimated that between 10,000 and 30,000 undocumented Mexican workers come to Idaho each year. Under the Immigration Reform and Control Act (IRCA) of 1986 approximately 11,000 undocumented Mexicans have applied for amnesty in Idaho.

When interviewing Mexican Americans, I asked them to share their daily life experiences and how they believe Mexican American life differs from that of the Anglos in Middlewest. I asked Mexican Americans particularly about their important cultural practices. As with any group, some respondents were more verbal, more articulate, and more thorough in their responses to interview questions. Many subjects needed some assistance, by way of examples, to enable them to analyze the taken-for-granted aspects of their lives.

Interviews with 210 Mexican Americans enabled me to construct a facsimile reproduction of Mexican American culture in Middlewest and Farm County. I am confident that although the following analysis is incomplete, it does represent the main features of Mexican American culture in Idaho. The accuracy of the cultural analysis derives from my discussions with key Mexican American informants willing to share in depth with me their knowledge of Mexican American cultural practices. It should be noted that this cultural analysis must be seen as an ideal type, meaning that no subject entirely participates in all the features of his/her culture. The existence of cultural traits does not preclude the existence of a multitude of unique personalities within this cultural framework. It is important to keep in mind that later in this chapter there will be a discussion of a typology of Mexican Americans.

Family Life

The most significant cultural trait among Mexican Americans of Middlewest is their family life. Most Mexican Americans I interviewed recognized the importance of this aspect of their lives. Mexican Americans spend much of their non-working time with their families. Many adult Mexican Americans call their parents every day and have dinner with them nearly every weekend. Mexican Americans report that their most frequent social activity is joining with relatives for activities. In the summer this generally means a family barbecue. The extended family celebrates both American and Mexican holidays together.

The intimacy of kin means that Mexican Americans are less individualistic than Anglos. Family loyalty and support goes unquestioned. Mexican Americans agree that they have the responsibility to support their extended family both financially and emotionally. Mexican Americans contend that Anglos do not appreciate the preeminence of family relations for Mexican Americans or the family solidarity that remains strong across generations. Davis (1990) believes that the almost sacred importance of the family derives from the influence of the indigenous peoples of Mexico.

In Mexican American families the children do not leave home when they become adults, as they commonly do in Anglo society. Some young married adults live with their parents, though this is in part due to economic factors. Mexican Americans perceive it as natural for single adults to live at home. Mexican American parents do not feel comfortable with the Anglo norm that has the single young adult being on his or her own. Four generations live together in some Mexican American households.

The primacy of family relations means that Mexican American children generally respect their parents. They do not question their parents' authority or talk back to them. Mexican American youths do not address their parents unless granted permission. One example of the value placed on respect for parents was provided by a young married Mexican American woman who said that, though her father passed away five years ago, she still turns off her car radio when she drives by his grave.

Mexican American culture holds a high regard for the elderly. Mexican Americans uniformly assert that they would never send their parents to nursing homes. The Mexican American migrant family does not leave the grandparents in Texas. In the labor camps, grandmothers take care of their grandchildren while the parents work in the fields. Most Mexican Americans believe that family loyalty can always be counted on despite one's transgressions.

An adjunct to Mexican American family life is the *comadre/ compadre* relationship. The comadre (female) or compadre (male) is a special friend, or it can also signify a god-parent. This relationship becomes an extension of the family support system. Such persons can be counted on for emotional and financial support. They have designated roles in baptismal and confirmation ceremonies, for which they often provide financial support. A family generally only has a few such friends, but in Middlewest this relationship has been extended because of the increased need for financial support.

Padrinos, a Spanish term that also refers to co-parents, are expected to contribute financially to the expenses of marriages and *Quinceañeras* (the celebration of a girl's fifteenth birthday). Most Mexican American families see padrinos as surrogate relatives.

Mexican American culture creates a number of intimate bonds that do not exist to the same extent in Anglo society. Mexican Americans view themselves as less individualistic than Anglos (Schaefer 1991). Mexican American life, as a consequence of the close social bonds, requires "sharing" among those close to each other. These types of relationships often allow Mexican Americans to express their emotions to a greater extent than Anglos. The intimacy developed in the extended family and compadres creates an intimate social atmosphere that affects all social interaction. Anglos place the highest value on individual success, whereas Mexican Americans will not sacrifice their social obligations for individual rewards. For example, Mexican American youth frequently quit school to work because their large families need the financial assistance.

Social Traits

The Mexican American community appears to emit more warmth than the "cooler" Anglo culture. Father Acuna told me that his Anglo parishioners requested him to stop hugging them after mass. In contrast, Mexican Americans regularly express an intimacy and warmth when they greet and mingle. For Mexican Americans it is not inappropriate to touch one another in a non-sexual manner; they are genuinely happy to see their friends and they express it.

Mexican American social relations rely more on personal relationships than on formal social structures. For example, Don Juarez asked me to be his advisor at the university because Sue Peña, a Mexican American leader, had recommended me. Many Anglo students at the university want the fastest possible interaction with their advisors and the university bureaucracy. All some want is a quick signature so that they may quickly depart. Don wanted me to know both him and his family. He also wanted to know me beyond my role as an academic advisor. He has been in to see me three times for a total of an hour and a half, enabling me to know Don as a real person and not just an advisee whose name I cannot remember.

In the Mexican American community people share limited resources. Mexican Americans know that they can rely on family, relatives, and sometimes padrinos if they need emergency financial assistance. Part of the sharing within the Mexican American community exists as an adaptation to the conditions of poverty. Sharing occurs regularly among Mexican Americans, in contrast to that among Anglos. The funerals of poor Mexican Americans provide good examples of the sharing trait. During my field research, on three occasions Mexican American leaders organized the collection of donations to finance funeral expenses. In one case, a Mexican American migrant family was passing through Middlewest when their sick child died. Although the family had no relatives or friends in town, the Idaho Migrant Council organized a fund-raising drive and collected enough money to pay the funeral expenses.

Father Acuna was born and raised in Mexico. He has given careful thought to how the Mexican culture differs from that of the United States. In his role as priest, he ministers to these two groups separately. Father Acuna thinks Mexicans "enjoy" life more than Americans. He said that Anglos go around looking "so serious" all the time. In Mexican culture, time is not such a controlling factor in a person's life as it is in the U.S. For Mexicans, personal relationships are more important than either time or money; it is not as important to be economically successful in Mexican culture.

Father Acuna went on to say that Anglos are "cold" when compared to Mexicans. However, Mexican Americans' retention of cultural traits appears to depend on their level of adaptation to American culture. Father Acuna said that to recognize the cultural difference one need only compare an Anglo church social with a Chicano church social. He explained that the Chicano event will have music, dancing, and singing that creates a "warm and happy" state of mind, while he sees the Anglo church social as a "dull and boring" affair because everyone remains serious.

Father Acuna cited Octavio Paz (1985) to claim that the Mexican American character reveals both a sense of inferiority and a sense of melancholy. This attitude leads to a certain sense of fatalism, which is hidden by a sense of privacy and a social mask worn to hide the emotions. This originated with the Mexicans having been conquered by the Spanish; it was then extenuated by the United States' conquest of half of Mexico. This sense of inferiority has been furthered by the subordination of the Mexican American population within the United States. A Mexican American social worker in Middlewest said that shame is a critical factor in his work with Mexican American clients; his continuous concern is to avoid shaming his clients.

Cultural Clashes

The closeness of family and kin results in some problems for Mexican Americans as they interact with Anglo society. Mexican American culture recognizes the extended family as one unit, whereas Anglo culture only recognizes the nuclear family. The Farmers Home Administration (FHA) limits the number of individuals who can live in one dwelling, and the labor camps for Mexican American migrant workers have regulations concerning housing occupancy. The Anglo managers of these labor camps are insensitive to Mexican American culture, and they evict extended Mexican American families because the rules allow only a nuclear family to reside in the apartments. Anglo managers often interpret the Mexican American living arrangements as being an attempt to "cheat on their rent." The managers are also indifferent to the poverty of Mexican American migrants that forces families to violate the regulation limiting the number of residents allowed to reside in an apartment.

A second problem arising from cultural differences develops from Anglo teachers believing Mexican American students to be disinterested in school because those students follow their culture's practice of subservient interaction with adults. Mexican American children and adolescents normally avert their eyes from adults and do not participate in class discussions. Many Anglo teachers infer from this that Mexican American youth do not respect them and that they lack intelligence because of their silence.

David Barrera, a former student at Boise State University whom I interviewed, has an excellent understanding of the problems and issues facing the Mexican American community. When he was a student in my class, David did not participate in class discussions even when they involved Idaho's Mexican Americans. I later commented on his lack of participation and how enriching his observations would have been for the class. His response was that it was just too uncomfortable for him to speak in class even though a considerable portion of the grade in this class depended on class participation.

A third problem involves Mexican American youth interacting in both the Mexican American and Anglo cultures. Mexican American adolescents typically want to participate and succeed in Anglo society; but first-generation, Spanish-speaking Mexican American parents find themselves at a disadvantage when they try to assist their children. The parents feel inadequate because they generally cannot afford the clothes and spending money needed, and these situations then can lead to intrafamilial conflicts for some Mexican American parents and their children. As a result, some youth look to their peers for behavioral cues, and the result of that can be antisocial behavior.

Some young Mexican American women resent the strict family control of their behavior. The Mexican tradition of protecting young women continues in many Mexican American families in Middlewest. Young women do not have the same freedoms as young men: many adolescent girls cannot date; sometimes an older brother will monitor the behavior and the friends of his sister. One adolescent girl said that her older brother monitors her telephone calls.

One aspect of family solidarity requires Mexican American youth to relinquish their paychecks to their parents. Mexican Americans do not consider this practice to be exploitative. Many Mexican American youths work because of their families' poverty; some Anglos consider this practice to be unfair.

Another feature of Mexican American life in Middlewest involves migrant workers "settling out," that is, deciding to live permanently in Middlewest. The presence of new residents from southern Texas and Mexico helps preserve Mexican American culture in Middlewest. However, new immigrants from Mexico, some legal and some undocumented, generally do not speak

English and many of them only have an elementary education. Many Anglos do not recognize this continuous migration. They believe these new immigrants have lived in the United States for many years, which then leads them to believe that Mexican Americans do not want to learn English and that they do not want to be educated. This erroneous perception leads many Anglos to think that Mexican Americans lack the intelligence to adapt to the dominant society.

While attending a Mexican American Issues Conference in Boise in the fall of 1992, I met a young Mexican American male attending Idaho State University. He made some insightful comments about the cultural shock he experienced returning to the university setting after spending three years in Mexico. He had grown up in Idaho but his family returned to Mexico because of a death in the family. He said he fell in love with Mexico; the effect of the country on his identity was profound and he became Mexican. The traditions and culture had some effect but the daily life and the closeness to nature most impressed him. Upon his return to the university, he found that he was unable to deal with the stress and the coldness of Anglo culture. He said it wasn't until he had been to Mexico that he could see how impersonal American social interaction was. He claimed that nobody knew him or cared about him at the university. He dropped out of college but returned to school after working in the fields for two years.

Machismo

Sociologists have a continuous debate over the authenticity of machismo as a trait of Mexican American males. Are Mexican American males more aggressive and tyrannical in their relationships with their families and with other Mexican American males as Paz (1985) suggests? Mirande (1985) believes that Anglo social scientists have helped to create a negative image of Mexican Americans and that they have inaccurately depicted the typical Chicano male as being violent and abusive.

However, two female social scientists, Blea (1980) and Horowitz (1986), report from their community studies that Mexican

American culture does indeed involve male dominance. The Chicano perspective of masculinity is one that views men and women as having distinct gender roles, with the male having a higher status in male-female relationships. The studies found that the Chicano father was perceived as being the head of the family and the person making the major decisions in the home. Blea and Horowitz agree with Mirande that male dominance does not include a license for violence and family abuse. This account would probably also be accurate for the majority of Anglo families.

Mexican American males and females I interviewed agreed that machismo does not condone violent behavior or family abuse. The analysis of machismo can be illuminated by viewing the father's behavior on a continuum. Those Mexican American males least assimilated into American culture exercise more control in their family decisions. For example, Sara Zabala grew up in Middlewest. She had worked for five years as a secretary prior to meeting her husband, who had only been in the U.S. for two years. After the couple married, Sara's husband did not think it appropriate for her to keep her credit cards or to go out unescorted in the evening.

The machismo factor is reduced when partners have long resided in the United States or when the wife works outside the home. The majority of Mexican American families interviewed did not think the term machismo was an accurate description of Mexican American males' behavior. They did say that older males are more likely to make decisions within the family. I interviewed several Mexican American males who had the responsibility for child care when their wives worked. Contrary to the machismo stereotype, most Mexican American males I interviewed were warm, gentle, and hospitable. My interviews with Mexican American males leads me to agree with Mirande's (1985) idea that the concept of machismo represents another negative stereotype of Mexican Americans that serves to justify the criminalization of Mexican American males who resist their oppressive conditions.

The Anglo community views adolescent Mexican American males who join gangs as examples of the machismo feature of

Mexican American culture. They condemn the physical violence practiced by these youths while denying the psychological violence that the schools have perpetrated against them. This point will be expanded upon in Chapter Nine.

Many Anglos believe that Mexican American culture and machismo force Mexican American males into fights. These Anglos acquire this perception from the police reports and the mass media; their knowledge of Mexican American culture often encompasses only what they see on television and read in the newspaper.

Language

Mexican Americans consider their language a crucial element of their culture; Spanish is a key source of identification and pride. Mexican Americans feel a sense of satisfaction when hearing their language spoken. Many Mexican American leaders who are fluent in English commented on their sense of relaxation and enjoyment when engaging in a Spanish conversation. One's language assists in creating and sustaining one's identity.

Language provides a way of seeing and understanding the world, and it cannot be separated from a people's culture. One cannot fully appreciate a culture unless its language is known. Mexican Americans told me that their ideas and feelings are not always translatable. One tangible verification of the importance of language is found in the fact that many Mexican Americans "code switch." In code switching a person uses both English and Spanish interchangeably because the languages do not always express the same things; different languages create different social realities.

Code switching is an interesting phenomenon that has been studied by Rosaura Sanchez (1983). As she sees it, the Mexican Americans who are most likely to use code switching are those who are concerned about their social mobility. She views code switching as a reaction to the subordinant/dominant relationship that exists between Mexican Americans and Anglos. Mexican Americans attempting to enhance their social standing use code switching. Code switching is viewed by Sanchez as a part of assimilation among its many additional functions that are not relevant to this analysis.

Language can function as an indicator of ethnicity. Some non-Spanish-speaking Mexican Americans lament their linguistic inability: whenever they attend Mexican American social events most of the conversation is in Spanish. It is interesting that Mexican American names such as Humberto, Julio, Francisco, Hermelinda, Serafina, Amalia are properly pronounced with a soft and romantic connotation. Some Anglos anglicize or harden the names of Mexican Americans, so that José becomes Joe.

Mexican Americans born and raised in Middlewest are unlikely to be fluent in Spanish. Many parents who want their children to succeed place an emphasis on their children learning English. However, the grandparents dislike the fact that their grandchildren cannot speak Spanish. Many Mexican American families in Middlewest have numerous children. In these homes it was not uncommon to find that the older children could speak Spanish while the younger ones could not. The children who begin grade school in Middlewest spend most of their time speaking English; it is difficult for these children to become fluent in Spanish.

Some Mexican American parents teach their children Spanish at home. There is a stigma attached to Mexican Americans who cannot speak Spanish. The adult Mexican Americans generally regret their inability to speak Spanish, but Mexican American adolescents often do not, because they see themselves as participating in the larger social domain. Nearly all Mexican Americans recognize the need to speak English if they are to be economically successful.

Liz Jarvez claimed that her daughters never spoke a word of English until they went to school. Her parents treated her and her siblings the same, always speaking Spanish in the home. Liz concluded, "My children had to learn Spanish; I didn't want them to forget who they are."

English Language Bill

An understanding of the racism in Middlewest requires an examination of the English language controversy. Anglos in Middlewest overwhelmingly support a bill introduced in the state legislature each year by their local legislator designating English as the official language of Idaho. They presented some of their reasons:

"If you are going to live in America you have to speak English."

"We don't want a situation like in Quebec."

"If I went to Mexico to live, I would learn Spanish."

"If these people are going to get ahead they have to learn how to speak English."

"Look at the other immigrants to America; they gave up their languages."

Anglos in Middlewest have an endless repertoire of complaints about Mexican Americans speaking Spanish. Anglos believe it to be impolite when Mexican Americans speak Spanish in the presence of Anglos. They also sometimes think Mexican Americans are talking about them. Many Anglos erroneously believe that all Mexican Americans have lived in Middlewest for a long time and, therefore, they all should be able to speak English.

Certain Anglos declare that Mexican Americans know how to speak English but refuse to do so. Many Anglos fail to recognize that many Mexican Americans understand English but feel embarrassed by their pronunciation. Anglos do not appreciate the fact that adults, especially those with limited formal education, have a difficult and intimidating experience when they attempt to learn a foreign language.

Some Anglos justify their demand for English by stating that the inability to speak English will interfere with the speedy transaction of business. They claim that they think job directives and safety become problematic if workers do not speak English.

Race relations are complicated social realities. On the one hand, one could interpret Anglo concerns about Mexican Americans speaking English as a matter of good will—they want

Mexican Americans to participate in society. However, Anglo decision makers regularly reject programs that would assist Mexican Americans to learn English. The rationalizations employed by Anglos contain a twisted logic that suggests empathy but often reveals a belief that Mexican American culture is inferior to the dominant culture.

Anglos do not believe the requirement to speak English is ethnocentric. However, most Mexican American subjects oppose this legislation. When interviewing Anglos in the latter part of my field research, I informed them of Mexican Americans' feelings about the English language bill. The Anglos did not then change their opinion; they continued to insist that English be the official language.

The English-only view is indirectly an Anglo demand for conformity. Anglos in Middlewest from the mayor and the ministers to the working class want Mexican Americans to assimilate. Mexican American culture is linked to social problems. The following quote comes from a Anglo civic leader and is representative of the dominant attitude about language and assimilation: "I support the English language view. I oppose the bilingual thing. If they [Mexican Americans] make a decision to live in America then they have to learn English. This is how America was formed. I don't want to sound like a redneck but immigrants have to meld."

School administrators in Middlewest support the English language bill and they have not provided leadership in creating bilingual programs for Mexican American students. The lack of adequate bilingual education for Mexican Americans is one of the major causes of the high Mexican American student dropout rate. The net result of the English-only view is that Mexican American youths do not graduate and will be relegated to the lower echelon job market. The exploitive model contends that Mexican Americans face oppressive conditions. Most Anglos do not understand this and scoff at the idea of oppression, but the failure to educate Mexican American youth means that most of them will be forced to live in poverty.

Language is a key feature of any culture. Many Anglos in Middlewest will not listen to the Mexican American point of view and, without recognizing it, are indirectly demanding that Mexican Americans change their identities and their culture. The intensity with which Anglos support the language bill suggests their high level of discomfort with the Mexican American people in Middlewest.

A minority whose culture is denied rarely adapts well to another culture. The demand for general assimilation into Anglo culture results in alienated people who do not know the appropriate behavior in either culture. The narrow interpretation of American history as basically Anglo-European misses the fact that America is fundamentally a multicultural society. This diversity provides rich cultural resources for enhancing our lives and enabling us to better understand the human condition and human diversity.

A sociological evaluation of the English language issue reveals a coded message: the English language bill represents a symbolic form of racism. Such a bill, if passed, would be unenforceable, impractical, and demeaning. Estella Medina said it best: "Language is what I am as a person. This English language bill is stepping on a person—an injury. They are telling us Mexican Americans that there is something wrong with us, that we are second-class citizens. It also assumes that we have no loyalty to America. The English language bill is a real slap in the face."

Mexican American leaders point out that many advantages accrue to those who are bilingual. The opportunities for employment are enhanced for those who speak more than one language. One sign of being an educated person is to be able to speak a foreign language.

Food

Mexican Americans have a distinctive cuisine, and the majority of Middlewest's Mexican American people said they eat Mexican food 75 percent of the time. However, the longer a Mexican American family lives in Idaho, the less likely they are to eat Mexican food. The Mexican food prepared in the homes of Mexican Americans is not the Mexican food served in Mexican restaurants. The most common daily dinner prepared by low-income Mexican Americans consists of beans, rice, and tortillas. Another common dinner has beef or chicken prepared in a hot sauce. Many Mexican American subjects joked about their hot and spicy food.

At fiestas, religious holidays, and important social events the Mexican American community serves special Mexican foods that are expensive and take longer to prepare. Four of the most popular foods are tamales, *buñuelos*, (a sugar-coated, deep-fried bread), *menudo* (a tripe soup), and *pan dulce* (sweet breads). Mexican Americans also eat *barbacoa de cabeza* on special occasions; this involves barbecuing a cow's head for twenty-four hours. It is considered a special treat that is eaten on special occasions; the cost is prohibitive for many low-income families. Ofilia Chávez, who operates the grocery store at the Middlewest Labor Camp, prepares beef heads, so too does a local Mexican American businessman.

The Rodriguez bakery truck from a nearby town in Oregon has a regular weekly route in the Mexican American districts of Middlewest, including deliveries to some of the businesses in town. The truck sells Mexican-style sweet breads and cookies.

Music and Dance

Music and dance have an important place in Mexican American culture. Many Middlewest Mexican Americans listen to Mexican American radio stations. A nearby town has the only regional full-time Spanish-language station; two other radio stations have an hour or two of Spanish broadcasts a day. A Mexican American Catholic priest has a weekly program, but the most popular programs play both traditional and contemporary Mexican American music. The local Mexican Americans enjoy several music styles, including the Ranchera (a type of polka), the Cumbia (a more Latin type of music from South America), the Hupango (a fast music from Mexico), and the Norteña (also from northern Mexico). The Norteña accentuates the guitar and the accordion.

Mariachi, a traditional form of Mexican music, thrives in the Mexican American community. Middlewest has two Mexican mariachi bands. These groups sometimes play at the Mexican American Catholic church; they also play for weddings, Quinceañeras, and fiestas. Some of the instruments used by the mariachi band come from Mexico.

A Mexican American teacher from a nearby small town has a contemporary Mexican band. This group plays for family celebrations and fiestas, but most of the time they play at a Mexican dance hall in Middlewest. The owner of the dance hall regularly hires Mexican bands from Texas, California, and Mexico. He charges admission of from ten to fifteen dollars per person. Most Mexican Americans earn a low income, but as many as 400 patrons attend these dances. The popularity of this dance hall, despite the high admission price, indicates the importance of music, song, and dance to the Mexican American community. One Mexican American exclaimed to me: "Oh, you won't be able to appreciate what music and dance means to us, it's not the same as Anglos going to a dance for a good time. Well, it is that, but it's more; the music and dance reminds us of the joys of being Mexican."

Few Anglos attend the Mexican dances, but many have a distinct image of this dance hall—the police and newspaper report on the fights that occur there. Rowdy and raucous behavior by some young men is not atypical of any group of working-class males. The high number of altercations at the Middlewest dances occur, in part, because of the number of young male migrant workers who have no community ties. The intense community focus on this dance hall creates a deviant image of the entire Mexican American community. Most Anglos of Middlewest have no knowledge of the solidarity and enjoyment that this dance hall provides for the local Mexican American community.

Mexican Americans have a distinctive style of dancing which calls for partners to dance side by side. The dance symbolically indicates the important role of the family in Mexican American life, because parents dance with their children and relatives. Mexican American teenagers are not embarrassed to be seen dancing with their adult relatives. This type of dancing also reveals the unity within the Mexican American community. The community dances together, side by side, not as couples. The family, kin, and friends dance together in a common closed circle. Mexican American community solidarity continues because these dances occur at weddings, Quinceañeras, and fiestas.

Within the Mexican American community of Middlewest there are several groups of men who sporadically come together to play music. Sometimes they become more serious about their music and play for local Mexican American bars and nightclubs. However, they primarily play for the enjoyment it brings. Most Mexican American musicians say that they learned to play from family or friends; many of them do not read music. They claim that music has always been part of their lives, because when the extended family has a social, someone will always sing and play guitar.

Fiesta

The two celebrations that involve the largest fiestas are Cinco de Mayo and Dieciseis de Septiembre. Cinco de Mayo commemorates the May 5, 1863, victory of the Mexican army over the French forces at Puebla. The September 16 celebration commemorates Mexican Independence Day. Fiestas and celebrations also are held in conjunction with weddings, baptisms, Quinceañeras, and Catholic church holidays.

All fiestas include food, music, dancing, and singing. The fiesta commonly features numerous booths that sell traditional Mexican piñatas, paper flowers, and crafts, although the main feature of a fiesta is the entertainment. Mexican American men and women dress in traditional Mexican clothes. Women's dresses generally are more colorful than those worn by Anglo women and combine colors that make for a vivid presence. Mexican American males wear black and dark-colored clothes that have a distinctive style and cut. Mexican American adolescents (these are not members of gangs) frequently wear all black clothing. The boys' favorite attire is L.A. Raiders jackets and hats. Mexican American women also wear black but they often wear dresses with black as the background color to increase the contrast with the vivid colors in their dresses.

Some fiestas have charros, Mexican American cowboys, in traditional Mexican dress with large sombreros, who ride horses and perform special tricks while riding. Some charros have extraordinary skill in the use of the lariat. The fiestas usually have several groups of dancers of different ages who perform traditional Mexican dances. The local dance instructor, José Muñoz, grew up in Mexico and graduated from the University of Mexico, majoring in dance and drama. For years he has volunteered his time to instruct younger dancers. The Mexican American community appreciates his work because the dancers represent an important aspect of Mexican American culture.

A successful fiesta requires many volunteers to organize all of the performers and to prepare the food and crafts for the booths. Mexican Americans commit their time and energy to fiestas because these events enhance community unity and help maintain the culture. Although the booths make money, no one in the Mexican American community works on a fiesta for profit. Jesse Torres and his wife have a booth at all of the fiestas where they sell buñuelos and piñatas. This retired couple donate their proceeds to their church. Most Middlewest Mexican Americans consider Jesse to be the most important local Mexican American leader, yet he is not above working at a booth for his community.

Fiestas in the broadest sense contain more facets of Mexican American culture than do any other events. A fiesta is the culmination of the efforts of many people. Leaders organize these events and serve as masters of ceremonies. Each person practices his/her craft to prepare for a successful fiesta. Women make costumes and prepare the food. Men haul material and set up the booths and equipment.

The fiesta celebrates some of the key elements of Mexican American culture: singing, dancing, and music. Many fiestas are held after church celebrations; Father Acuna sang several songs with a mariachi band at one fiesta. Estella Medina, who works at the county courthouse, exclaimed to me: "This fiesta is wonderful. It renews my faith in our people. Look at all these good people; and the entertainment is fantastic. I feel bad because all you [Anglos] see is crime by our people."

Religion

Most Mexican Americans in Middlewest practice Roman Catholicism. St. Mary's, the Middlewest Catholic church, has a separate Spanish-language mass on Sundays and observes Catholic church holidays as practiced in Mexico. The most important Mexican holy day is December 12, the Feast of Our Lady of Guadalupe. A special mass said on this day commemorates the appearance of the Virgin Mary to an Indian, Juan Diego, in 1531. She asked that a church be built on the spot where the temple of an Aztec goddess once stood and she performed a miracle: although it was winter, she produced blooming rose bushes to induce the bishop to build the church. This religious holiday attempts to integrate Catholicism with native religions because the Virgin is portrayed wearing traditional Indian garments.

On the Feast of Our Lady of Guadalupe, Middlewest Mexican Americans fill the church for a mass which includes both music and song. Mexican American girls, dressed in traditional Mexican garments, perform a ritual dance. Father Correro presented roses to the women at the conclusion of the service. No Anglos attended this mass, other than myself.

A fiesta followed in the church auditorium. The entertainment included several groups of singers and dancers. A group of Mexican American adolescents even performed a rap dance, revealing the integration of Mexican culture with the popular culture of the United States. Mrs. Estella Medina acted as the mistress of ceremonies; her leadership position in the community in part derives from her involvement in church activities. The Mexican American church auxiliary sold buñuelos, tamales, and soft drinks.

For most Mexican Americans, religion is an integral part of everyday life. Sal Trevino, who ran for the state legislature, said to me that to be a Mexican American leader you must take an active role in the church. Jesús Martínez provided an example of religion permeating a person's dialogue. In response to those promoting the English language bill, he said, "Those people better talk to God; God made the languages and I think he knew what he was doing."

Weddings

Mexican American weddings feature many of the cultural practices discussed above. A Mexican American wedding ceremony in the local Catholic church lasted two hours. A mariachi band played both religious and secular music. Several religious songs accompanied the wedding. The bride had six bridesmaids whose dresses of vivid gold and black conveyed a beauty and vitality distinctively Mexican American. Two small girls served as flower girls and they had dresses with the same colors. Several grade-school girls, relatives of the wedding party, also wore gold and black dresses.

In addition to the marriage vows, the ceremony involved placing a lasso over the couple to symbolize their bonding and unity. The couple received a rosary, a Bible, and a set of coins to symbolize a life of prosperity. The coins also signify the couple's ability to survive the good and bad times. The wedding ceremony is another example of the interweaving of Catholicism and Mexican American culture.

A traditional Mexican American wedding is an expensive affair. As part of the wedding ceremony, padrinos and relatives pledged their emotional and financial support for the couple. Padrinos received recognition for the gift they provided for the wedding. Several compadres addressed those attending concerning their support for the newly wedded couple and their future children. Following the service, the family and relatives were photographed. This activity lasted a half hour because of the large number of relatives involved. The grand finale included seventy-five relatives being photographed together.

Later in the afternoon, the relatives and close friends assembled for a formal dinner. A Mexican American band played for those in attendance. Brief speeches and several toasts accompanied the dinner for the newlyweds. A national guard armory served as the site of an evening dance. The decorations included gold and black crepe paper and balloons. Some small children played among a pile of balloons. The evening began with another ceremony. The band played a slow march to accompany the formal entrance of the bridesmaids, groomsmen, and the newlyweds. The couple then danced alone. Following this dance, the bridesmaids and groomsmen joined the couple and all danced in a circle of unity.

An additional ritual is the dollar dance in which guests pay a dollar to dance with the bride or groom. The dollar is pinned on the clothes of the couple. One subject reported that she had $156 dollars pinned to her wedding dress at the end of the evening. The money is meant to provide assistance for the couple's honeymoon. The wedding couple also received the standard wedding cake, presents, and champagne.

The evening dance involved the entire Mexican American community. People did not need an invitation to attend this dance. A Mexican American wedding is a community cultural event that incorporates many key elements of Mexican American culture, all of which promote community solidarity. Approximately 400 Mexican Americans of all ages attended the dance I witnessed; it was a joyous celebration of community.

Quinceañeras

The Quinceañera is another Mexican American cultural ceremony. This ceremony, at a girl's fifteenth birthday, celebrates the rite of passage for Mexican American girls. Not all Mexican American girls have Quinceañeras; the family's economic status and degree of assimilation are the determining influences on the family's decision to hold this ceremony. The elaborateness of the ceremony depends on the financial status of the family.

Paula's ceremony began with a Catholic mass in which she renewed her pledge to Catholicism. Paula wore a formal dress, as did also the fourteen girls in attendance. The fourteen boys in the ceremony wore tuxedos. A Mexican American woman made the girls' dresses.

Father Correra lectured Paula on her new responsibilities. He instructed her to find a role model to guide her in her new adult responsibilities. The priest told Paula that the Mother of Christ would serve as the appropriate model. He then lectured all of the adolescents in attendance, urging them to avoid being self-centered. He lectured the parents concerning their parental responsibilities. The priest finished his admonishments by telling those gathered that, "I will be by God's side. When you die, if you attempt to tell God that you did not know how to behave as God wants, that you did not know better, I will go 'psst, psst.' I will whisper in God's ear, 'I told them.' You will not have any excuses."

After the mass, a photographer took pictures of Paula with her family and friends. Approximately 150 people attended the mass and dinner at the family's home where seven women were preparing food. Father Correra received special attention: he and the men ate first. Most ate outside under makeshift shades constructed of tarps to protect the guests from the sun. Paula's working-class family could not afford all of the expenses for this ceremony, so the family's padrinos shared in these expenses.

An evening dance serves as the culminating event of the Quinceañera. The masters of ceremony introduced all of the padrinos and noted the gifts they brought for Paula. These included a cake, a rosary, a Bible, a kneeling cushion, flowers, a necklace, rings, and a veil, among other gifts. Additionally, more than fifty sponsors contributed money for the celebration.

The specific events of the Quinceañera included the father and daughter dancing the first dance together. The attendants then performed two dances. Paula later returned in a plain dress to dance with a doll. At the end of this dance she threw the doll into a crowd of small girls. Throwing away the doll symbolized Paula's departure from childhood. Approximately 350 people attended this Quinceañera. A Mexican American band played for the dancers well into the night. People of all ages participated in the dancing. The Quinceañera represents another traditional Mexican American ceremony that unites the people and preserves the culture.

Other Cultural Events

Héctor Manzanares lives in the country. In the field next to his house nearly one hundred large drums rest on the ground. In front of each drum a colorful rooster is attached by a cord to a stake in the ground. The drums provide makeshift shelters for the roosters. Hector raises and trains several special breeds of fighting cocks. He claims to have special knowledge on how to breed and train the best cocks. The cockfights occur on a regular basis during the summer.

Mexican American males, having been notified by word-of-mouth, gather at designated areas to wager and watch the fights. Cockfights and the attendant betting are illegal, but few arrests occur. Hector claims that he has won as much as $20,000 in a year. Attached to each leg of the roosters are razor blades to hasten the death of one of the combatants. The cheering, betting, and the bloody fights fill the air and the senses with excitement, similar to a boxing match. Feathers, dust, and blood fly.

Some older Mexican Americans reported on another cultural practice—*curanderismo*. They prefer traditional female healers (*curanderas*) over medical doctors. Curanderas' techniques include the use of herbal teas, artifacts, bits of colored cloth, and certain incantations to cure physical and psychological problems. My interviewees had a limited knowledge of these practices. Most Middlewest Mexican Americans view folk healing as an old-fashioned practice.

Housing

Culture also refers to the mundane aspects of life. The pattern and style of Middlewest's Mexican American housing reveal aspects of culture, economic status, and degree of adaptation to the dominant culture. A high concentration of Mexican Americans is found in three areas of Middlewest. The area's first Mexican American residents lived in the labor camp, which provides substandard housing that is the equivalent of a ghetto. Local farmers and government built these housing units.

Across the proverbial tracks in Middlewest is the "Chicago District" where most Mexican Americans live. This section of town generally has the poorest quality of housing; few Anglos live there. Small, overcrowded houses dot the landscape in various states of disrepair. This section of Middlewest, in the classic minority tradition, has a reputation for violence, gangs, and drug trafficking. According to one real estate agent, the average price of homes in the Chicago district is $15,000. The interiors feature inexpensive second-hand appliances and furnishings. Many run-down trailer houses are scattered throughout the district. The city has not provided curbs and gutters. Because the houses are small, the area's children spend most of their time on the streets.

Mexican American houses here generally lack garages, which results in a visible clutter of cars in the neighborhood. Most Mexican Americans drive large, older American cars; few drive foreign or compact cars. Assuredly, the financial situation of most Mexican Americans accounts for the well-worn appearance of their cars. Some young Mexican American men drive "low riders." The name derives from the fact the car's shock absorbers have been modified to allow the car's frame to be close to the ground. These cars have little chrome and their metallic paint presents a sharp contrast to the dull and rusted colors of most cars in the neighborhood.

A few small businesses exist in the Chicago district, including a grocery store, a TV-repair shop, a laundromat, a gas station, and two tiny Mexican restaurants. Several homes in the district function as small fundamentalist churches. Some Anglos will not walk in the Chicago district after dark, and pizza companies will not deliver there after dark. The barrio of Middlewest is unlike its urban counterpart because of its small size and limited services.

A third Mexican American section of town is called "Little Mexico." This is a small subdivision built with federal housing funds under the direction of the Idaho Migrant Council. The project required that families assist in building each other's houses. These modest homes have a quality superior to those in the Chicago district.

Not all Mexican Americans live in these three sections of Middlewest. Some of the more affluent Mexican American families rent or own homes in the Anglo sections of Middlewest.

The walls of most Mexican American homes contain two symbolic displays: religious artifacts such as inexpensive biblical-scene paintings, crosses, and pictures of Jesus; and family photos, primarily of weddings and children. These interiors reaffirm the importance of family and church in Mexican American culture.

Most Mexican Americans do not believe that divisions exist within the Mexican American community, but some see a division between migrant and permanent resident Mexican Americans. Some resident Mexican Americans dislike the migrant workers; they feel that the migrants give all Mexican Americans a bad image. They also believe that the migrants take their jobs and depress the wage scale. Nevertheless, most Mexican Americans in Middlewest have a family history of being migrant workers, so considerable solidarity exists within the Mexican American community.

"Oreos"

Mexican Americans, because they live in a predominantly Anglo community, cannot escape being influenced by Anglo perceptions of Mexican Americans. For example, the predominantly marginal Mexican American students resent the few Mexican American students who excel. Marginal Mexican American students often view teachers and administrators as enemies; they may not be able to articulate their grievances, but a latent hostility smolders in these students. Having little ability to alter their status or attack the Anglo school personnel, these students label a successful Mexican American student an "Oreo," a chocolate cookie with white (Anglo) filling. (Many people associate the use of the term Oreo with an African American who has become assimilated.) The logic generally fits: the successful Mexican American students have Anglo friends, they like their teachers, and they have a higher degree of assimilation. This leads to their being criticized for rejecting their ethnic roots.

During the course of my field research, two local Mexican American high school girls transferred to a country school because they were distraught over the resentment of their fellow Mexican Americans.

Mexican American professionals and businessmen also can be targets of attack. They also have Anglo friends and professional contacts. These Mexican Americans are commonly classified as "wanabes," persons wanting to be something they are not. Mexican American leaders who have dedicated their lives to assisting the Mexican American community become targets of many forms of criticism that vary from comments that they are "only working for their own self-interests" to they "think they are better" than their fellow Mexican Americans. Sadly, the poverty-stricken Mexican Americans misdirect their hostility toward Mexican Americans who have become successful. Displaced anger occurs because it is difficult to hate abstractions such as the Anglo system. Mexican Americans recognize that they have a subordinate position in Middlewest, but they lack the vocabulary to articulate their grievances.

Types of Adaptations

Some Mexican Americans internalize the stereotypes that Anglos have of Mexican Americans. For example, certain Mexican Americans accept the dominant view that their culture promotes crime and poverty. Mary Archuleta works for the state. She has a defeated demeanor because unconsciously she perceives Mexican Americans to be inferior. In a public meeting she voluntarily apologized for the criminal activity of Mexican Americans in Middlewest. A Mexican American laborer criticized his fellow Mexican American workers for being too pushy; Armando Castillo, who works for a feed company, said that he never has any problems at work because he knows his place.

Several Mexican American women I met had very low self-esteem. Lupe Pantoja has worked on the trim line of a potato processing plant for fifteen years. She expressed interest in obtaining a GED certificate and enrolling in a vocational program. Lupe said her husband tries to encourage her and she hates her five dollar per hour job, yet her lack of confidence immobilizes her.

Mexican American culture in Middlewest lacks uniformity. The Mexican American community is continuously being renewed by new arrivals from Texas and Mexico. Their ethnicity can be measured on a continuum similar to that described in the work of Keefe and Padilla (1987). At one end of the continuum are those Mexican Americans who retain a high degree of ethnicity that closely parallels the traditions of Mexico. These people usually are older, were born in Mexico, have relatives in Mexico, have less formal education, speak mostly Spanish, and have migrated from the Rio Grande Valley of Texas. They have a high level of participation in Mexican American cultural activities.

A few Mexican Americans who have a high level of assimilation are found at the other end of the continuum. Their characteristics include younger age, more formal education, less speaking of Spanish, middle-class employment, fewer ties to Mexico, long residence in Middlewest, more Anglo friends, and less participation in the Mexican American cultural activities.

Many Mexican American leaders become bicultural because of their high interaction with people of both races. They feel comfortable in both Mexican American and Anglo settings. The Mexican American community of Middlewest commonly recognizes three types of Mexican American ethnicity, corresponding to the three generations of Mexican Americans living in Middlewest. Mexican Americans believe that each generation has become less Mexican American, but they think that even the third generation retains considerable ethnicity. The most visible difference in ethnicity occurs when grandparents who speak only Spanish are unable to communicate with their English-speaking grandchildren. Mexican American teenagers enjoy the popular culture of the dominant society, which causes some conflict with their more traditional parents. Migrants tend to have a higher level of Mexican American ethnicity than resident Mexican Americans. While walking in the Middlewest Labor Camp, one hears primarily Spanish music on the radios; but in the other Mexican American sections of town English-language stations are heard.

An important factor in the retention of Mexican American culture is the colonial status and subordinate position of most Mexican Americans in Middlewest. A key feature of the social relations in Middlewest and Farm County is the Anglo community's control of the important social institutions of society. The Anglo community, though it does not acknowledge it, effectively prevents most Mexican Americans from participating in Anglo institutions. Most Mexican Americans work in the secondary job market. Their lower class position results in a unifying of the Mexican American community; thus their culture works to protect their self-image.

Anglo Perspective

Among Anglos in Middlewest, knowledge of the Mexican American community often consists of a deviant image created by the criminal justice system and the mass media. Most do not know or care to know about Mexican American culture. An Anglo minister commented:

> Race relations are not good; I am not sure they will get better. Some of the churches are concerned about it, but [there has been] not much success. The gang culture makes it hard; lot of prejudice, just a lot of prejudice against the Spanish. We don't know what to do; you hear things like I am sure you would have heard like the South with blacks. People resent a Spanish person buying a house in their neighborhood or even renting a house. This person across the street is Spanish. He keeps his place immaculate; in fact, that place had a number of Anglo renters, it was a trash heap. Since he has been in it, it is clean. People comment on how unusual it is, he is a clean Mexican.

Idaho commemorated its statehood centennial in 1990. In Boise, the state capital, there were several days of celebration. The gala event consisted of an evening of entertainment. All the minority groups in Idaho participated, except the Mexican Americans, who are by far the largest minority group in Idaho.

Basque dancers performed. This ethnic group from Spain has a longer history in Idaho than do the Mexican Americans, and the Basques have become highly assimilated. Juan Celedón, a Mexican American leader, said, "It is as though we [Mexican Americans] do not exist in Idaho. The state has never recognized our contributions to Idaho. It is as though we don't exist."

Assimilation

Approximately 20 percent of the Anglos in Middlewest report that they have Mexican American friends. Yet when asked to elaborate on the degree and closeness of the friendship, the interviews reveal that most of these friendships lack intimacy and closeness. The Mexican American friend commonly is not invited to dinner.

The typical interracial friendship occurs as the result of the Mexican American person having achieved a high level of assimilation. The Mexican American who is most "eligible" for friendship has more education, a better job, speaks fluent English without an accent, and has a lighter skin color than the majority. Many Mexican Americans claimed their Anglo friends did not see them as Mexican American, and some maintained that their Anglo friends commonly commit faux pas by talking derogatorily about Mexicans. A Mexican American women commented: "I am driving my son and his three Anglo friends to their soccer game in Boise. They are in the back seat and they begin talking about the other team and one of the Anglo boys says that the other team has a lot of mean and dirty Mexicans on it. They did not see my son as a Mexican."

Such incidents reveal the irony of race and ethnic relations–Anglos can have Mexican American friends and yet remain intolerant. Also since they have a Mexican American friend, they can more easily maintain a self-perception of being non-racist.

Separate Communities

While in many ways Middlewest has two separate communities, one Anglo and one Mexican American, some social and cultural events attract both races. Most Mexican Americans who live permanently in Middlewest consider themselves Americans and celebrate American holidays. They participate to a greater degree than Anglos in the celebration of the local Christmas parade and the Fourth of July celebration.

The Middlewest park and swimming pool attract many people in the summer. Both races use the swimming pool but the childrens' play often remains separated by race. Picnics in the park typically are divided by race.

Sports

The people of Middlewest avidly participate in sports activities. Mexican Americans participate in sports more than in any other Anglo social institution, including little league baseball, high school sports, and adult softball teams. Mexican Americans generally feel less discriminated against in sports; Mexican Americans and Anglos play on integrated teams. Mexican American players, however, do not participate proportionally to their percentage of the town's population. Some Mexican American parents cannot afford to buy their children the necessary sports equipment.

The schools reward and the local newspaper reports the accomplishments of Mexican American athletes. However, some Mexican American parents believe that the Mexican American athlete has to be significantly better in order to receive an opportunity to play. Mexican American parents think their children do not receive as much encouragement as do Anglo children.

Sports provides another example of the situational nature of racism. I observed two young Anglo men I had interviewed playing softball in the park with teams that included Mexican American members. These Anglo athletes interacted in a congenial fashion with their Mexican American teammates although in their interviews they had both spoken disparagingly about Mexican Americans.

Some sports still basically lack integration. Mexican Americans account for less than two percent of the membership in the local golf clubs. Golf remains a middle-class sport and Mexican American golfers are from that social class.

Many Mexican American males in Middlewest enjoy boxing. Several Mexican American teenagers participate in Tony Ocha's boxing program. Boxing and minority status seem to go together; boxers attempt to exchange their poverty status for esteem through the sport. Ocha, a former boxer, coaches Mexican American boxers in his garage. He has coached for years, without pay, because he feels that someone has to work with the kids and help keep them out of trouble. He believes the sport improves the boys' self-esteem, while he and the boys also have fun participating in the sport.

Conclusions

My field research on the Mexican American community reflects findings that are similar to those found in the ethnographic work of Blea (1980) and Horowitz (1986). The material in this chapter also supports the conclusions of Keefe and Padilla (1987), who found that Chicanos in their community studies retained a strong sense of ethnicity. As many previous sociological researchers have noted, the vitality of the Mexican American community is sustained by family life, religious rituals, cultural celebrations, and community life.

The Mexican American community provides an ongoing set of social, religious, and artistic events that bring the community together, while at the same time these activities reinforce ethnic traditions. The Mexican American family is the primary social institution that carries on the day-to-day features of the culture. The family setting is the arena in which children learn Spanish, eat Mexican food, attend church with their parents, and learn the values and attitudes of their culture.

Mexican Americans commonly have large families and close relationships with their relatives. A Mexican American easily can have an extended family approaching thirty people. This individual will also have a set of compadres and padrinos who function as surrogate relatives. This means that most Mexican Americans in Middlewest have a strong support system of people who regularly join together for social and religious activities.

Many Mexican American cultural activities are religious in nature. Weddings, funerals, baptisms, and Quinceañeras all take place in a religious setting. Religion influences the day-to-day life of most Mexican Americans. The religious values along with the typically large families place a greater emphasis on the group than on the individual. Benefits include the sharing of resources and the providing of emotional support. It is taken for granted that assistance is to be provided to any member of the extended family. Warmth and intimacy are readily created by the extended family, and this intimacy is extended beyond the family setting into the larger cultural group.

The life of Mexican Americans in Middlewest and Farm County is punctuated with cultural activities that include singing, dancing, and music. These activities include family gatherings with guitar music; going to a weekend dance with a Mexican band; a group of girls organized to perform traditional dances; and the more elaborate performances of music, dance, and singing that accompany weddings, Quinceañeras, Cinco de Mayo, and September the Sixteenth celebrations.

Mexican American life has a set of values that sometimes sharply contrast with those of the Anglo culture. Mexican Americans place less value on individualism, competition, and economic success. Mexican American life in some ways is similar to the more traditional Anglo culture of the past, when religion and family played a larger role in people's lives. Many Americans yearn for a revival of those traditional values.

A considerable portion of Mexican American life in Middlewest is shaped by the treatment the people receive from the dominant society. Many in the Anglo community have stereotyped Mexican Americans as criminals and welfare cheats. If Anglos would get beyond these stereotypes and learn about Mexican American culture, it is likely that they would gain a respect for the Mexican American people. Most Mexican Americans live in poverty because they work in the secondary job market.

The social interaction between Mexican Americans and Anglos fluctuates. Members of both races get involved in activities to improve race relations. Each race, at times, alienates the other. The problem is that once Middlewest has created two essentially separate communities, many individuals, social groups, and local institutions then unconsciously perpetuate the divisions within the community.

The social nature of human beings in many ways inhibits positive race relations. People naturally become friends with their work associates and with those who belong to the same church, and they have difficulty relating to those of a different social class. People naturally assist those most similar to themselves. People today have to work hard to survive and they feel as though they have little time to work at improving race relations. Ironically, Anglos demand conformity and assimilation, but their behavior and institutions often deny or inhibit the active participation of Mexican Americans. Anglos say, "Assimilate and we will accept you," but Mexican Americans can only become assimilated when they are allowed to have opportunities to participate fully in the schools, employment, politics, and religious services of Anglo Middlewest.

Race relations between Anglos and Mexican Americans in Middlewest would improve if there was a significant increase in the social interaction between them. Racial harmony would be enhanced if Mexican Americans were to have the same opportunities as Anglos to gain an education, obtain a job, and have political representation. In such a situation, Mexican Americans would become more fully bicultural—participating in the Anglo culture while still retaining their cultural roots.

Mexican Americans come to Idaho because they want to work and make a decent living for their families. Many come with limited formal education and without the ability to speak fluent English. Instead of assisting these new arrivals to their community, Anglos too often respond with avoidance and derision.

Anglos in Middlewest need to recognize that they are part of the problem. It is not Mexican American culture that causes poverty and crime; instead, it is people in social institutions and situations. Anglos would do well to stop demanding that

Mexican Americans change and become like them; they need to learn that if they truly start to educate Mexican American kids instead of unintentionally pushing them out of the schools, there will be greater racial harmony and social justice. Mexican Americans need to be paid living wages; police and courts must stop using selective enforcement of the laws against Mexican Americans; the media should work to create a positive image of Mexican Americans; the churches should stop having separate services for Mexican Americans; politicians should endeavor to provide adequate social services for Mexican Americans. When any or all of these things are done, there will be more racial harmony and social justice in Middlewest.

The tragedy in Middlewest is that in general Anglos reject, demean, and victimize the Mexican American community and then compound the tragedy by blaming the victim.

Chapter 4

MEXICAN AMERICAN LEADERS DEFEND THEIR CULTURE AND PEOPLE

And I learned quickly that there is no real appreciation. Whatever you do, and no matter what reasons you may give to others, you do it because you want to see it done, or maybe because you want power. And there shouldn't be any appreciation, understandably. I know good organizers who were destroyed, washed out, because they expected people to appreciate what they'd done. Things don't work that way.

–César Chávez

Introduction

From the previous chapter we saw that the Mexican Americans of Middlewest have their own culture. Most Mexican Americans work for Anglo owners and managers of businesses, factories, and government departments. Mexican American children attend schools controlled by Anglo teachers and administrators. During their leisure time, Mexican Americans interact mostly with one another. My field research interviews and observations indicate that Mexican Americans generally face institutionalized racism when they leave their own culture to interact with the dominant Anglo society.

Most Mexican American leaders operate biculturally—they are comfortable interacting within both the Anglo and the Mexican American cultures. Their leadership positions derive from years of dedicated service maintaining their Mexican American

93

culture, assisting Mexican Americans living in poverty, and attempting to defend Mexican Americans against racism. Most of the Mexican American leaders have experienced the migrant lifestyle and have worked in the fields.

Middlewest's Mexican American leaders generally have achieved more education, greater income, and higher-status employment than their fellow Mexican Americans. These leaders assist the community because they have experienced poverty and discrimination and, consequently, often feel compelled to pay back something to others. As one expressed it: "You get skills, you have to help others. I made it, now I have to help my people; I owe it; that is just the way it works."

In many ways, all of the Mexican Americans in southwestern Idaho are part of one large ethnic community. The Mexican American community of Middlewest, especially its leadership, cannot be separated from a larger Mexican American community that is spread throughout seven towns in southwestern Idaho, all in close proximity to Middlewest.

Each community has its own grass roots leaders. Some local leaders participate in one of three important Mexican American organizations. Not only do the Mexican American leaders all know one another but also they have worked together on many projects. Many Mexican Americans of Middlewest have relatives and friends in the surrounding communities. Fiestas and conferences are attended by Mexican Americans from all seven communities. However, the migrants living in the three labor camps in the area do not participate as much as those living permanently in the area.

Poverty

Nearly all Mexican American migrant workers and their families live at or near the poverty level. Social services personnel and Mexican American leaders estimate that between 35 and 45 percent of the permanent Mexican American residents earn an income below the poverty level. Poverty has horrendous effects on Mexican American families. Many families do not have access to health care. Jesús Fernández, a Mexican American elementary school principal in Middlewest, reported that some Mexican American children come to school unable to concentrate on their studies because of their health problems. Recently, an eleven-year-old girl came to school with a 3.5-inch cut on her foot that required six stitches. The accident had occurred four days earlier. In another case, a twelve-year-old boy needed dental care for severely abscessed teeth but his parents could not afford the necessary dental care.

Francisco Hernández and his family know the consequences of poverty. He works seasonally at the sugar factory and works in the fields during the summer. His income qualifies him for unemployment compensation and food stamps; still, he has no money to repair the family car, and the gas company sends threatening letters for non-payment of their heating bill. The stress caused by the family's precarious economic standing doubled after Francisco's wife, Maria, sustained multiple injuries in a serious automobile accident. The other driver's insurance will eventually pay all of Maria's health bills, but this takes time. When Francisco took Maria for her second visit to the doctor, she was refused treatment until payment could be made. Francisco did not have cash or credit cards for this payment and, although Maria needed a prescription drug, she was turned away. As Francisco neared the end of this story, his pain, anguish, and outrage intensified. His voice quivered and his facial expressions told a story that my narrative cannot capture. Three days later, Maria received treatment for her broken collarbone and broken ribs at a low-income medical center in a neighboring town.

It is difficult to measure the percentage of Mexican Americans in Middlewest and in Farm County who face the myriad problems associated with poverty. The Idaho Department of Employment (1991a) recorded that 33 percent of the permanent resident Mexican Americans were in the poverty category. The department's 1988 data revealed a 14 percent unemployment rate for Mexican Americans. The seriousness of the problem is underscored when it is realized that governmental agencies typically undercount minority problems. The average local Mexican American migrant family lives on only half the income set by the federal government as the poverty standard.

Marta Pérez experienced what happens to many Mexican Americans living in poverty. Her earliest memories are of her family being on the road and working the fields, and she recalls feeling like an outsider at school because she attended so many different schools. She quit school in the eighth grade and went to work in the fields. She married at the age of fourteen, and by the time she was twenty-two she had four children. When Marta's husband left her, she moved in with her parents. The home had two bedrooms and Marta slept on the sofa. She claimed that one who has not experienced it cannot appreciate how poverty wears a person down. Marta felt as though she could never get ahead; she had more bills than money; she could not afford to buy her children clothes. Marta said, "Everywhere you go the Anglos sneer at you, they don't want you around. You work hard and you still can't make a living. I got angry, then I started drinking to ease the pain; before long I was drinking all the time."

I asked Marta about Mexican American poverty. She said:

> It's the system. Mostly, Mexican Americans work in the local factories. They get laid off. They have not worked long enough to get benefits. Most Mexican Americans' income only averages out to about $500 a month. You go to Health and Welfare and they don't give you food stamps because you made too much money last month. Always poverty, always; I have to pay the bills for the months I have no work. The system is bad. Yes, I have a lot of anger at the way the system works. We have to tolerate this; we never get ahead.

Marta began associating with other Mexican Americans who had succumbed to poverty. She and her friends led chaotic lives that included intermittent work, petty crimes, and drug use. Her kids had to raise themselves as she became what she called "dysfunctional." The more she drank, the worse it got. Her oldest son and daughter turned to their peers for acceptance and support. The son now resides in a home for delinquent boys and the daughter became a teenage mother.

Marta feels enormous guilt for her failure as a parent. After years of this lifestyle, Marta hit rock bottom; then she turned to religion. The Mexican American Assembly of God church became an integral part of her life; she attends church four times a week, and she has not had a drink in a year and a half. Many Mexican Americans with alcohol and/or family problems turn to fundamentalist churches for assistance.

Marta believes the grinding poverty has a greater effect on Mexican American men than it does on women. She thinks that much of the macho image is a defense against a self-esteem under attack. The men work seasonally for minimum wage; wives then berate their husbands for not being good providers. Men in these circumstances turn to drinking and to other women. Fragile egos will fight for little reason, as men desperately attempt to shore up their self-esteem. Some Mexican American men have many driving violations including DUI (Driving Under the Influence) citations. Marta described her life during her dysfunctional period as one of hopelessness.

In a later interview I asked Marta why most Mexican Americans don't vote. She laughed, "You have to get serious; people have to find a job, get assistance, fix the car; voting is a luxury; the people are just too busy trying to survive." Some men on the down side of poverty feel anger and frustration. Their families become the victims of psychological and physical abuse. Marta said, "When you try to change, then the peer group works against you. They don't want you to make it, to get control of your life, because where does that leave them? . . . It only intensifies their failure."

A group of secondary Mexican American leaders consists of ministers of fundamentalist churches such as the Assembly of God and Pentecostal churches. These denominations hold services several times a week. They are commonly quite puritanical, and the congregations are admonished to refrain from deviant behavior. The ministers crusade against drinking, drugs, and adultery during each service. These frequent admonishments and calls to self-examination provide a strong support system for those facing problems. Most of these churches are made up of small congregations that provide more intimacy and support than the larger and more impersonal Catholic church.

Mexican American Organizations

Four Mexican American organizations have their headquarters in southwestern Idaho. They include the Idaho Commission on Mexican American Affairs, the Idaho Migrant Council, the Mexican American Businessmen's Association, and Image de Idaho. Mexican American leaders from Middlewest participate in each of these organizations. Raul Rodríquez chairs the Commission on Mexican American Affairs and has worked on Mexican American issues for more than twenty years. Raul lives in Boise, the state capital; this has enabled him to develop contacts with leaders in both major political parties. He also has developed liaisons with the major corporations based in Boise.

Raul leads the lobbying efforts in the state legislature when proposals arise that will either assist or hurt the Mexican American community. He can quickly mobilize the Mexican American leadership when necessary. With other leaders, Raul engineered legislation to require farmers to provide portable toilets for field workers. For years, Raul and other Mexican American leaders have had to work hard to defeat attempts to pass a bill establishing English as the official language of Idaho. He and other Mexican American leaders are proud of their successful effort in lobbying the legislature to establish a $100,000 college scholarship fund for minority students. Mexican American leaders praise Raul for his lobbying ability, which requires incredible restraint and patience on his part. He spent an enormous amount of his time pressuring the state legislature to create the Mexican American Commission.

Raul made the following comments on the problems facing Mexican Americans:

I was fired by a local college and pushed out of state employment. The establishment does not like Mexican

Americans talking about prejudice and discrimination in Idaho. As chairperson of the Mexican American Commission, I regularly receive calls from across the state about Mexican Americans being treated unfairly. It is frustrating because we have no staff or authority to intervene. Nobody in state government is advocating for the Mexican American community. The state's affirmative action program is a joke.... The two areas where Mexican Americans are having the most problems in Idaho are the schools and the criminal justice system. When three Mexican American male youths get together, they are seen as a gang. It is always the Mexican kids' fault. The schools, even if it is unintentional, destroy the self-esteem of most Mexican American kids. The parents are becoming very upset but they have a hard time articulating their views. When you listen closely, you understand the teachers and especially the counselors are prejudiced against Mexican American kids.... We cannot take issues straight on, the farmers, factory owners have too much power; not even the Democrats will assist us.

In a later interview Raul informed me, "You know, I have been working with the Mexican American caucus on our version of a reapportionment bill. Now, several people asked me if I have heard the rumor that I will not be reappointed to the Mexican American Commission."

I attended several board meetings of the Mexican American Commission on which Raul serves without compensation. He has made the commission a viable entity though it operates with minimal funding. Raul has written three grant proposals that will provide funding to record part of the oral history, art, and culture of Mexican Americans in Idaho. His commitment and dedication provide an outstanding example of what civic responsibilities entail.

The Mexican American Commission has eight members—four Mexican American leaders and four members of the state legislature. Two of the legislative members often do not attend the meetings; the other two showed little enthusiasm for their appointed task. They seldom participated in the discussions and their demeanor projected an attitude of cool indifference. During one commission meeting in which a federal official reviewed national minority policy, one of the legislative members of the board fell asleep. Mexican American leaders said that one of the legislative members of the commission voted for a bill that the Mexican American Commission wanted to defeat. Members of the state legislature who are sympathetic to Mexican American issues said that the legislature resists any legislation that would assist Mexican Americans in Idaho.

During the winter of 1991 the commission did not have its own office space; meetings had to be held in an unused portion of another agency's office. The heating did not function and the commissioners had to wear heavy winter coats throughout the meeting. The office furniture was constructed from cardboard. This arrangement could be seen to symbolize society's treatment of Mexican Americans in Idaho.

The Commission on Mexican American Affairs serves as a sounding board for Mexican Americans facing racial conflicts throughout Idaho. The commission has no authority or staff to investigate or enforce settlements. The Mexican Americans on the Commission feel frustrated because they believe that the attorney general's office does not act vigorously to investigate complaints. The Mexican American commissioners informally telephone or travel to meet with the police, school administrators, state agencies, and political figures in an attempt to resolve racial conflicts.

The year I observed commission meetings, Mexican American citizens logged the following concerns: (1) The lack of Mexican Americans employed in state government; (2) The expulsion of Mexican American youth from schools; (3) a school district dropping a $500,000 grant for bilingual education; (4) a county establishing a separate court for Mexican American offenders; (5) inappropriate evictions of migrant workers from designated labor camps; (6) selective enforcement of laws against Mexican American offenders; (7) Mexican Americans being evicted from apartments and houses because of their race; (8) discrimination against Mexican Americans in job hirings, promotions, and terminations; and (9) the Idaho Department of

Agriculture certifying H2A workers from Mexico while local Mexican Americans were unemployed.

For the most part, the Mexican American community and leaders support the Democratic party; yet the Democratic party rarely supports Mexican American issues and candidates. In 1991 twenty-two Mexican American leaders, including those from Middlewest, invited Tim Robertson, the governor's assistant, to meet with them. The leaders wanted to express their concerns about lack of support for them from the Democratic party. One complaint focused on the small number of Mexican American employees in state government. Mexican American leaders expressed their concern that the Idaho Department of Education has no Mexican Americans on its staff and the department has failed to provide leadership in developing bilingual education. The leaders believe the Department of Education has little concern for the Mexican American school dropout rate. A third complaint involved the issue of racial conflict. Mexican Americans feel that Democrats avoid meaningful involvement with these issues.

Image de Idaho

Image de Idaho is a statewide organization of Mexican Americans, several members of which live in Middlewest. Image de Idaho has approximately 300 members and a fifteen-member board of directors. It operates without a paid staff. Its leaders devote long hours to insure the success of Image de Idaho programs. The board's primary activities include providing scholarships to Mexican American students; sponsoring conferences; and functioning, unofficially, as the public-relations committee for the Mexican American community.

The Image de Idaho board plays an essential role in organizing an annual Mexican American Issues Conference and a Mexican American Women's Conference. These conferences enable the Mexican American leaders to network and maintain Mexican American solidarity. The conference workshops create a forum for interaction between the Mexican American community and various government agencies. Exciting keynote speakers stimulate the pride and unity of those Mexican Americans working for "la raza." The culminating event of the Mexican American Issues Conference in Boise is a celebration of the Septiembre 16 holiday.

The Mexican American leaders and their organizations work together on many projects. A review of minority literature reveals that serious fractions often occur among minority leaders. Mexican American leaders in Idaho have avoided this problem; they recognize the need to present a united front if they are to be successful.

Mexican American Businessmen's Association

The Mexican American Businessmen's Association is a recent creation. These businessmen live in communities throughout southwestern Idaho and most have not previously participated in community activities. Their primary mission is to promote the success of Mexican American youth. They believe it important to provide positive role models for youth. They supported a Mexican American individual's campaign for election to the state legislature. This association has an energetic and expanding membership. It is creating a college scholarship fund and its members make a practice of hiring Mexican American college students for their part-time workers.

Idaho Migrant Council

The Idaho Migrant Council (IMC) remains the most important Mexican American organization in Idaho. It has existed for twenty years and has the largest membership. As a nonprofit organization, IMC operates on a budget of approximately $4 million and provides services to Mexican American migrant workers. The IMC maintains its state headquarters in Middlewest and has approximately 100 full-time employees. Its funding comes from federal grants. Two hundred additional teachers and staff operate the Migrant Head Start programs during the six-month migrant season.

The IMC operates three major programs statewide, including the Head Start program, the employment and training program, and the housing program. The Migrant Head Start program enrolls more than 500 students each year. In 1991 the IMC received additional monies to operate Head Start programs in Wyoming and Montana. Teresa Medina has directed this program for over fifteen years and has become an important Mexican American leader.

Mexican American leaders also experience racism. Teresa Medina became agitated as she told me how the Middlewest schools treat her children. She said that both her son and daughter have been labeled as non-achievers by the local public schools. Teresa related how her children became increasingly alienated from school. She concluded, "I will never forgive the school for what they have done to my children."

Head Start has enabled many local Mexican American women to obtain an education and employment. Mexican American women must enroll in a preschool training program and receive fifteen hours of training to gain employment in Head Start. The IMC programs demonstrate that, given an opportunity, Mexican Americans are eager to advance themselves. For example, Veronica Ortiz started out as a field worker with an elementary education. She became a member of the IMC and learned about their programs. She completed a Child Development Associate (CDA) program sponsored by the IMC and became a teacher's aide. After gaining experience, she became a teacher. Veronica has dramatically improved her self-confidence. She lost eighty pounds and now has a positive sense of self. Veronica has the distinction of being one of the few Mexican Americans elected to a school board in Idaho.

Sally Rivera also had an elementary school education and completed the CDA training to work in IMC's Head Start program. Because her husband did not approve of her working, Sally's success illustrates the determination of Mexican Americans to succeed. Despite his strong disapproval, she persevered to become the director of the Migrant Head Start program at the Middlewest Labor Camp. Sally went from being a field worker to becoming the supervisor of ten workers.

IMC manages a statewide employment and training program which provides training in the basic skills of applying for and maintaining a job. The program tests the academic and vocational interests of Mexican American migrants. The IMC staff assists Mexican Americans to enroll in high school equivalency programs and vocational programs. The major source of funding for these programs comes from the Job Training and Partnership Act (JTPA). Over the years, many Mexican Americans who now live permanently in Middlewest have received vocational training from the IMC that has enhanced their standard of living.

The IMC also operates a housing program. For several years IMC has received grants for Housing and Urban Development (HUD) programs to restore low-income housing and to weatherize low-income houses. The housing program has several significant accomplishments to its credit, including the remodeling and management of a labor camp. Several years ago, HUD funded a grant that enabled the IMC to supervise the building of twenty low-income houses for Mexican American families in Middlewest.

Few Anglos in Middlewest have any knowledge of the services provided by the Idaho Migrant Council. The IMC has done more to train, educate, house, feed, and provide employment for Mexican Americans than any entity in the state of Idaho. However, many Anglos see the IMC as an unnecessary "welfare program." The gulf between the Anglo and Mexican American communities of Middlewest is evidenced by the lack of information Anglos have about the IMC.

Many Mexican American leaders started their careers by working for the IMC. The keynote speaker at the 1991 Mexican American Issues Conference, Julio García, an administrator with the Southwest Private Industry Council, said: "Most of us Mexican Americans gathered here tonight to celebrate the twentieth anniversary of the IMC know the importance of the Idaho Migrant Council. Because for us, it was the equivalent of college; we obtained our leadership skills through working for the IMC."

Another contribution of the IMC to the Mexican American community is its sponsorship of an annual Mexican American Youth Conference. Approximately 400 Mexican American high school students from across Idaho receive assistance to attend the conference. The adolescents listen to motivational speeches by successful Mexican Americans. They also attend two days of participatory workshops. In these workshops the young people learn how to apply for and receive financial assistance to attend colleges and vocational schools. Mexican American leaders and professionals serve as role models for the youth. A recent keynote speaker, Tony Gallegos, a commissioner of the U.S. Equal Employment Opportunity Commission, described his own impoverished background and how he overcame this to become successful. Gallegos told the assembled youth, "I am not here to advise you to go to college. No, I am telling you that you have to go to college."

The Mexican American youth receive the message that they have a responsibility to become the leaders of tomorrow. Juan Celedón, the director of the IMC, told me: "There are not enough Mexican American leaders; that's why we started the youth conference. We need more leaders. We [leaders] meet with school administrators, the police, we just met with university people. Last week we met with the newspaper because of their bias in reporting Mexican American crime. The community needs more leaders, there is much that needs to be done."

Louis Iberra, an accomplished motivational speaker, captured his adolescent audience with a complex mix of serious motivation, jokes, and student participation. His manner and message allow the young people to relax, get to know one another, and talk seriously about their futures. The conference includes a queen's contest, talent show, and speech contest, and it concludes with a dinner and dance.

Two important Mexican American leaders work for the Idaho Migrant Council. The director, Juan Celedón, founded the IMC some twenty years ago and it survived the Reagan years. Celedon began by organizing students in the 1960s. He admits that as a young activist he had some rough edges and used unsophisticated tactics; he has matured with the IMC.

The IMC has had two major crises during its twenty-year existence. A major conflict developed between the IMC and a medical group. The two agencies jointly created a low-income community health clinic but they differed on how its services should be administered. The two organizations went their separate ways, but not without some scars. The second problem involved the accountability of the budget to federal funding guidelines. This dispute involved both financial accountability and the types of programs the federal government would fund. The problem of meeting federal guidelines hampers most nonprofit organizations. The end result of this dispute was the elimination of some personnel and programs. Also, the government has restricted the IMC from becoming involved in advocacy programs for the Mexican American community.

Some in the Mexican American community complain that the IMC has become a bureaucracy and that the agency "plays favorites." During my field research, I spent many days observing the managers of the IMC. They work in a dedicated and professional manner. The IMC leaders do receive many requests for assistance that do not fit within the guidelines of the programs they administer. Their inability to grant those requests naturally lead to disappointments and "sour grapes" complaints from some.

Most Mexican American migrants have positive views of the IMC. The managers of the IMC have gained community leadership because they assist Mexican Americans after their regular working days are finished. The Mexican American migrant workers appreciate the emergency rent, food, and gas money supplied by the IMC. The IMC also provides migrants with assistance to gain access to social services. The director and deputy director have reputations for assisting low-income Mexican Americans. Celedón reviewed some of the success of the IMC: "We have made progress in the last twenty years. The community has more Mexican American professionals now. The leadership of Image de Idaho and the Mexican American Commission work with us. We stick together. The people in our community had no success, they felt defeated. Now every success builds and prepares for more success for our community. We operate four farm labor camps; we also remodeled these facilities. We built and own an office building here in Middlewest. We have had some victories in the legislature."

Juan Celedón is a member of three of the principal Mexican American organizations in Idaho. Through years of experience he has become accomplished in delivering speeches, in working with agencies to increase their support for Mexican Americans, and in organizing his fellow Mexican Americans to accomplish special projects. For example, Juan created the Mexican American Caucus, a group of Mexican American leaders, to develop and lobby for a Mexican American reapportionment plan. One key feature of the Mexican American Caucus's reapportionment plan establishes a voting district in Middlewest and Farm County that enhances the influence of the Mexican American vote. Federal law dictates that minority areas should not be gerrymandered, but the Mexican American Caucus plan may not withstand a court judgment. However, the Mexican American demand that they be players along with the state legislature has had positive effects. The Republican party recently hired a Mexican American to work toward increasing the number of Mexican American Republicans. The governor recently appointed a Mexican American to fill a vacant seat as county commissioner of Farm County.

Mexican American leaders organize fiestas, assist the poor, support other Mexican Americans in court hearings, and meet with governmental leaders to prod them into providing services to the Mexican American community. A prime example is Armando Acquirre, the deputy director of the IMC. His career began with the IMC nineteen years ago. He serves on the governing boards of several organizations such as the community mental health association. He knows many of the personnel and administrators of social service programs on both the local and state levels. He actively explores possibilities to create or extend programs to serve the Mexican American community. For example, while attending the Chamber of Commerce Leadership Program, he heard the chief administrator for the city of Middlewest mention that the city had a $200,000 grant for housing development that had not been spent. Within days, Armando had begun exploring the possibilities of using these monies for low-income housing for Mexican Americans.

Acquirre has energy and persistence; he ardently explores any possible avenue to gain grants, programs, and assistance for the Mexican American community. He wants to establish a government lending program to foster small business development. Armando seems to know all of the people, both Anglo and Mexican American, as he attempts to establish a drug and alcohol prevention program for Mexican Americans in Farm County. He also hopes to develop a paraprofessional program for young Mexican Americans. He said the following about race relations in Middlewest: "In ways, the Anglos are afraid of us; I suppose because we speak another language and our skin color is different. But we want the same things they do. Our people want a good job, a house, and a good place to raise their kids. We want our kids to get an education, to have a better life than we have. Isn't that the American way?... We will have to help ourselves. The Anglos sure are not going to give us much help."

Armando Acquirre organized the Farm County Mexican American Political Awareness Committee, which encourages Mexican Americans to become involved in the political process. The group conducts drives to register Mexican American voters and it also assists Mexican Americans who run for office. In the past few years more Mexican Americans have run for political office, but with limited success. Still, they have gained some political influence.

Other Leaders

Many local Mexican Americans consider Ricco Gómez to be their most important leader. He has received several awards for his community service work. He lives in a town close to Middlewest and has a statewide reputation among the Mexican Americans of Idaho. He has served on many prestigious boards of directors. Ricco began assisting Mexican American migrant workers in the 1950s. He has worked to reduce police abuse and to develop better educational opportunities for Mexican Americans. Gómez has been on state boards that enhance the access of Mexican Americans to jobs and social services. Whenever a Mexican American cultural event is scheduled, he works to make it a success.

The state and federal governments have honored Ricco Gómez for his community service. He played a key role in the successful efforts to create the Mexican American Commission and the Human Rights Commission as state agencies. He also assisted in the drive to establish Image de Idaho. Ricco has not lost his roots; he knows many working-class Mexican Americans. No one I interviewed maligned the character of Gomez, because they recognize that he has spent his life in service to the Mexican American community.

Estella Medina is the quintessential grass roots Mexican American leader of Middlewest. She arrived in Middlewest as a girl via the migrant trail. Her husband works in farm labor as a truck contractor. Estella actively participates on the Catholic church's Mexican American Council and is a tireless worker on behalf of the Mexican American community. For example, in 1990 she acted as the mistress of ceremonies at the fiesta honoring the Virgin of Guadalupe. In 1991 she organized the church council to hold a special dinner honoring the migrant workers. She ran unsuccessfully for the school board in 1992 and has encouraged other Mexican Americans to run for office. Whenever an issue of concern to Mexican Americans arises in Middlewest, it is certain that Estella Medina will be present.

Estella works for the Farm County court system as a juvenile officer and as a court interpreter for Mexican American offenders. She believes that some judges assign Mexican Americans harsher sentences. During the period of my field research, Estella attended more community meetings than did any other person; she attended more city council meetings and school board meetings than any other person in Middlewest. The chief of police requested her services on the interracial committee to solve the Mexican American gang problem. She is an active member of all the local Mexican American organizations. When the RUDAT study recommended the establishment of a committee to implement its recommendations, Estella went to the committee, requesting to be a member. Like many other Mexican American leaders, she does not have a college education. I asked her why she participates in all the community activities. She responded: "I care what happens to people. They need a push in the right direction, so they can make it, so they don't have to stay in the same position forever. I care what happens to my community. Things won't get better if you don't get involved. It's the love of the people." By her voluntary service, Estella represents the essence of good citizenship.

Mexican American Leaders/Professionals

The leadership of the Mexican American community in Middlewest consists of teachers, lawyers, criminal justice personnel, a few businesspeople, social services professionals, and two Catholic priests. Most of these people started as migrant workers and overcame their limited opportunities, limited education, and their backgrounds of poverty. They have traveled a long and arduous trail, in part because they are self-taught, and have gained their skills by trying to solve the problems of their fellow Mexican Americans.

Most Mexican American professionals in Middlewest become community leaders. One way these leaders assist other Mexican Americans is through their jobs. Most Mexican American teachers participate in the migrant and bilingual education programs in the public schools and alternative schools. In their capacity as teachers they serve both as role models and motivators to encourage Mexican American youth to pursue their education.

Alberto and Maria Garza typify the Mexican American teacher. They started as migrant workers. They became teacher aides but soon realized the need for a college degree. They became teachers to assist Mexican Americans, but they recognized the need to serve in Mexican American organizations, because so few leaders exist. Alberto has recently accepted an elementary school principal position. During the field research, Alberto was a guest speaker at several forums; he served on the committee organizing the Cinco de Mayo fiesta, he worked on the Mexican American voter registration drive, and he is a member of the Mexican American Caucus.

Lawyers constitute another group of Mexican American professionals. Each Mexican American lawyer has a practice or governmental position that enables him or her to assist the Mexican American community. The four lawyers residing in southwestern Idaho believe from their experiences that the criminal justice system discriminates against Mexican American offenders. The two Mexican American legal aid lawyers say that most of their Mexican American clients' cases involve not receiving payment for one's work, having checks garnisheed, or being denied social services.

Middlewest has two Mexican American lawyers in private practice. Tony DeRose has a civil practice and Roberto Torres a criminal practice. They primarily serve Mexican American clients. Tony has a reputation for being the most radical Mexican American in Middlewest. He attends many community meetings, including the city council meetings, where he criticizes Anglo leaders for their prejudiced attitudes. Most Anglo business and civic leaders in Middlewest dislike Tony; they believe that his charges of racism are "unfounded" and "border on hysteria."

In the past, DeRose has fostered a radical image by wearing a black beret and black leather jacket. He writes articles for the Idaho *Law Review* and at one time had a regular column in Boise's daily newspaper. Tony articulates one viewpoint on the problems facing Mexican Americans in Middlewest; yet most Anglos in town immediately dismiss his views. Most of Tony's practice involves low-income Mexican Americans, and he has worked with many clients seeking amnesty. The mayor recently appointed him to the Middlewest Housing Authority. Most of Tony's fellow Mexican American leaders believe that his radical tactics are counterproductive because of the conservative orientation of Middlewest.

Rose García has become the most important female Mexican American leader because she writes a weekly column in the Boise newspaper. Her column has educated and informed many Anglos in Idaho about the issues and problems facing the Mexican Americans of Idaho; however, many Anglos in Middlewest dislike her "biased" editorials. Rose, because of her visibility, receives many requests to lecture and participate in issue-oriented conferences. She also serves on many citizen committees.

García works for the IMC as the director of a mental health project that receives state money to assist Mexican American clients. She says that the mental health problems of Mexican Americans are not being met because the state of Idaho does not provide adequate staff and resources to meet their needs. The problem is intensified because Mexican American culture inhibits clients from discussing their personal problems. Only a few Spanish-speaking Mexican Americans in Idaho have social work or counseling credentials. Rose says the state's Department of Employment should recruit Mexican American social workers from other states in the region.

Mexican American Business Leaders

The local Mexican American businesspeople and professionals not only make financial donations for cultural celebrations but also participate in fiestas by playing musical instruments, singing, and preparing food. Rodolfo Cortez operates two Mexican restaurants, one in Middlewest and one in Boise. He sings and plays in a mariachi band. Mexican American leaders frequently use his restaurants as meeting places. The most common business for Mexican Americans is operating Mexican restaurants. Mexican Americans own seven restaurants in southwestern Idaho, which, for the most part, are small establishments that only provide a family living. The next most common Mexican American businesses are small auto-repair shops and bars.

Don Flores has a small contracting business in Middlewest which he started twenty years ago. Flores began as a construction worker. He built his own house, and that led to the realization that he could operate a construction company. He provides financial assistance to many Mexican American projects. Flores said that being Mexican American has not hurt his business, because he has light skin and also does not use his name in his business operations. He does believe, however, that he lost a significant small-business loan because of his race. He shared the following story:

> My two sons were moving their furniture from our old house to a new one I had just purchased. A relative called me and told me my boys were being arrested. By the time I arrived on the scene, both boys, ages 13 and 15, were in the back of the police car in handcuffs. Apparently, a person in the neighborhood called and reported a burglary underway. The police thought the boys were robbing their own house. Both my sons were crying because of the rough treatment from the police.

Flores claimed that the police only treat Mexican kids that way and that he had never been so mad in his life. The police later apologized for their mistake, but Flores was still angry as he told me the story.

The only Mexican American with a large business in Middlewest is Oscar Mireles. He started in the fields and now has a tortilla factory with forty employees. He and his son have plans to open another plant in the state of Washington. Mireles shared with me an account of the difficulties of establishing his business. The whole family made tortillas while he went to the stores seeking accounts. He now has his own trucks and several large accounts. Oscar Mireles belongs to many Anglo community organizations but he has not forgotten his heritage—the Mexican American community counts on his generous donations. His family cooks the beef-head barbecue that is sold on Sundays.

Priests

The two local Mexican American Catholic priests, one from Middlewest and the other from a nearby town, automatically have leadership positions in the Mexican American community of southwestern Idaho. They conduct a separate Spanish-language mass on Sundays and they preside over Mexican American weddings, Quinceañeras, and the Virgin of Guadalupe mass. Mexican Americans frequently rely on their priests to assist them in times of crisis. Both priests said that attempts to integrate masses among Anglos and Mexican Americans failed, having caused stress and discomfort. Many Anglo Catholics do not want to attend church with Mexican Americans. Both priests said that many Anglo Catholics hold prejudiced views about Mexican Americans.

Father Acuna came from Mexico a few years ago. He has a gregarious nature and enjoys interacting at the socials and fiestas of the Mexican American community. Occasionally he sings with the mariachi band at a fiesta. Father Acuna more actively pursues a social agenda for the people. He has the respect of the people and their leaders. Father Acuna has a regular Spanish-language radio program in which he criticizes the Anglo community for its racist treatment of the Mexican American people. I asked him how the church hierarchy views his editorials. Father Acuna laughed and said they do not speak Spanish.

Because of his work with Mexican American Catholics, Father Acuna has no doubts about the discrimination facing Mexican Americans. He said that less of the church's resources matriculate to Mexican American parishes than to Anglo parishes. He feels that Anglo priests demand assimilation, and he thinks that Anglo priests reject the use of Spanish and do not respect Mexican American culture.

Father Acuna believes that the Catholic church remains important to Mexican Americans because religion is in their blood and the church operates as a support system against racism. He thinks that the situation of rural Mexican Americans resembles that in South Africa. Father Acuna regrets that Mexican Americans have so few opportunities. He claimed that the police and courts operate in a racist fashion. He has received two citations for driving violations, and he said that the arrests occurred because he was Mexican. He has spent many hours in court and at the jail supporting Mexican American offenders. Father Acuna concluded by stating that Mexican Americans in southwestern Idaho face systematic exploitation.

Father Correro heads the Catholic church in Middlewest. He does not approve of priests becoming involved in social and political issues. However, being a Catholic priest automatically places him in a leadership role. He believes that as a Mexican American priest he must teach Mexican Americans the rules of the church and how their faith can sustain them.

Father Correro conceded that race relations is a serious problem in Middlewest. He claimed to hear many racist comments from his Anglo parishioners. He said Anglos think Mexican Americans do not have a work ethic and that the Mexican Americans cannot help but feel the rejection. His Anglo parishioners keep demanding that Mexican Americans speak English. He recognizes that the Anglos and Mexican Americans of Middlewest live in separate communities.

Father Correro became incensed when discussing how the Anglos of Middlewest refuse to provide adequate social services to disadvantaged Mexican Americans. He said, "Anglo attitudes are the problem. They feel no responsibility to help others. In America, people place too much emphasis on consumerism and too little on Christian charity."

The observations of Mexican American Catholic priests have special significance because these priests are in a unique position of observing and interacting intimately with both Anglos and Mexican Americans. Both priests agreed that Middlewest and Farm County have a high degree of racism. I asked them about solutions to this problem. They both replied that a major increase in resources must be provided for disadvantaged Mexican Americans. They focused on social services, education, and employment-training programs. They called upon government officials to provide the leadership to improve race relations in Idaho.

Conclusions

This chapter reveals the need for immediate programs to improve the position of Mexican Americans in Middlewest. A national health-care program would be of great benefit to many in the Mexican American community. That community needs to increase its efforts to register voters. Anglo business and government leaders need to create more college scholarships for Mexican Americans.

In my opinion, there need to be established cultural awareness workshops for Anglo farmers, factory owners, businessmen, school personnel, criminal-justice employees, and community leaders in general.   The city council should create a community race-relations committee which would ensure affirmative action in hiring practices.   This committee could have a grievance subcommittee trained in conflict resolution to handle racial disputes in the community. Factory and farm workers need to develop strong unions. The Catholic church needs to support a more liberal theology; Catholic masses should be integrated.   Mexican Americans need to be educated about the types of federal assistance available.

My research on Mexican American leaders supports the theoretical orientation of Mirande (1985) and Blea (1988), who recommend creating a Chicano paradigm. The Chicano paradigm recognizes that the Mexican American community is not passive but actively resists the oppression of Anglo society.   Middlewest's Mexican American leaders and organizations came to the defense of individual Mexican Americans being mistreated by the criminal-justice system; they also interceded on the behalf of Mexican Americans to enable them to gain access to social services. The Mexican American leaders also challenged the dominant social institutions for not providing more opportunities for members of the Mexican American community. For example, to assist Mexican American youth the leaders created conferences, scholarships, and programs to encourage and support the education of their youth.

I asked the Mexican American leaders who in the Anglo community they trust, who they could count on for assistance. Their response: "Not many." The Mexican American community represents less than six percent of the population of Idaho and, consequently, it has little political power. My respect for the Mexican American leaders grew as I began to appreciate the precarious situation of many Mexican Americans in Idaho. My respect increased for their efforts to pursue social justice for the Mexican American community.   I soon understood their frustrations, as one race crisis after another flared across southern Idaho. These racial conflicts generally happened without response from the politicians, the media, and the government entities that have a responsibility to address these problems. The Mexican American leaders have extraordinary commitment, tenacity, and dedication. Anglo Middlewest, Anglo Idaho has little perception of their efforts and contribution to the community and state.

I interviewed several Anglo government bureaucrats who did not want to be quoted, who did not want to speak out, because their superiors and the public were known not to be sympathetic to Mexican American problems. They presented themselves as concerned persons, empathetic to Mexican American problems, but they were afraid to challenge the status quo. The mood and social environment inhibit them from speaking out because of the potential for being labelled a radical. Apparently in Idaho you are a radical if you support bilingual education, defend civil rights, demand affirmative-action programs, request access to medical care, believe in decent housing for all, and address the need for a living wage for the Mexican American people of the state.

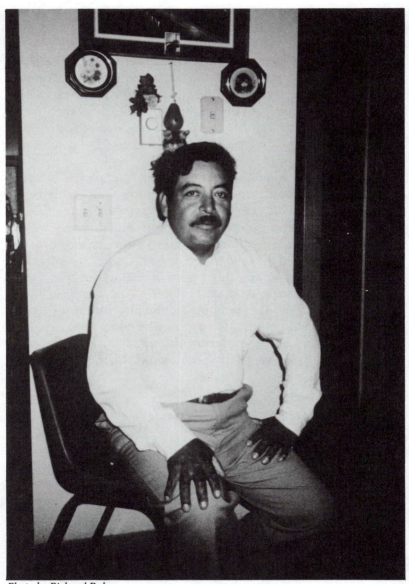

Mr. Ángeles, a migrant worker, attempted to organize the residents of a local labor camp.

Chapter 5

THE ANGLO
WORKING CLASS AND
ANGLO FARMERS

*Those who don't know any better come into our neighborhood
scared. They think we're dangerous. They think we will attack them
with shiny knives.... But we aren't afraid. We know the guy with the
crooked eye is Davey the Baby's brother ... and the big one that looks
like a dumb grown man, he's Fat Boy, though he's not fat anymore nor
a boy.*

*All brown all around, we are safe. But watch us drive into a neigh-
borhood of another color and our knees go shakity-shake and our car
windows get rolled up tight and our eyes look straight. Yeah. That is
how it goes and goes.*

–Sandra Cisneros

Anglo Workers

During the fourth phase of my field research, I interviewed
thirty-five Anglo working-class residents of Middlewest. Most
worked in factories or in unskilled occupations; however, I
attempted to obtain interviews from as many different working-
class occupations as possible. Most of the subjects interviewed
worked in food processing plants, trailer factories, wood-
products mills, and other small construction-related businesses.
Additional interviews involved subjects from the following occupations: firefighter, gravedigger, mailman, grocery clerk, dairy
worker, and sales clerk. The working-class women represented

119

the following occupations: secretary, bookkeeper, beautician, real estate sales, sales clerk, and factory worker.

The Anglo male working-class subjects can be divided into two groups, those earning a modest but adequate income and the working poor. The working poor have the common characteristics of being young and unskilled. Most of them believe that they earn inadequate wages yet they dislike unions. The majority do not vote; their political rhetoric sounds conservative, primarily because of their fierce notions of individualism and independence.

Most of these workers grew up in Middlewest or in the small towns near Middlewest. Many of the men served in the military; most do not belong to clubs or organizations. Some workers participate in youth programs, such as sports and scouting. The males list camping, fishing, and hunting as their favorite leisure-time activities. They complain about their financial status and commonly live in modest apartments and homes.

Some younger Anglo male workers have hostile feelings toward management, which they claim does not treat them with respect. They also complain about inadequate fringe benefits; many cannot afford medical insurance. Many low-income workers dropped out of school, but not in as high a rate as did Mexican American workers. Young Anglo workers as a group experience a high divorce rate, have drinking problems, and do not commonly attend church.

The Anglo blue-collar workers who earn more than $8.00 an hour tend to be older, more skilled workers. These workers usually have adequate benefits. They participate more in community activities and many belong to the Elks or Moose lodges. More of them attend church regularly. Their favorite leisure-time activities involve outdoor sports. The majority of these workers vote on a regular basis.

Anglo workers like living in Middlewest. They prefer small-town life and like Middlewest because it does not have the problems of urban life. The negative aspects of Middlewest, to them, involve the decline of the downtown businesses and the fact that Middlewest has too many Mexicans. One worker commented:

We're an agricultural-based community. I was raised here. People are laid back. People do what their fathers did, because that's all they know. We're not high-tech here, playing all those modern games. I tell you what, in Boise, they don't live life nearly as full. Everything is done high speed; Boise doesn't seem to have time to play Monopoly with the kids. So maybe they go out to the movies and theater, maybe other entertainment, but no time to lay around, to play catch with the kids. I don't see this in Boise, they [have a] gotta-be-doing-something mentality.

Approximately 25 percent of the Anglo workers—the same proportion as Mexican American workers—want to be their own boss and establish their own businesses. Most do not have a definite plan or specific business in mind. They dislike having someone telling them what to do; they dream of escaping the hierarchical workplace.

I did interview a few Anglo workers who have definite plans to advance their economic standing. For example, Terry Hunter works as an assistant manager of the meat department of a local grocery store. He works overtime and enrolls in all of the store's training programs. His motivation derives from his desire to become a manager of a large store in Boise. Another example is Phil Todd. He is the purchasing agent for a small business. He received his business training in the army. Phil has completed three years of college by taking evening courses. He plans to complete a master's degree in business administration that he hopes will lead to a high-paying position.

Most of the workers interviewed share a conservative political perspective. They oppose taxes and welfare. Most oppose gun control because they like hunting. Working-class men often conduct a rite of passage for their sons that involves hunting achievements; killing a deer becomes a merit badge in many working-class families. They believe freedom exists because of the right to bear arms. Their anti-government orientation has a western flavor. One worker typified the sentiment: "We value independence and we don't like anyone telling us what to do!"

Most Anglo male workers have some negative attitudes about Mexican Americans. Their attitudes have a harsher and more emotional tone than do those of the Anglo middle class. They say such things as, "The Mexicans are on welfare but they drive new cars."

Jake Jackson has a second job as a horse trader. Jake enjoyed sharing his expertise. His father was also a horse trader. The day I interviewed him he had purchased six horses. He drove about 300 miles to examine, analyze, and trade the horses. For Jake, horse trading is not a hobby; he makes good money at it. Jake said that the secret to making money is knowing horses: "Most people spoil their horses, they're city folk, and they don't know the value of a horse." He reviewed the most important aspects in evaluating a horse, which include appearance, past injuries, gait, and responsiveness to commands. This last trait has great importance, because Jake can retrain an unresponsive horse. He speaks with a western drawl and has the easygoing manner of a rural cowboy; but when the discussion concerned Mexican Americans his discourse became bitter:

> The Mexicans are on so many government subsidies, food, housing, clothing, health, everything is gave to them. It doesn't cost them anything for all that stuff. The money they are able to earn is minimum wage, but they put it in their pocket or they put it in their cars. You know, when they leave here in the fall and go back to Texas or Mexico or wherever they go, they live pretty well, as well as they want to. The younger crowd, they spend as much money on their cars and stereos that it would feed a Mexican family for a year. Just with the money they spend on a stereo outfit. I talked to a guy at a wreck, a guy who sells stereo equipment. I says how much would you say this stereo cost? He named it off. This Mexican kid had three thousand dollars of stereo equipment in his car. Can you believe that?

Roger, a fifty-year-old construction worker, has the discourse of a blue-collar philosopher. He feels abused because for the past five years he has earned $11,000 a year. He once owned a small construction business and most of his jobs came from subcontracting for larger firms. He lost his business when a contractor defaulted on his payments to Roger for materials and work already completed. He still does some home remodeling work for people.

Roger thinks Idaho "stinks" when it comes to paying the working class. He claimed that he barely survives. He doesn't own a house, and he drives an old pickup. He likes Middlewest because his family and relatives live in town. He believes the community disdains status seekers. He regularly plays golf with local businessmen. Roger said that people don't waste their money on clothes in Middlewest: "My wife is a shop-a-holic. I finally told her I am never going to the shopping center again because there is absolutely nothing there I would buy and I no longer get a kick out of seeing the things people will buy."

Working-class couples recognize that they both must work to avoid poverty. Most Anglo women work as secretaries, receptionists, and bookkeepers. Local women workers generally earn lower incomes than do the men. They can be found in the lowest-paying positions. In the offices of Middlewest the men are the managers and the women do the office work.

This pattern is repeated in all the large companies in town. For example, at the local dairy the women do the office work and the men do the line work and hold the managerial positions. The division of work resembles that of the workplace of the 1950s. Take Patty Burke, for example—she has twenty years of experience at the local five-and-ten. The store needs remodeling. The toys, knick-knacks, and display cases would make a modern merchandiser cringe, but Patty claimed that the store has healthy profits. She said that all the women salesclerks in the store are friends. Patty has conservative political views, but she is dissatisfied with having been the assistant manager for ten years while the company continues to hire inexperienced men to manage the store. Patty feels she will always be the assistant manager.

Patty and her husband grew up in Middlewest and married while they were in high school. Patty's husband is a welder for a horse-trailer company. She said that they both love living in Middlewest. She likes knowing many people in town and having lots of friends, and she said that her family has a good life. They like to go camping; they attend church most Sundays; and they vote Republican. Her husband only cares about one political issue—"He just goes crazy when someone comes on TV saying people shouldn't be allowed to have guns anymore."

Patty does not like welfare because, as she said, "those people should have to work like the rest of us." Patty claimed that Middlewest is a great town in which to raise children. She and her husband attend all the high school games because their daughter is a cheerleader; their son has enrolled in a vocational school. Both children plan to live in Middlewest.

Patty's rural small-town life appears warm and folksy but, again, her mood changed when the interview turned to the Mexican American community. I asked Patty to assess the Mexican American community. She said:

> There is kind of a split. Many of the migrants find they can get welfare, food stamps fairly easy.... There might be a resentment about them moving into our community. Seems like there is almost more of them than there is Anglos. There are gangs here in town, which is bad.... There is quite a bit of shoplifting in our store. It's almost a job to them.... A lot of Mexican Americans think we owe them something. They are not very friendly. They have a chip on their shoulder. The drug problem is horrendous. When you go down to Chicago street—that's the lower part of town—some of those houses are known drug houses. You see the same people sitting on the corner. They don't work; they drive dogs for cars. I wonder how they make it?

I asked Patty her thoughts on the English language bill. She said, "We shouldn't have to learn Spanish to keep our jobs. If they want to live here, I feel they should learn to speak English. If I went to Mexico I would learn Spanish."

Martha Palmer, a divorced woman, sells real estate and has lived most of her life in Middlewest. Her grandparents came to Middlewest as pioneers. She likes Middlewest because see never feels alone there. Martha likes the town as a place to raise her children, who belong to the Boy Scouts and play Little League baseball. Martha has a paternalistic attitude towards Mexican Americans:

> More and more of the Mexican Americans are staying in Middlewest. We went overboard with bilingual education. They were a humble-type people when I was growing up. They were quiet and never made waves. They stayed in their own neighborhood. But the school made a mistake by encouraging bilingual education. They [Mexican Americans] need to blend into the community. You know, they need to change and adapt. They come here from Mexico to live. I don't see why things need to be written in Spanish. This is the United States, they should speak English.... I rent one unit of my duplex to a Mexican American girl. All the neighbors want her out. They say she is no good.... Yes, there's a lot of bigotry here in Middlewest but, you know, human nature is bigoted.

This interview typifies the inconsistencies in Anglo attitudes toward the Mexican Americans of Middlewest. Martha sees herself as having a progressive attitude concerning Mexican Americans, but she seems to have no insight into her lack of acceptance of cultural diversity.

Other interviews of working-class women included a bookkeeper, a waitress, a payroll clerk, and several salesclerks. The women attended church more than their husbands. They liked Middlewest as a place to raise their children. None of the women identified with feminists and most opposed abortion. Their biggest complaint involved the lack of places to shop in town. Geri Arnold likes Middlewest because it never changes. She has a daughter in high school, and she thinks it's wonderful that the school has not changed. Geri said that she and her husband have the same friends they had in high school. She felt that women have a hard time finding work in Middlewest, and she had this to say about Mexican Americans: "The Mexicans have bad values. They don't take care of their property, their part of town is so run down. I am afraid of them because there are so many shootings and knifings. The only negative thing about Middlewest is the influx of Mexicans. They're rude. I don't like them speaking Spanish. They drive new cars but they're on welfare and food stamps. They don't pay their bills. All they do is take, take, take."

Ken Moore works for the city of Middlewest as a laborer and has lived all his life in Middlewest. Ken's wife has left him. His hobbies include riding motorcycles, going to rodeos, and bear hunting. He believes his values are pretty much like everybody else's. He does not like women taking jobs away from men; he opposes environmentalists because they "come up with all these little rules that threaten my right to trap and hunt." Ken had the following observations concerning Mexican Americans:

> Through the years they just keep coming, more and more Mexicans. They're involved in all the crime and drugs. They got gangs, the Crips, they are spray painting everything in town and there don't seem to be anything people can do about it; its bad.... In school, now, they have to teach Mexican stuff for one month. They got a whole month dedicated to Mexicans. I don't think that's right.... I think they oughta be more strict on that welfare. You be down at the store and you see a Mexican with a new car, new clothes; he goes to the register with a cart full of food and he pays with food stamps. And then he gaves his buddy a twenty or thirty or one-hundred dollar bill to buy a six-pack of beer.

The image of Mexican Americans of most of the Anglo working class has two primary components. First, they stereotype Mexican Americans as criminals and welfare cheaters. They have no explanation of why Mexican Americans exhibit these traits and they have little curiosity concerning the causes of the alleged antisocial behavior. Second, the Anglo workers view

Mexican Americans as not appreciating the "important values" of cleanliness, ownership of property, and economic success. This leads to their criticism of Mexican Americans because they drive old cars, have run-down houses, and do not exhibit a work ethic. This is a classic case of blaming the victim, in which the Mexican American population is condemned for being forced to live in poverty.

Randy Kemp has had a variety of jobs and recently lost his job at the dairy plant. Randy said: "The big problem around here is Mexicans. See those apartments? The owner was renting to migrants. They don't care, they are breaking into places; they broke into my garage. They stole a stereo from my car. They cause a lot of problems. I got tired of them. I talks with the owner; he's gonna keep the migrants out. The Mexican kids party all the time; they destroy everything. Our daughter is in a girls' home. Her problem was hanging around with those Mexicans. She takes off with them, drinks beer with them, and does not come home for a week. The judge says he can't do anything about it."

Larry Jones also has little use for Mexicans. He says, "When I was unemployed I went to the welfare people for help. They made me fill out all this paper work. Then they said I had too many assets. Assets, my ass; I told those bastards that I bet they woulda helped me if my name was Mexican." Larry did not complete high school. He has drifted from one job to another. His supervisors fired him from some of those jobs. Larry does not like bosses; he resents the fact that at his current job, in a trailer factory, the bosses get the bonuses. Larry cannot afford health insurance on his $5.50 an hour job. He believes the company treats the machines better than it does the workers. According to Larry, the company regularly lays off workers, who never know how many hours they will work a week.

Jones wants his own business and he looks forward to being able to tell the bosses to "kiss my ass." He did not hesitate to share his personal problems, which include a messy divorce and a serious drinking problem. He is "pissed-off" because his former wife got their house and because he cannot afford to pay the child support. Larry said that the credit company reclaimed his truck. He lamented, "I cannot even afford to go out for a beer on Friday night. Sometimes I feel like giving up because I will never be able to get ahead."

Larry estimated that 35 percent of the workers at the trailer factory are Mexican American, and he feels that each group keeps to itself. Larry claimed Anglos have a joking relationship with the Mexican Americans, making such remarks as, "I hope my friends don't hear that I am taking orders from a Mexican." Larry said that he and his friends used to get into fights with the Mexicans, but that does not happen much anymore. It is quite common for people in Larry's economic position to blame an ethnic group as a way to vent their frustrations.

Jimmy Carlson, who grew up in Middlewest, said that he has had nothing but bad experiences with Mexican Americans. He attends church services three times a week and participates in the administration and charity work of his church. Nevertheless, he claimed, "I had to fight them all the time in school. I tell my children to avoid the Mexicans." Carlson works for an electrical repair shop that employs two Mexican American workers; Jimmy said that they are good people and good workers but claimed that they are an exception.

Sociologists (Livingston 1979) have known for a long time that increasing social interaction on an equal basis improves race relations. Jimmy Carlson likes the Mexican Americans with whom he works—stereotypes can lose their force when people actually associate with those from a different ethnic background.

A Summing Up: Anglo Worker Attitudes

Many Anglo workers believe that too many Mexican Americans live in Middlewest. They want Mexican Americans to adapt to their way of life. They have a limited knowledge of Mexican American culture, and that makes it easier to stereotype Mexican Americans as criminals and welfare cheaters. One minister summed up Anglo sentiments: "The treatment of Mexican Americans in this town is similar to how the blacks must have been treated in the past in the South."

Anglos in Middlewest have a narrow interpretation of American history as being fundamentally that of Anglo Europeans; they miss the fact that America is actually a multicultural society. This diversity provides a rich resource for the enhancement of our lives, enabling us to better understand ourselves. Instead of ignoring Mexican Americans or questioning their very presence in America, Anglos would do well to appreciate and enjoy the rich tapestry of Mexican American culture in Idaho. A tragedy here is the distancing of Anglos from the Mexican American population. The Anglos of Middlewest lack the empathy to appreciate the problems facing the Mexican American community.

Anglo Farmers

The family histories of most of the area's farmers show that most have been farming in Farm County for two or three generations. There are approximately 3,300 farmers in the county. Most farms operate on between 300 and 800 acres of land; some farmers have as many as 3,000 acres while others farm as few as 40 acres. The small farmers have second jobs as an economic necessity. I interviewed twelve farmers whose ages ranged from thirty-two to sixty-seven. Though an experienced interviewer, I have never interviewed a group with such a consistently common set of shared beliefs.

To gain an appreciation for farm life and attitudes, I also interviewed agricultural officials with the state and federal governments. In addition, I interviewed the owner of an onion shed and the manager of an apple packing plant, both of whom employ many Mexican American migrant workers.

Local farmers grow some thirty-five different crops but only six to eight in any one year. Some farmers specialize with particular crops such as onions, asparagus, mint, corn seed, sugar beets, and hops; others concentrate on fruits, with apples being by far the most commonly grown. Fruit farmers also grow pears, apricots, plums, and peaches. Perhaps surprisingly, farmers do not grow many potatoes in this part of Idaho.

Agricultural statistics indicate that Farm County ranks as the thirty-fifth largest agricultural producing county in the United States. According to experts, Farm County has an ideal climate for many crops. The harsh winters destroy diseases that attack crops and the summers are long and hot. Farm County produces 90 percent of the corn seed for the United States, and the county has the largest sugar plant in the country. In the fall, hills of harvested sugar beets twenty-five feet high and twenty-five yards wide extend for a quarter of a mile.

The local farmers uniformly agree that they like to farm, and they cannot imagine doing any other type of work. They most value the independence that goes with farming; they like being their own boss. A good way to get a farmer talking is to ask him what he thinks of the government—each farmer I interviewed reacted with grimaces to the mention of the government. They deplore government intervention and they hate having the government tell them how to farm. They believe the federal bureaucrats create unnecessary policies and laws because they do not understand farming, and the farmers believe that government policies reduce their profits.

Middlewest farmers intensely dislike the Environmental Protection Agency (EPA), which they believe creates too many restrictions. Each farmer interviewed presented as proof the EPA's decision to ban the pesticide ALAR. To the farmers, the EPA only listened to "those crazy environmentalists" when, in reality, no harm or danger occurred to consumers because of the farmers' use of ALAR on their apple crops. The farmers believe that consumers don't appreciate how hard they work and that the consumer just takes for granted that American farmers produce the best and safest food in the world. One retired farmer concluded his critique of the government with the statement, "Hell, I used to take baths in DDT; there are no problems with the farmers' use of chemicals."

Area farmers also disapprove of OSHA, the Occupational Safety and Health Administration, which, according to the farmers, has no idea of how work must be organized on a farm. They think the rules and regulations of OSHA harm farm productivity;

most agree with the statement, "If we followed their [OSHA] rules we would never get the work done."

The INS, Immigration and Naturalization Service, is one of a host of government agencies criticized by farmers for creating too much paperwork and recordkeeping. A typical remark was, "All of these government rules from bookkeeping to telling us what we can grow are ridiculous. I don't like the government telling me how to farm."

To say that farmers are conservative would be an understatement. The farmers deny that they have political influence, but all the legislators from Farm County support a conservative Republican agenda. Both farmers and the Farm Bureau have considerable political influence in the state. In Farm County, farmers serve as state legislators and as county commissioners. The family of one of the most conservative U.S. senators operates a farm in the county; the current chairman of the state Republican party owns a farm in the county. In a recent session of the Idaho state legislature, the Farm Bureau successfully opposed all proposed environmental legislation.

Enormous inconsistencies exist in the political perspective of farmers. They dislike government spending and welfare, but they receive the benefits of many government programs—which they of course do not define as welfare. At the core of the farmers' political views is a belief in the benefits of the free-enterprise system and a belief that everyone has an equal chance for success in America.

Farmers do not perceive a contradiction in the fact that they have inherited their family farms while the average person could not enter farming without a quarter of a million dollars of capital. Also, the idea that farmers receive "welfare" has legitimacy: there is the price-support system; the University of Idaho's agricultural extension service provides basic research for local farmers; irrigation water comes from dams and canals built by government funds; and farmers receive benefits from a tax policy that significantly reduces their taxes.

The farmers' values reflect those of Middlewest in general. However, they emphasize even more the basic view that farmers live a more simple and traditional life. Farmers believe that farm families care about and help one another more than do other people. They enjoy the variety of skills and activities required to operate a farm. Farmers assert that farm life allows for a slower-paced life.

Few if any challenge farmers about their attitudes toward Mexican Americans. Consequently, they present their views about race as matters of fact, and they present a harsh and narrow set of negative views about Mexican Americans. The local farmers deny that they are prejudiced but then proceed to denigrate Mexican American migrant workers. They dislike the Idaho Migrant Council and the legal aid organization for "meddling" in the farmer's relations with his workers. The farmers' sense of community and social responsibility does not seem to extend to migrant workers. Farmers do not perceive their behavior as being racist when they send their children to schools outside their own districts in order to avoid the children having to attend schools with Mexican American students.

Farmers claim they cannot pay their migrants a higher wage because of their meager profits. Though nothing could be more inaccurate, the farmers maintain that the migrant workers earn a decent living. Fred Fisher's view is typical: "In my opinion, the migrants are no more in poverty than we farmers are." The farmers believe that Mexican American migrant workers are not good workers—they are not dependable, they prefer to live on welfare, and they the lack motivation to get ahead.

A farmer's life consists of hard work and long hours. Much of the year farmers work on weekends. They have to know how to plant, grow, and harvest the crops. The successful farmer knows when and how to use chemicals on the fields and when to irrigate, recognizes the condition of the soil, understands the effects of the weather on crops, knows how to repair farm equipment, and has a fair number of financial skills. A farmer also has to have the ability to adapt to changing conditions: consumers' tastes may change; the market might become more competitive; uncertainties abound.

The most significant changes in modern farming involve technological improvements. Farmers now can achieve greater efficiency and productivity; to compete, however, the farmer has to have a large farm. Some older farmers regret the new specialization in farming and the loss of the family farm with its chickens, pigs, and milk cows. The technology has forced them to adapt to the agribusiness way of farming. The farmers interviewed said they have become like any other business. Several had computers to assist them in maintaining records for the government and in keeping track of business expenses and labor costs. Spouses generally are in charge of the accounting system for the family's farm. The farmers are quite unhappy about government regulations that require them to maintain extensive records regarding farm labor. The INS requires that the farmer have two forms of identification from each farm worker, and it uses this documentation as a means to control undocumented workers. The farmers uniformly agree that after the Amnesty Law of 1986 and the new identification rules, few undocumented workers are to be found in Idaho. Mexican American leaders, however, believe that, despite amnesty, there are still high numbers of undocumented workers.

Almost all the farmers said they prefer to hire migrant workers from Mexico. They believe these men work hard and do not complain while the Mexican American migrant workers are too soft, which they attribute to their having been spoiled by living in America. Many farmers posit that Mexican American migrant workers would prefer being on welfare.

Bill Black, the local manager of the Agricultural Stabilization and Conservation Service (ASCS) for Farm County, knows most of the local farmers. Black said that it is the nature of farmers constantly to complain. Farmers never admit to having a good year; they dress in plain work clothes but most have land and equipment worth at least a quarter of a million dollars. They legitimately complain about the unpredictability associated with farming; they never know what the weather has in store for the season. For several years now, Idaho farmers have been coping with a drought. The farmers do not control the market, so they never know in advance for what price a crop will sell. In 1992 most of Farm County fruit growers lost their crops due to freezing spring temperatures. Sometimes farmers do have to sell their crops without making a profit.

The farmers I interviewed would not reveal their profits. They claimed they did not know their profits for last year because they reinvest their money in new equipment and land. However, they did know, in detail, the exact cost of producing each crop. Bill Black said that the average farmer in the county makes approximately $40,000 to $50,000 in profit a year but some years does well while in others has no profits. According to Bill, a key to understanding the farmers' complaints is to realize that most capitalists earn at least ten percent on their investments; the farmer only averages about five percent. The farmer has a big investment yet does not earn a great rate on that property and equipment.

My interviews with farmers took place in their homes or in their fields. A couple of interviews occurred in pickups as the farmers took me on a tour of their farms. The view from the top of Benson Butte reveals scattered farmhouses and farm roads spread across a spacious valley with orchards and crops showing as different shades and patches of green. The Snake River meanders through the valley. In the distance, the Owyhee Mountains with their snow-capped peaks rise modestly. The valley attracts a considerable bird population: ducks, cranes, and geese claim the riparian areas while pheasants and hawks keep watch in and above the fields. In the midst of such serene and lovely surroundings, it is easy to appreciate the farmers' claim that they enjoy a better way of life. They examine the weather, land, and nature each day, in contrast to urbanites, who often only notice the extremes in weather and only see apples and onions in grocery bins.

Farmers postulate that a farm has the best environment to raise a family. Farm children learn responsibility and how to work hard. Farmers believe that their children do not think life is boring or that they have nothing to do as do many city kids. George Kirby said, "My sons both belonged to 4-H. The older boy had 300 laying hens and his younger brother raised hogs. The boys had lots of chores and they made their own money. It taught them to be hard-working and independent."

Andy Lyons's parents came to Farm County in the 1920s. Recently retired, Andy has lived his whole life on the family farm. He has a high school education and claims that a person does not need to go to college to be a farmer. Andy said he never wanted to do anything but farm: "It's in the blood; you don't do it for the money." Andy said he just loved farming and couldn't wait for spring to arrive. He spent much of the interview talking about the good old days:

> Farm communities aren't like they used to be. For one thing, there used to be more operators. We were family farms then. In the old days it took twenty-three people to run a threshing crew. It was about seven families working together threshing for ten days to two weeks. It was a ball. Every place you went, the women would try to outcook the one before. When I was fifteen, there were about six kids my age and we worked together. It was a ball; we loved it. Today, there is no trading help. Oh, we do a little. The biggest change in farming is we don't work together as much as we used to.

Andy owns 160 acres and used to rent another 600 acres. He said that for his last five years of farming, he averaged $30,000 profit a year on 350 acres. Andy said he let his farm equipment get old along with him, and when he retired he auctioned it off for $115,000. He currently rents his land for $32,000 a year; he could sell it for several hundred thousand dollars.

Andy has participated in migrant farm housing since its beginning. During the 1940s the migrant workers lived in tents. Later, the farmers organized a Farm Labor Sponsoring Committee that built 300 cinder-block housing units. Then the federal government began to regulate farm labor housing. Andy said that the government always insisted that the committee's housing was inadequate. Finally, after so much harassment, Andy said the farmers just closed it down. "We [farmers] were providing adequate housing. The people were satisfied. Then the government had to meddle. You know, the Hilton Hotel in Chicago would not qualify for migrant housing."

Andy claimed that farmers in Idaho do not participate in the farm subsidy programs, but he did receive $10,000 a year for not planting wheat. For the last several years he said he raised onions. His sons went off to college and now live in different states; they have no interest in farming.

Farmers operate an uncertain business which requires that they control costs wherever possible. Still, the exploitation of migrant workers has become extreme. In a later chapter, Mexican American migrant work life will be more closely examined. For now, it should be noted that the income of migrant families averages half of the federal government's standard for poverty. Middlewest farmers justify paying Mexican American migrant workers a poverty wage by blaming the victim. Andy's comments are representative: "I don't know how to say this—a lot of the time migrant workers aren't worth a damn. They don't work on Sunday and you don't know how many will show up on Monday. Come Monday they may come but not be capable of working. . . . There is an element among 'em, their fingers are pretty sticky. I've had several episodes where they have taken things—gas, oil, tools."

I asked Andy what he thought about the labor camp housing. He replied, "Those people [Mexican American migrant workers] get into trouble and they are not truthful. They just can't get along; you ought to see how they live. They leave the houses in a mess. They tear things up just awful."

I then asked Andy if farmers exploit their workers. He said, "They are not paid that poorly. I never had any trouble getting workers. I am satisfied. Why are they here? They're always willing to work for me. They are in no more poverty than we are."

These excerpts from the interview with Andy Lyons illustrate two important features of ideological colonialism. First, the Anglo farmers have nothing positive to say about Mexican Americans and, secondly, they deny the extreme poverty of their workers. The views of the farmers are somewhat contradictory because they claim that migrant workers have decent pay and yet they often use the workers' poverty status as testimony to their inferiority.

Farmers absolutely deny any responsibility for the poverty of their workers. The farmers have little empathy for their workers. It is difficult to understand how the farmers can be blind to such obvious poverty. However, the migrant has a different color and culture and, of course, "everyone knows" that Mexican Americans do not live as Anglos do. Most farmers have one to three Mexican Americans who work for them most of the year. The farmers work beside these Mexican Americans and consider them friends; they even provide homes for some of these contractors. The farmers volunteer this information as evidence that they do not exploit or hold racist views about migrant workers.

Michael Hawk represents his family's fourth generation of farming in the county. He also has several uncles and brothers who farm. Hawk specializes in growing several varieties of hops. He just turned thirty-five years old and farms a thousand acres. Michael says his land and equipment could be sold for more than one million dollars; but he said he would never sell the land because he has the responsibility to care for the land for the next generation to be able to farm it. I attended a farm auction where he sold $100,000 worth of old farm equipment. Michael has farmed all his life; he says farming is like a fever that just will not go away. Michael likes being the boss and being independent; he claims he gets great satisfaction from operating a successful farm.

Michael and the other farmers I interviewed agreed that what makes one farmer more successful than another is "luck." Yet these same farmers espouse a credo of individualism and competition as the ingredients that enable one to triumph economically. Michael's response to the question of whether or not he exploits migrant workers sounded paternalistic:

> I do what I can for these people. We farmers are concerned about our workers; there is just no solution. . . . I give them a soda now and then, sometimes a party; I provide a turkey when I can. . . . They are not educated and motivated like we are. . . . Yes, migrants have a lower standard of living, but it's the risk/gain factor. I would love to

go out and just sit on a tractor, not have to think; it would
be so relaxing. They don't have the risk factor. When I
have a bad year, they are the lucky ones.

Michael owns a small brewery that produces expensive quality beer. He also has part ownership in a wilderness resort, but
he just doesn't see how he could possibly pay migrant workers
a higher salary. Farmers often may lack the ability to present
a strong case when attempting to explain the economic relationship between themselves and their workers; however, they
have a group of political front men who impugn the patriotism
of anyone who might question the munificence of our capitalist
economy.

A crew boss, Jesse Gómez, was a key informant for me. His
family has migrated to Idaho from Texas for more than fifteen
years. He claimed that Ted Dryer, compared to the other farmers, is the best farmer and treats his workers well. My interview
with Ted Dryer, however, revealed his perspective. He said:

> We need them.... Let's face it, there are bad apples
> in every race. The Mexican Americans are more visible
> getting into trouble. They are getting into trouble where
> they shouldn't be. They don't have much use for anything
> outside their family, sometimes not even within the family.
> It's the way they are brought up, getting into trouble. Some
> say they are picked on, I don't know. Well, it's the way
> they live. When we were young, our folks, you never
> spend more money than you make. We also saved; it's not
> in their vocabulary. I could be wrong; to me they just work
> day to day. If they make $100 dollars today, they spend
> $100. If they want a gallon of ice cream they go buy it—
> that's their attitude. I was brought up different. We weren't
> satisfied just to be a laborer. We became independent.
> Most Mexican Americans, seems that's the life they want to
> lead. Mexican Americans don't like steady jobs; they prefer
> to spend their time on welfare. Food stamps hurt because
> they come to rely on it. Instead of subsistence food they

spend it on expensive food. They eat more T-bone steak than I do.

Sometimes a somewhat quirky person can provide insights into social relations. One young farmer, Randy Jacobson, whose father farms more than 3,000 acres, has what is to me a crude and offensive personality. His social behavior lacks the normal social conventions of courtesy and tact. Jacobson's obnoxious behavior embarrassed me; though we had just met, he asked me questions about my sexual and drug habits. However, my interview with Randy produced many insights because he was without inhibition in his analysis of Mexican American migrant workers. For example, he complained that OSHA was after him because a "dumb Mexican" had turned over his tractor and killed himself. Despite the circumstances, Jacobson placed little value on the lives of Mexican American workers. This young, wealthy, arrogant farmer reeked of ethnocentrism as he explained how it was a form of theft for migrant families to take the money their children earn in the fields. He had no understanding of either the economic necessity for such action or the lack of resentment by Mexican American youth at having to contribute their earnings to the family. Randy concluded by saying that he had to watch his workers all the time because "they will steal you blind."

Ernie Rogers manages his father-in-law's apple-packing plant. The family also owns several large apple orchards. Rogers belongs to several grower associations and has been appointed by the governor to the state apple commission. The plant employs thirty-five workers, most of them Mexican Americans. Ernie Rogers has not very much positive to say about his Mexican American workers; he views them as undependable and thinks it is a crime that they do not speak English. He says the parents do not supervise their kids and that this is just one example of how Mexican American culture produces crime. Another characteristic Ernie perceives is that Mexican Americans lack the desire to better themselves; he thinks they would rather receive welfare than hold down a job.

I asked Ernie what he thought of race relations in Farm County. He replied:

What I think, one of the biggest problems they have is a lot of the problems come from the Mexican American community itself. They have the highest school dropout rate of anybody in the state. I think they live in poverty and are not getting ahead—it stems from not getting an education. I am concerned about it. If you know them like I do, some of them are wonderful people. They just are not exercising the opportunities they have to get ahead. . . . The Idaho Migrant Council, in my personal opinion, the Mexican American community needs a spokesman; but the people who manage it, I think they make lopsided demands. They are extremely vocal and obnoxious, but, well, sometimes a group has to do this.

Ernie's pauses, facial expressions, and his non-verbal communication in some ways expressed more than his verbal statements. He recognized that his views toward Mexican Americans were harsh, and I felt that his concern was how he could express his negative views without sounding racist.

The local farmers said they prefer to hire temporary workers from Mexico because they are "better" workers. The Idaho Department of Employment assists farmers in obtaining workers from Mexico. Many Mexican Americans view the government's H2A program as legalized slavery. These Mexican nationals work in a precarious environment with few worker safeguards. Many Mexican Americans, both permanent and migrant, shared with me accounts of farmers not paying workers or paying them less than expected, and a Mexican national is more vulnerable to these problems.

Local Mexican American leaders believe that area farmers do not make a genuine effort to hire local workers. Undocumented workers are even more vulnerable to abuse. An Anglo Middlewest lawyer said, "The farmers want it both ways; politically, they say we don't want foreigners taking jobs from Americans, while many hire the cheap foreign workers, legal and illegal."

The unwillingness of many Americans to recognize exploitation and discrimination has tragic consequences for Mexican American migrant workers. Most Anglos in Idaho do not know that labor camps exist. An interview only provides a glimpse of a subject's inner self, so it is difficult to assess what effect this rural ghetto has on the self-esteem of the people living there.

The Anglo farmers and citizens of Middlewest do not consider the demoralization and alienation that must be felt by these unfortunate inhabitants. One interview was unforgettable. In response to a question about the scale of life satisfaction, Rosalinda González responded with the lowest possible score. When she was asked to explain, she cried for ten minutes without stopping.   It was only necessary to look around to understand her grief. José, her husband, was periodically unemployed and, despite several stays in alcohol-treatment programs, had failed to control his drinking problem. The family was living in an apartment that most likely would not meet the standards for a prison cell. Rosalinda cried for her children because she fears that they too will have to live their lives in a migrant labor camp where nobody cares.

Summary

The local farmers avoid discussions and interactions with Mexican American migrant workers. They reviewed many of the problems that they face—the cost of fertilizer, the lack of water, and adverse government policy, to name only a few—but none viewed the poverty of the migrant worker as a problem or concern. Yet despite this indifference, Mexican American migrant poverty does exist. It is a harsh reality, hidden along the farm roads across southern Idaho. The farmers send their children to separate schools to prevent their having contact with Mexican Americans. Few politicians, few newspaper articles, and few civic leaders question this social arrangement. Few Anglos will say directly that they think Mexican Americans are inferior, but they do say that Mexican Americans lack ambition, the desire for education, and a work ethic.

The Middlewest Labor Camp should be closed, but currently no alternatives to it exist. The farmers prefer to tear down their migrant housing rather than fix it to meet government standards. The farmers condone and defend labor camp managers under their employ who deny tenant rights and exceed their authority. Farmers effectively control housing authorities that tacitly view their tenants as prisoners.

Farmers have to learn many skills and must gain much knowledge to become successful farmers. Farming is a valued and respected vocation. The moral values espoused by the farmers would be commendable if they didn't apply them only to their fellow Anglos. The mystery is how skilled farmers could be so ill-informed and have such misinformation concerning migrant workers. The priests and some ministers wonder why Anglos limit their Christian charity to fellow Anglos. Pastor Blaine said, "The farmers have no souls."

Assuredly, rural isolation contributes to the farmers' single-minded, self-assured beliefs about Mexican Americans. Another contributing factor is the separation of the Mexican American and Anglo communities; Anglos minimize their social interaction with Mexican Americans. A social environment that labels and ignores a minority group becomes the breeding ground for the dehumanization of that minority group.

Chapter 6

PERMANENT WORKING CLASS MEXICAN AMERICANS

They are the only ones who understand me. I am the only one who understands them. Four skinny trees with skinny necks and pointy elbows like mine. Four who do not belong here but are here. . . . When I am too sad and too skinny to keep keeping, when I am a tiny thing against so many bricks, then it is I look at trees. When there is nothing left to look at on this street. Four who grew despite concrete. Four who reach and do not forget to reach. Four whose only reason is to be and be.

–Sandra Cisneros

Introduction

This chapter will examine the three types of working-class Mexican Americans who live permanently in Middlewest: seasonal workers, factory workers, and the working poor.

The family histories of permanent Mexican Americans in Middlewest show that most families first came to Idaho as migrant workers. Only three generations of Mexican Americans have lived in Idaho. I asked local Mexican Americans how and why they exited the migrant stream. Most migrant parents responded that a life of migration had a negative effect on their children's education. They recognized that their children missed significant periods of school at both the beginning and the end of the school year. One Anglo myth contends that Mexican Americans do not value education, but I found that the goal and dream of most Mexican American parents is that their children will not have to work in the fields. Other migrants said that they just got exhausted migrating and felt they could not continue the migrant lifestyle. Several migrant families said they had no choice—they did not have the money to return to Texas.

Many subjects said that the key factor in establishing permanent residency is finding full-time employment. For many migrants, finding steady work occurred as the consequence of having family and relatives who had already "settled-out." A Mexican American's relatives are a valuable resource because they may provide their homes as temporary housing and assist their migrant relatives in securing work. When necessary, resident Mexican Americans provide the necessities of life to their exiting relatives.

Seasonal Workers

The seasonal farm worker has not left field work, but the family now lives year-round in Middlewest or in a labor camp. The men often work nearly year-round for one farmer, participating in many types of farm labor and working closely with the Anglo farmer. This work includes repairing farm equipment, driving tractors, and irrigating the land. Sometimes the farmer provides these workers with a pickup truck and a modest house.

Seasonal workers usually still face a period of unemployment during part of the winter. Only the larger farms require seasonal workers, but Farm County has many of these among its more than 3,300 farms. The income for seasonal workers on these farms ranges from $8,000 to $15,000 a year. Many have worked for the same farmer for ten to fifteen years, yet their wages remain only slightly above the minimum wage standard. Considering the fact that many Mexican Americans have large families, most seasonal workers' incomes do not rise above the government's poverty category. Most seasonal workers have no health insurance or retirement benefits.

Rolando Salinas has been a seasonal worker for many years. He first came to Idaho in the 1950s in a large canvas-covered truck with twenty-five other men to work in the beet fields. His family was among the first Mexican Americans to settle permanently in Middlewest. Rolando works for one farmer about ten months a year for $10,000. His wife Carmen works part-time for a seed company; she earns $6,000 a year. The couple has nine children, whose ages range from nine to thirty years old.

Rolando's son Ruben was born in Middlewest. He claimed that his junior high school teachers told him and his friends to stop coming to school. Ruben said that most of the teachers think Mexican Americans are not intelligent. In junior high school many Mexican American children do drop out of school. Both the father and son believe that racism is a serious problem in Middlewest. As an example, Ruben said that he and his friends got into a fight with some Anglo boys. He reported that he and his Mexican American friends had to go to court, where they were placed on probation, but the Anglo boys did not receive any punishment. Ruben has had several part-time jobs, including working in the fields. He also works for the Bureau of Land Management (BLM) for eight to ten weeks in the summer fighting fires. Ruben feels that he only earns a decent wage when he is working as a fire fighter.

Rolando dislikes the government's program to bring H2A workers from Mexico, because he thinks it reduces his wages. These H2A workers are brought in from Mexico with government assistance, by the request of farmers, when local workers are not available. He adamantly opposes the English language bill. He says, "My brother was killed in World War II and they [Anglos] think we are not loyal to America unless we speak English."

Rolando's younger children speak more English than they do Spanish. They go to Sunday mass less frequently and think that some Mexican American traditions are "old-fashioned." Nevertheless, Rolando thinks his younger children retain their ethnicity and that the family still has close ties. They gather almost every weekend for dinner. Rolando has served on the board of the IMC and also has served on the Middlewest school board.

Raul Soto, another seasonal worker, has worked for the same farmer for twenty years and in 1990 earned $12,000 with no benefits. Raul said that his family has kept their traditional Mexican way of life—they speak Spanish at home and they mostly eat Mexican food. Raul said, "God made the man the head of the household." The family of one of Raul's married daughters lives with Raul's family. Juanita met her husband in the fields. He came to Idaho as a migrant worker from Mexico and he speaks little English. Most of Raul's family works in the fields; he has one daughter, Maria, who commutes to Boise to work for a computer company. Maria said she misses the fields because she likes being able to work with the whole family. Eva, Raul's youngest daughter, talked about her school experience: "I graduated with one of the highest grade averages in school. My favorite teacher said I would be receiving several awards at the awards assembly. I was very anxious during the ceremonies. I waited and waited; I never got an award. It was the saddest day of my life.... I attended the university last year, but I knew I could never be somebody; so I dropped out."

Arnold Cordova is a seasonal worker; his wife, Carol, works as a teacher's aide. In 1990 they earned $13,000 combined. At fourteen years of age Arnold quit school and got married. During the months when Arnold and Carol are unemployed, they have to live with Arnold's parents. Carol dislikes the frequent moves. She claims that Anglos intimidate Arnold. As an example, Carol mentioned that the farmer for whom Arnold works has him working in fields recently sprayed with pesticides. Arnold has been coming home with a terrible rash but refuses to talk to the farmer about this problem.

Carol's family has lived in Middlewest for much longer than has Arnold's family. She has a higher degree of assimilation, whereas Arnold prefers to speak Spanish and eat Mexican food. Carol received assistance from the Idaho Migrant Council to obtain her GED (high school equivalency diploma) and CDA (Child Development Associate) certificate. Her first employment, as is the case with many young Mexican American women, was as a teacher's aide with the IMC. Carol wants her family to have better jobs and become economically successful. She says that she intends to enroll in college when Arnold obtains a factory job. The Cordovas have one daughter and do not plan to have more children because they want their daughter to have a better chance to become successful.

At the time of my interview, the hospital had garnisheed Arnold's check because he had not paid his daughter's bill for having her appendix removed. The spring farm work had not begun and, consequently, the family had not made its past two car payments. Carol and Arnold believe that Mexican Americans face a harsh racial climate in Middlewest. As an example, Carol said that a school bus driver kept their daughter, but not the Anglo children, on the bus after school for being noisy. The driver then inadvertently left the girl on the bus in the garage. When Carol and a school administrator found her several hours later, she was crying and had urinated on herself. The school principal did not take any disciplinary action against the bus driver. The school never offered an apology and the family had no money to hire a lawyer. Carol is a teacher's aide in a local elementary school. She reported that some Anglo youth call Mexican Americans names and that some Anglo teachers do not like Mexican American children. "They don't say it, but you can just tell, they talk to and help the Anglo kids more."

Carol concluded her remarks on race relations as follows: "It's hard not to dislike Anglos. The way they look at us, the way they treat our children in school. The newspapers just give the Anglos a reason to dislike us and look down on us. The police see us as troublemakers. They pull you over to see if they can get you for anything."

Coco and José Gómez are both in their forties. Coco grew up in Texas and José in Mexico. They have lived twenty-two years in Middlewest. Coco and José feel pride knowing that they own their home. They said the Idaho Migrant Council has been a blessing. The IMC weatherized their small home with insulation and new windows. José is not a United States citizen; he cannot read or write English. He has always worked in the fields. Coco has worked for seventeen years for a seed company where she earns $18,000 a year. She has had several promotions; most of the company's Mexican American women earn far less. Coco and José perceive racism to be a problem in Middlewest. Coco claims that her company hires and promotes Anglos first. The Gómez children have had problems in school. The high school suspended a son and a daughter; the school authorities claimed that the son stole school property and that the daughter had a knife at school. Coco said they took the school to court and won in both cases. She said that her brother-in-law had recently lost his job with a seed company because the supervisor maintained he came to work under the influence of drugs; Coco claimed that her brother-in-law has never taken drugs, however.

José works seasonally for a prominent farmer who has related agricultural businesses and whose family has a high profile in Republican party politics. José earns less than minimum wage and works six days a week. He claims that the Anglo workers receive turkeys and beef as gifts, but the Mexican Americans do not, and he thinks the bosses consistently treat the Anglo workers better.

A subset of seasonal workers can be classified as temporary/seasonal workers. These workers have an unstable work life; they work periodically in the fields, but for no one farmer. They also try to obtain work in the packing sheds and in the sugar factory. Both jobs last approximately four months. Some summers they fight fires for the Bureau of Land Management. These workers generally have long periods of unemployment. Thus their incomes seldom rise above the poverty level. Many temporary/seasonal workers live in the farm labor camps.

I interviewed Jesse and Carlota Ortego in the Middlewest labor camp in the early spring. The apartment was freezing cold though Carlota had turned on all the gas burners on the stove. We sat with our coats on. Sally, the couple's youngest daughter, had just come home from the hospital, where she had been treated for pneumonia. The apartments at the labor camp have no insulation and inadequate heat. I wondered if the doctor would have released Sally if he was aware of her housing situation.

Jesse once had five jobs in one year. At the time of the interview he did not have a job but anticipated returning to the fields later in the spring. He receives $180 a month in unemployment compensation and the family receives $370 in food stamps each month. In 1990 their combined income was less than $11,000. The Ortegos have little money to pay their bills. A Middlewest loan company required additional payments beyond the contract period because of late payments on their loan; the Ortegos had made payments for seven months longer than stated in the original contract. They did not know the name and address of the local legal aid office.

The police arrested Jesse twice in 1990 on DUI (driving under the influence of alcohol) charges. He no longer had a valid driver's license and he had just completed a rehabilitation program. Carlota had recently pled guilty to a charge of shoplifting. I interviewed several other young Mexican American families in similar circumstances. The bleak and painful effects of poverty became all too real for me. As I left the labor camp, I wondered what would happen to the Ortegos and their three small children. None of the local politicians seem to be talking about finding a solution to this problem.

Factory Workers

During my field research I interviewed fifty working-class Mexican American families in Middlewest. Most worked in food processing plants that employ large numbers of Mexican American workers. Their salaries ranged from $9,000 to $25,000 a year. The local Mexican American male factory worker's salary averages $15,000; the Mexican American female factory worker's salary averages $9,000. In many Mexican American families both the husband and wife work in a factory, which means that some working-class families have a combined income of $25,000. Most of the factory families have four or five children and own modest homes.

A few of the Mexican American factory workers have become supervisors and two have achieved management status. Most Mexican American workers think that Mexican Americans have not received promotions to supervisory positions or management positions in anywhere near the proportion as have Anglo workers.

José Medina has worked in a food-processing plant for twenty-one years. He has the responsibility for production on the night shift and earns $33,000 a year. His wife also works in the plant; she earns $12,000. José said his job involves supervising the foremen and making sure production remains as efficient as possible. He has a high school education and has learned everything on the job. He said he obtained his position by working harder than anybody else and by having common sense.

All of the local factories have special categories of work for most of the women. They do the lighter work, which they commonly describe as being boring, mundane, and unskilled. They have much less opportunity for promotion to higher paying jobs. I interviewed several Mexican American women who had worked fifteen years for their companies and still earn less than $12,000 dollars a year.

Drive to Success

Approximately 25 percent of the Mexican American factory workers I interviewed want to own a business or advance into managerial positions despite their limited opportunities. Several of these workers have two jobs. Roberto Ramos and his brother-in-law both are blue-collar workers at a local potato-processing plant. They work different shifts to allow them to manage their restaurant. Their wives and older children also work at the restaurant, which has succeeded to the point that the brothers can anticipate becoming full-time businessmen. Roberto's wife, Sara, has enrolled in a business-management program at a vocational school. She has learned computer and accounting skills that will enhance the management of the restaurant. Roberto went to night school to obtain his GED. The Ramos families told me they work as hard as possible because they want their children to attend college.

Both Roberto and Sara believe that Middlewest has a horrendous race problem and that their three children have suffered from discrimination at school. They moved their son to another school because they believe his teacher had systematically discriminated against him. The final incident occurred when this teacher took a picture of each child for the bulletin board; she did not take their son's picture.

Emilda Sota projects an intense demeanor. Emilda shared

with me her work strategies that led to her promotion to a supervisory position at a local factory. She wants to advance further but she only has a high school education. This young woman radiates enthusiasm and intelligence. I could not help but speculate on the career she might achieve if she is given the opportunities.

A third example of the drive for economic success comes from Tino Ruiz. He works days as a factory worker and remodels houses in the evenings and on his days off. He and his wife buy inexpensive run-down houses and remodel them. They then sell the homes for a profit. They are making good money and intend to expand this work into a full-time business. Tino said, "Yes, there is prejudice in Middlewest, but I am too busy to worry about it."

Dual-Income Factory Workers

Joe and Juanita Cedano are in their late thirties; they both arrived in Middlewest as children of migrant workers. Their combined income approaches $40,000 a year. Joe works in a local factory and Juanita works as a government examiner. They each have worked for their present employers for more than fifteen years. Their lifestyle resembles that of Anglos to a greater extent than does the lifestyle of most other local Mexican American families. They have more Anglo friends and they live in a Anglo neighborhood. Joe plays golf and softball; Juanita likes to go out to dinner and to the movies. They are members of the Catholic church, but they seldom attend mass. They recognize that not many Mexican American families can afford their lifestyle; however, they believe that it is the parents' fault for taking their kids to the fields. Their own parents made sure they graduated from high school. They think that some Mexican Americans cause their own problems.

The Cedanos take pride in the fact that their oldest son is a college student. They recognize that their children have become assimilated more than have most Mexican American children. The youths' grandparents dislike the fact that the youngsters do not speak fluent Spanish. The oldest boy encountered resentment from his fellow Mexican Americans in high school because of his good grades and Anglo friends.

The Cedanos do not perceive as high a level of racism as do most Mexican Americans in Middlewest. They also do not participate as much in the Mexican American culture of Middlewest; however, they do know the Mexican American leaders. They voted for the Mexican American candidates to the state legislature and they make contributions to Mexican American organizations. In spite of their success, this family has not been able to avoid some racist experiences. Juanita works for a government agency where some Anglos refuse to be assisted by a Mexican American. The police arrested their youngest son at a football game for fighting. Joe said: "There was this hassle between the Anglo boys and the Mexican American boys. The police just arrested the Mexican American boys. They handcuffed my son like a common criminal. I can tell you we were pretty upset parents. They think all Mexicans are criminals."

Ricardo and Sara Nuñez have both worked at a food-processing plant for more than fifteen years. Together, they earn $38,000 a year. They live in a middle-class Anglo neighborhood and drive a Volvo. They and their children have mostly Anglo friends. They have fretted over the arrest of a relative because they believe it gives the whole family a bad name. Ricardo says that the family spends most of its leisure time participating in sports: the boys participate in several sports and Ricardo coaches baseball. They attend most of the high school and college games in Middlewest.

When the discussion turns to Mexican American ethnicity and racism, the family recognizes that their family has become assimilated more than most. The children do not speak fluent Spanish and they do not attend mass regularly. However, the family does participate in most of the regular socials with their relatives. They donated money to Juan Celedón's political campaign and voted for him.

The Nuñez family has had its share of racist encounters. Ricardo reported that Anglo parents sometimes hurl racial comments at him when he is coaching baseball. At work, his employers hire Anglos first and he has to work twice as hard because the supervisors think all Mexicans are lazy. During breaks at work, the Mexican American and Anglos workers stay segregated by race. Ricardo likes living in Middlewest because all of his family and relatives live in Middlewest. He summed up his sense of race relations: "It is OK if you [a Mexican American] succeed as long as you don't get beyond the Anglos. If you do, you are not a good Mexican."

Economically successful Mexican Americans almost always are those who have lived and worked longer in Middlewest. Their parents and relatives generally have stable employment. More successful Mexican Americans commonly graduate from high school. They perceive less racism than do most Mexican Americans; they speak less Spanish at home and they have more Anglo friends. They have fewer children on average, and their children have a higher degree of assimilation. They seldom live in the barrio district. They usually attend church less frequently and they often have contacts with people who work in personnel offices for companies and government employment agencies—which enables them to be apprised of the job market. They are more likely to enter interracial marriages. They also often speak English without an accent.

Accounting for Economic Success

The ethnic literature (Feagin 1989; Schaefer 1991) reveals that when a minority remains small, the dominant community feels less threatened and therefore the minority group faces less racism and has increased employment opportunities. The Mexican Americans who first settled in the Middlewest area generally have the most secure and highest paying factory jobs.

Does the employment success described above mean that any Mexican American can succeed if he or she only tries? Unfortunately, not necessarily. First, the success of Mexican American factory workers has limitations—most factory-worker families have an income that would classify them as lower working class. Their lack of access to educational opportunities means that they also lack access to most middle-class professions. Also, most Mexican Americans in and near Middlewest do not have factory jobs, and their incomes barely rise above the poverty line. Critical factors in the local economy are the lack of good jobs and the overabundance of workers.

The interviews I conducted do not easily illuminate the causes of economic success for Mexican Americans. Does the more economically successful Mexican American person participate in assimilative behavior that leads to a better job, or does the better job enable the person holding it to assimilate? Obviously, the two factors are interrelated and reinforce one another. Children whose parents have better jobs and a higher degree of assimilation undoubtedly have a higher probability for success. If a Mexican American has been successful in school and has a better job then he or she will have increased social interaction with Anglos, which will increase assimilation. The assimilation under discussion has limitations, because most Mexican Americans retain an "ethnic loyalty," as Keefe and Padilla (1987) found in their research. How much does Mexican American ethnicity impede economic success? I think that Anglo racism is a critical variable, and it helps explain the high level of poverty of Mexican Americans in Middlewest. The vast majority of resident Mexican American adults work in the secondary job market for low wages and part-time employment.

I interviewed several Mexican Americans who had dropped out of school but later attended an alternative school in order to obtain their high school equivalency diploma. Many Mexican American youths have attended the Center for Employment Training, the Idaho Migrant Council training programs, and/or the local vocational training school. Mexican Americans in Middlewest have received training as welders, secretaries, teacher's aides, bookkeepers, and mechanics, to name some of the popular programs. The fact that they obtained these credentials indicates the high motivation and determination of some Mexican Americans, since most of the Mexican Americans that I interviewed completed these programs while working and maintaining their family responsibilities.

José Pardo, for example, came to Middlewest for many years as a son of a migrant family. Eventually he married, but he remained on the migrant trail. He finally settled-out because he wanted his children to obtain an education. The IMC enrolled José in a local vocational-technical welding program. He now is earning $18,000 in a machine shop. He also works part-time, training Mexican American welders in a program sponsored by the IMC. Jose remarked, "The IMC changed my life; I serve on their board now, I do all I can to support them."

Working Poor

Another group of Mexican Americans work in a variety of jobs. The common characteristic of these families is that their income barely exceeds the poverty level. The working poor frequently slip into poverty. The most common economic situation involves the wife working as a paraprofessional and the husband having a low-income factory job.

Norma and Lorenzo Cortez represent this type of family. Norma started her work career in the fields after she dropped out of high school. Norma later completed her GED and a secretarial program with the assistance of the Idaho Migrant Council. Upon graduation Norma worked for the IMC, but since then she has had several jobs. Her low income stimulated her to enroll in a vocational program to become a medical assistant.

Lorenzo has also held many working-class positions. His work record indicates that he often has been laid off because he lacks seniority. He currently works at a food-processing plant, but the company wants to fire him because they think he drinks on the job. Lorenzo says his life has become miserable; because of the harassment of the Anglo supervisor and Anglo workers, he does not know how much longer he can continue this work. Lorenzo receives the worst job assignments at the plant. He plans to quit and enroll in a vocational training program once Norma has a job.

Isabel Jiménez works part-time in the fields and her husband, Abel, works for a local seed company. Abel often goes several months a year without work. Their combined income for 1990 was less than $15,000. They live in a broken-down trailer in the Chicago district of Middlewest. Isabel does not like living in the Chicago district. One of her neighbors sold drugs, which led to a police raid on the house. She fears letting her girls walk to school because some single migrant Mexican Americans have been harassing girls. The couple has five children; the two oldest dropped out of school when the junior high school vice-principal told them they would not graduate because they engaged in disruptive behavior at school. Isabel began to cry, "We stopped migrating from Texas, for the kids, [so they] would have a better life. Now I am afraid to let them go outside because of the gangs. And my kids—we wanted better—are going to end up in the fields."

Amalia Vásquez and her husband believe that they both lost their factory jobs because of their Mexican heritage. They think the employers always favor Anglo workers. Amalia had several jobs the year following the loss of her factory job. She worked as a cook, a laborer in an apple shed, and as a teacher's aide. Her husband worked four months at the sugar factory and then had a series of minimum-wage jobs. Their combined income for 1990 was $17,000—counting their unemployment money.

The couple has nine children. She said that most of her kids hate going to school because the teachers think they cannot do the assignments. Amalia reported that Jesse, the third-oldest son, came home crying from school and said he never wanted to go back because the teacher made fun of him. His parents made him go back, but he quit school in the eighth grade. Amalia said she could not blame her son. However, Jesse could not find work because of his age. Amalia said that he started running around with the wrong crowd, and that led to his imprisonment.

Amalia reported that her daughter Victoria also had problems at school. She failed all her courses and had a baby by the time she was fifteen years old. Amalia takes care of her granddaughter while Victoria attends a vocational school. Amalia laments the long hours she and her husband must work, which diminishes their parental guidance. Amalia shared her frustration: "When they expelled my son, the principal threw him on the floor.... I went to the other mothers, but the other mothers were afraid—if you put wood on the fire you will only get a bigger fire.... We all had younger children that had to go to the junior high school. I was mad; but what can you do?"

Amalia believes that Mexican Americans face a hard life in Middlewest. She said that an Anglo neighbor thinks Mexican Americans want to take over the town, because of their increasing number. Amalia claims that Anglos complain about everything Mexican Americans do. Her Anglo neighbors have called the police to complain about noise. She feels that any time Mexican Americans get together, Anglos fear disruptive behavior. Amalia said that the particular disruptive behavior consisted of a family barbecue with two relatives playing guitars. The police came by to tell them to keep the noise down.

Maria Alimeda obtained assistance from the IMC after her divorce. She attended a vocational school and graduated with secretarial training. She works for a local government agency as a deputy clerk. Her income places her just above the poverty level. Maria does not like her work environment—she is the only Mexican American worker in the office. The other women do not talk to her and office communications frequently bypass her desk. Maria claimed that her supervisor had tried to get her fired. By chance, I had interviewed the manager of the office. She considered herself a liberal and a supporter of Mexican Americans, but she was not aware of Maria's problems.

Maria presented me with many examples of racist experiences she has faced in Middlewest. The worst experience happened to her son at school. "My son drew a picture of a woman. The art teacher said it was very good. My son never got his picture back; they said it was lost. Later, an Anglo boy had a similar picture ... my son said it was a copy of his drawing.... The Anglo boy got an award and a scholarship.... My son loved to paint, but he quit his art classes."

Critique of the Pluralistic Model

Mexican Americans in Middlewest seem to have become less assimilated, had less occupational advancement, and achieved less education than would have been predicted by the pluralistic model of Keefe and Padilla (1987). Mexican Americans in Middlewest appear to maintain their culture and language, and they have not become assimilated as a group. The different goals of Anglos and Mexican Americans produce a situation with considerable social conflict. The Anglos of Middlewest want Mexican Americans to become assimilated while the Mexican Americans want employment and the right to retain their ethnicity.

I believe that the major weakness of the Keefe and Padilla study results from their discounting of their subjects' accounts of discrimination and racism. They fail to examine the relationship of Mexican Americans to Anglo-controlled social institutions. The present study attempts to overcome this deficiency by examining Anglo attitudes and by listening to the Mexican Americans describe what they believe to be their racist encounters with Anglos.   The data of this research reveals that the pluralistic/assimilation model fails, and indicates that only a theory that includes elements of the exploitive model can explain its findings.

Conclusions

This chapter has revealed four major features of the Mexican American community in Middlewest. The first is that many second- and third-generation Mexican Americans still work in the fields. Many young Mexican American adults in Middlewest have grandparents who were born in Texas and migrated annually to Idaho. Many of these young Mexican American adults were born in Middlewest, yet most of these second- and third-generation Mexican Americans have incomes below or close to the poverty level. The low-income jobs and poverty of the Mexican Americans' derives from the structure of the economy, which limits their opportunities.

Second, the stereotype of Mexican Americans as being lazy and lacking in motivation cannot be supported, because of the significant number of working-class Mexican Americans who have attempted to establish a business or who have attended a vocational school.

Third, the interviews with working-class Mexican Americans demonstrate that they face a considerable amount of racism. The extensive racism described by permanent Mexican Americans living in Middlewest rebuts the position held by some sociologists who use the concept of cultural capital deficiency as the cause of the under-class position of some minorities (Stolzenberg 1990; Reimer 1985). These sociologists contend that the major problem facing minorities is the changing nature of the American economy and that race discrimination only plays a small role in maintaining minorities in the under class.

The fourth important finding is the fact that many of these families have children who have dropped out of school, seriously jeopardizing their employment opportunities. Chapter Nine will examine in detail how the Middlewest high school seems to be organized to educate middle-class Anglos but not lower-class Anglos and Mexican Americans.

Many Mexican Americans I met had completed a vocational or technical training program and still could only secure employment in the fields. Maggie González, a young Mexican American woman, successfully completed a medical vocational program and felt relieved that she obtained employment at the district health department. Maggie has two brothers and several Mexican American friends who have successfully completed vocational programs but remain unemployed.

Mexican Americans, because of their own personal experiences or from the experiences of relatives and friends, soon learn that they have limited opportunities to secure employment that pays a decent wage. Faced with this negative employment situation, some Mexican Americans stop searching for employment.

Photo by Richard Baker

Migrant workers topping onions near Middlewest.

Photo by Richard Baker

Scene in the Middlewest Labor Camp. One myth that many Anglos
believe is that migrant workers drive new cars.

Chapter 7

MEXICAN AMERICAN MIGRANT WORKERS

We pick
  the bittersweet grapes
  at harvest
  one
    by
      one
with leather worn hands
    as they pick
      at our dignity
      and wipe our pride
      away

We pick
  with a desire
  that only survival
  inspires
While the end
  of each day only brings
  a tired night
  that waits for the sun
  and the land
  that in turn waits
for us. . . .

          –Ana Castillo

Introduction

Research and publications concerning Mexican Americans in Idaho are nearly nonexistent. The research amounts to an M.A. thesis (Reilly 1976) on Mexican American dropouts in one school in addition to a few state and federal reports on the housing conditions of Mexican American migrant workers. Historians, including Ourada (1979) and Gamboa (1990), have also examined the circumstances of Mexican American migrant workers in Idaho, but this was not the primary focus of their research.

The Idaho Ethnic Heritage Project (Mercier and Simon-Smolinski 1990) and the Idaho Human Rights Commission (Mabbutt 1990) produced reports on Mexican Americans in Idaho. The authors of these reports could find no major studies examining the Mexican American population of Idaho. Most of the Heritage Project's data came from articles in Idaho newspapers, and the Human Rights Commission project concluded that the lack of research on Idaho's Mexican American population reflects the low status of the Mexican American community in Idaho.

The reports listed above agree that the primary reason that Mexican Americans came to Idaho was to fill the need of Idaho farmers for field workers. In the early 1900s Idaho sugar factories advertised in south Texas and in Mexico for farm workers. The Bracero program, an agreement between the American and Mexican governments, brought Mexican males to Idaho's fields to fill the labor shortage caused by World War II (Gamboa 1990). However, in 1960 only 3,300 Mexican Americans resided in Idaho on a year-round basis. The available literature reveals that Mexican American migrant workers have faced a consistent pattern of abuse. Historically they received low wages, lived in very poor housing, and faced intense discrimination. The Heritage Project (Mercier and Simon-Smolinski 1990) concludes that, "Idaho had the most notorious reputation for discrimination."

The Gamboa (1990) study reveals that several strikes were organized by the Mexican workers of the Bracero program during the early 1940s in southwestern Idaho to protest the poor housing, food, and working conditions. The Mexican Consulate in Portland barred Mexican workers from coming to Idaho for two years because of the intense bigotry.

The few documented studies available show that little has been done to change the circumstances of the Mexican American workers in Idaho. Almost all Mexican American migrant families in Idaho live in poverty. The average migrant family earns approximately half the poverty level income. Most live in substandard housing and have inadequate access to medical care. The summary that can be drawn from the existing data is that Mexican American migrant workers, both historically and currently, are exploited. Yet the work they do is essential for the agricultural industry of Idaho.

The Idaho Department of Employment (1991b) estimates that 7,691 Mexican American farm workers migrated to Farm County in 1989. The Idaho State Economic Opportunity Office (1991) reports that an additional 4,500 Mexican American farm workers permanently reside in Farm County. López (1989) estimates that 10,000 undocumented Mexicans migrate yearly to Farm County. However, most governmental officials and Mexican American leaders think the number of undocumented workers is significantly lower than the 10,000 figure. Yet the Immigration and Naturalization Service arrested and charged a farmer from Farm County with twenty-two counts of knowingly creating and supplying false immigration documents for Mexican Americans working on his ranch. The *Idaho Statesman*, Boise's daily newspaper, in its May 29, 1991, issue further reported that this same farmer employed 1,000 farm workers.

Because of the mobility of migrant workers, no one has been able to determine an accurate figure on the number of Mexican American farm workers in Farm County. The figures given above suggest that during the six-month farm season Farm County's Mexican American population is perhaps double the official figures. This means that for half of the year 20 percent of the work force in Farm County is Mexican American—obviously a significant contribution to the Idaho economy.

Radical Exploitive Model

A strong case for the radical exploitive model comes from examining the social and economic position of Mexican American migrant and seasonal farm workers. As mentioned, Idaho's Mexican American migrant workers earn, on the average, less than half the federal poverty standard. The wages of seasonal workers are only slightly better. Economic exploitation is possible because of the excessive number of workers who can only secure intermittent employment. Since they have traveled a great distance to seek work, migrants essentially become a captive labor force. The situation of Mexican American migrant workers in Farm County can be described as one of hard-core poverty. They survive on a limited diet that consists primarily of beans, potatoes, and tortillas. Migrant workers have few possessions, and most drive old cars that frequently break down. Their families generally do not have adequate access to health care. It is a fact that only Mexican Americans primarily work as laborers in the fields, and it is common knowledge that nobody else looks to do this work. These Mexican American workers do among the hardest types of work for the lowest pay. The situation could be viewed as one of occupational apartheid.

A core element facilitating the exploitation is the ideological justification for the subordination of Mexican Americans. Middlewest and Farm County Anglos hold a set of beliefs that effectively serve to blame the victim. A key component is that poverty occurs because of individual deficiencies; therefore, migrant workers do not deserve assistance. The victimization of Mexican American migrant workers involves a standard rhetoric and a set of myths that includes the following: the migrant workers drive new cars; they cheat on welfare; they make good money; they prefer field work; they lack motivation; and they do not value education.

The capitalistic ideology contends that workers are free to select the type of work that they want, and that each person's attributes or "character" will determine his/her occupation, income, and social status. Such a belief system inhibits Anglos in recognizing flagrant inequality. Only a small percentage of Anglos viewed Mexican American poverty as a social problem.

As temporary residents, Mexican American migrant workers are not eligible to vote in Idaho. The result is that they have virtually no influence on government policies, whereas their employers, the Anglo farmers, have significant political influence at all political levels. One consequence of having no political voice is that governmental agencies that are supposed to provide services can bypass the Mexican American community. Parts of this chapter and the next will document the political oppression of Mexican American migrant workers. One result of political impotence is that the criminal justice system can easily abuse the civil rights of migrant Mexican Americans. The next chapter will examine the oppressive treatment of Mexican Americans within the judicial system.

Nothing could support more effectively the view that Mexican American farm workers face oppressive conditions in Idaho than the report on the migrant-seasonal worker farm survey conducted by the Idaho Department of Employment (1991). It found that 30 percent of these workers were unemployed at the time of the survey. More than 30 percent of the workers were from Mexico and approximately 33 percent of those surveyed were unmarried. The average level of workers' schooling was the sixth grade, and most of their children will undoubtedly receive far less education than the national average. Eighty percent of those interviewed said that finding work and housing was a serious problem. The survey found an oversupply of farm workers. It also found that these workers often do not apply for government assistance programs; less than half even applied for food stamps. It is a sociological truism that the conditions listed above will result in a myriad of social problems. Contrary to the Anglo stereotype, the survey found that Mexican American migrant workers would prefer to exit the migrant stream and have full-time work other than farm labor.

Migrant Life

Most Mexican American migrant workers come from Texas—from towns such as Eagle Pass, Pharr, and McAllen near the border. They migrate because they are unable to find work in their own area. Some of these workers travel a circuit through Arizona, California, Oregon, and Washington. Most of them drive straight through from Texas to southwestern Idaho, arriving in May and leaving in October. They may stop for short breaks or to nap, but they do not stay in motels and they seldom eat in restaurants. Their worst fear is having car trouble.

I interviewed twenty-five Mexican American families who migrated to Farm County to do field work. My key-informant migrant family came to Idaho in a Ford van and a Mercury coupe. The previous fall, they had only traveled 100 miles when the transmission failed; it took several days to repair the car. The family had no choice but to sleep in the van. If auto repairs are too expensive, migrant workers sell their vehicles for junk.

Two of the most popular myths believed by Anglos are that migrant workers drive new cars and that they earn good wages. Generally, nothing could be further from the truth. A new car is an exception, and, while migrant workers may sometimes receive decent paychecks for a period of time, they regularly live in poverty—not because they don't know how to manage their money but, rather, because of their general economic circumstances.

A few young male Mexican Americans have older automobiles that they modify into "lowriders," cars that they have adjusted to ride lower to the ground. The cars receive a coat of metallic paint and the owner removes much of the chrome. Mufflers are adjusted for a noisy rumble. Some owners reupholster and modify the interior of their cars. To a labor camp visitor, these cars can provide an intriguing introduction to a different culture.

The Sánchez family has been migrating for twenty-two years. They come to Idaho because they cannot find full-time employment in south Texas. The family includes seven children, whose ages range from two to nineteen years old, as well as the children's grandmother. The group had a difficult winter because Elena Sánchez and two of the boys had worked for a fast-food restaurant that cheated them out of their pay. They arrived at the Middlewest Labor Camp broke. They sought the assistance of the Idaho Migrant Council, which has a federal grant to provide a small amount of assistance for migrant families for gas, rent, and food. The director of this program informed me that many migrant families arrive in Idaho with little or no money.

To understand better the migrant work system, one must start with the labor contractor or "crew boss." The crew bosses work for the farmers and recruit the necessary labor to do the field work. A crew boss operates as a foreman who has the responsibility of supervising the field workers. A crew boss will generally have two or three crews working in the fields. Some bosses work exclusively for one large farm, and the crew bosses who manage the labor for big farms live year-round in Farm County. Other crew bosses for smaller farms are migrants.

Many migrants and seasonal workers claim that the crew bosses cheat them. They say that the farmer pays their money to the crew boss, who then takes some of their earnings. Also, farmers frequently award the crew bosses a bonus which they do not share with the workers. The low pay workers receive, coupled with the privileged position of the crew boss they witness, often results in the laborers' resentment toward these labor contractors.

The farmer bears the responsibility for the low pay of the Mexican American migrant worker, but the crew boss, usually another Mexican American, serves as a buffer between the owner and the worker. On the one hand, the crew boss represents a success story. A crew boss for a large farm can earn over $25,000 a year. This position offers an avenue out of poverty for the migrant worker. On the other hand, the crew boss sometimes acquires and displays the same negative attitudes as the farmer; and even if they do not take advantage of their fellow Mexican American workers, crew bosses generally will be resented and viewed as being disloyal to the Mexican American community.

Everado Villa is a labor contractor for one of the large farms in Farm County. His father was also a crew boss. He dislikes workers from Texas because they do not work hard enough; and he prefers workers straight from Mexico because "they work hard and keep their mouths shut." He claimed that he has to keep his eyes on the Texas migrants to make sure they work and do not steal anything. He said that he absolutely hates the Legal Aid people because they take the farmers to court for no legitimate reason. Everado earns more than $30,000 a year and his family has experienced a high degree of assimilation. He was proud that he does not live like the other Mexicans. He and his wife plan to have just one child, so that they can afford to send her to college. Most of their friends are Anglo and their leisure time activities include boating and snow skiing.

Flora and Salvador Enríquez are also crew bosses, and they too arrived in Farm County via the migrant trail. They have become bicultural by developing friendships with both Anglos and Mexican Americans. Flora is on a bowling team in which the rest of the team is Anglo. Salvador has served on the board of directors of the IMC. Both of their children have college degrees, and they said that this is the land of opportunity. Yet they also believe that Mexican Americans receive "unfair" treatment from Anglos. They believe the schools and the police "mistreat" Mexican American youth. Salvador believes that the farmers pay their workers as much as they can. Flora said "we [her family] want to keep our culture and get ahead." She said that the couple supports the Mexican American community because "we know what it is like to be poor."

The farmers in Farm County are dependent on migrant labor. Their labor needs include the following: weeding, thinning, and irrigating crops; picking fruit; detassling corn; harvesting; repairing machinery; applying fertilizers and pesticides—to name only some jobs. However, the farmer requires many workers only intermittently. Local farmers generally have one or two Mexican Americans who work for them most of the year; one of these might be the crew boss and the other a seasonal worker.

The migrant workers earn a minimum wage of $4.25 an hour, or sometimes less. Some jobs pay by piece work. In the fall of 1991, apple pickers in Farm County received 22 cents a bucket for picked apples. The fastest workers made up to sixty-six dollars a day. Only young males could earn this much, and they had to work at incredible speed. With a ladder and a bucket, these men worked without breaks in order to pick 300 buckets in a day.

In topping onions, the fastest workers could make $100 a day by working rapidly for long hours. The work quickly becomes backbreaking, since the worker must bend over all day pulling onions from the ground and cutting off the dried tops. The laborer must then stack the onions in rows for the harvester to convey them into trucks. Topping onions takes place in the early fall on hot, dry, and dusty days. Spending a day working in the onion fields would be a great experience for those who believe in the myth that Mexicans are lazy.

If the field workers only picked fruit and topped onions regularly they could make a decent living, but these jobs are only of brief duration. The typical migrant worker goes many days without work. Also, a person does not remain young and fit forever.

I spent two weeks with Elena and Gilbert Sánchez and their family to gain a better sense of the life of a migrant farm laborer family. They informed me that their religion plays a significant role in their family life. They belong to the Mennonite Church and attend services three times a week; they joined this church because Gilbert needed help to overcome a drinking problem. Each morning at 6:00 A.M. as I joined the family in their van, they said a prayer before leaving for the day's work.

Gilbert shared with me his views on the difficulties of migrant life and of his inability to get ahead financially. In 1991 the yearly earnings of Gilbert, Elena, and their two older sons amounted to $12,000. They needed to make car payments and they also had expensive car repairs. They cannot afford to go to the low-income medical clinic when a family member becomes ill. Gilbert and Elena hope that their seven children will have a better life; they remain happy because of their faith in the Lord.

The following summer, I spent another week with the Sanchez family. Elena is a crew boss, and I wanted to observe her organizing and supervising her workers. Elena had two crews of twenty workers each in the fields. Most of the workers in one crew were relatives of Elena's. Her family and Gilbert's brother's family work together in the fields. This extended family has a very congenial relationship with one another. When Elena checks on the other crew, Gilbert takes charge of the number one crew. Elena's crews spent the week thinning crops, which does not require the speed of piece work; but the workers kept a steady pace. The crews work six days a week and take a fifteen-minute lunch break.

One of the reasons migrant families earn a low income is that there are many days when they do not have work. In the fall of 1990 the workers could not top onions for ten days because of hot weather and the danger of the high temperatures scalding the exposed onions. In the spring of 1991 the workers could not thin and weed crops for a week because of rain. Even without weather problems, migrant workers lose many days of work because farmers do not need them regularly.

Another type of migrant work involves working in the sheds, the places where fruit and vegetables are sorted and packed. I spent a week observing and interviewing people employed at an onion shed and at an apple packing plant in Farm County. These facilities employ approximately forty workers. Farm produce can be stored there until it is delivered to food wholesalers. The supervisors and managers are Anglo and they generally hold negative opinions of their Mexican American workers, who include a mixture of migrant and seasonal workers. These people earn minimum wage or close to minimum wage, work irregular hours, and must be available for work at the time of day and for the number of hours specified by the manager. The number of hours worked ranged from zero to as much as twelve hours a day. The manager of the onion shed had an exceedingly high rate of firings, with well over 50 percent of his workers being fired in a season. The sheds and plants operate only four or five months out of the year, yet this work is held in higher esteem than is field work.

The Anglo foreman works year-round, receives benefits, and earns five times the amount paid to the Mexican American workers. The manager earns twenty times as much as the Mexican American workers. The three Anglo farmers who owned the shed declined to disclose to me their average annual profits from this business. The Mexican American migrant workers, earning low wages and with little control over their working hours and conditions, have few resources and few allies, which makes them easy targets for abuse.

The children of migrant laborers start to work in the fields when they reach the age of twelve to fourteen, depending on their strength and how much the family needs the additional income. The younger children generally attend migrant Head Start programs operated by the IMC. The children too old for the Head Start program stay in the local labor camp, where grandparents, an older child, or a neighbor look after them.

The migrant children I talked with do not attend school in Middlewest. The schools in Texas arrange for migrant youth to make up the days of school they miss because of migrating. These children miss a month of school in both the fall and spring, and I suspect that the quality of their education must be seriously diminished. Migrant parents usually value education, but their way of life contributes to many of their children becoming school dropouts.

When the Sanchez's daughter Tina failed to pass the seventh grade, Elena and Gilbert had her working in the fields to teach her a lesson. They believe the hard work will convince her to study. However, when the children of migrant workers go to the fields, they join their family and friends who also are working there. The youths' most important role models often work in the fields, and adolescents generally want to achieve adulthood as soon as possible. Field work actually can be an attractive option to young people who are doing poorly in school and who never plan on being sick or getting old. Yet with the loss of these young minds and their creativity from the schools, the Mexican American community loses many potential teachers, social workers, and doctors.

Health Care Problems

Mexican American migrant workers frequently do not have health insurance or enough cash to pay for medical care. Several migrants said that they could not afford the low-income medical clinic. This situation forces many migrant families to forego needed medical care. Some migrants informed me that the Middlewest hospital has refused to provide services to them. Liz Jarvez, who lives in the Middlewest Labor Camp, said: "My neighbor Sherry, her daughter was playing—she turned a pot of boiling water on herself. Sherry took Maria to the emergency ward in Middlewest. I got there an hour later. Those people hadn't treated Maria. I was so mad I started yelling and screaming for someone to help this little girl. They finally treated her; but if I wouldn't of come, Sherry was ready to leave."

One day I observed Elena Sánchez rubbing the sides of her face; I asked her what the problem was. She informed me that her teeth ached constantly. I asked if she had seen a dentist, and she replied that they were behind on the rent at the labor camp and could not afford any dental bills. I checked with various social service agencies, inquiring about low-income dental assistance in Middlewest. Each agency referred me to another agency. The low-income medical clinic finally informed me that they have one dentist who works part-time for the clinic. I asked for an appointment for Elena; they said they would place her name on a waiting list. I declined to make the appointment for Elena when I learned that she would have to wait one year for it.

Carlos Cortez, a young adult migrant worker, shared the following experience. His father, Juan, had serious ulcer problems. Carlos had to take his father to the emergency ward at the Middlewest hospital, which refused to treat him because he had no insurance or cash. Juan underwent surgery for a bleeding ulcer in a Texas hospital three weeks later.

Migrant Field Workers

Mexican American migrant workers have different attitudes and perceptions of migrant life, which can be depicted as an uneven continuum. On one end of the continuum are a few migrants such as eighteen-year-old Sid Guzmán. He represents the small number who enjoy working in the fields. He feels like an adult because he has a paycheck, a wife, a pickup, and a new baby. He likes making his own decisions, and he feels important because he has more money than the local residents when he spends the winter in Mexico.

At the other end of the migrant continuum are many more people, such as Benita Diaz. She hates all the traveling involved in the migrant way of life and recognizes its negative impact on her children's education. She works in the bakery of a grocery store and also has a part-time job as a secretary at the labor camp. Benita has worked at the grocery store during several migrant seasons and has been offered the opportunity to work there permanently. She has asked her husband to let the family stay in Middlewest year-round because it would allow their children to do better in school. He would like to exit the migrant trail but he owns a house and has family in Texas; however, his main concern comes from his doubts about being able to find a permanent job.

Miguel and Beatrice Flores both grew up in migrant families

and have become migrant workers themselves. They live in the Middlewest Labor Camp with their daughter. The parents of the couple also live in the camp. Beatrice's family has lived in the camp for several years. Beatrice spent some time attending the high school in Middlewest but she dropped out in the tenth grade because she hated school and the teachers. Miguel's family has migrated from southern California for the past fifteen years.

Miguel and Beatrice together earned $8,000 in 1991; they also receive rental assistance and food stamps. They spend most of their leisure time in the labor camp, where they like living because they have family and friends there. Miguel enjoys sports and drinks an occasional beer with the other men in the camp. The Flores do not have much contact with Anglos, but they dislike how Anglos treat them in Middlewest. The local police have arrested Miguel several times for driving violations, including not having a driver's license, not having insurance, and driving under the influence of alcohol. Miguel thinks that the police only arrest the Mexicans. The couple claim that Anglos stare at them and look down on them when they go to the local stores; they say some Anglos call them "wetbacks."

The Flores do not feel optimistic about their future. They want their children to speak Spanish and to be proud of being Mexican, but they hope that the children will not have to do farm work. The couple have more hostility about their inability to escape field work than do some of the older Mexican American migrant workers. They told me: "The field work is in the hot sun and it's dirty work. They pay you less money. The Anglos have everything, air conditioning. No Anglos work in the fields. This is not a way to live; we can't pay our bills.... We would like to work in the nice office, same rights, be able to get loans, and be treated more the same as the Anglos."

Romero and Eva Vásquez also live in the Middlewest Labor Camp with their daughter. They both grew up in migrant families and they met in the fields. Both dropped out of school because they could not keep up with the non-migrant youths. They earned $7,000 working in the fields during the summer of 1990. Romero said that he could not find enough work because of the high number of migrants seeking work. The Vasquezes experienced financial problems when they bought a car. Romero paid $1,300 cash for a 1979 Ford and then he and a friend had to rebuild the engine. Romero reported that he only had a part-time construction job during the winter in Texas and Eva could not find work. They borrowed money from a relative to finance the 1990 trip to Farm County. They arrived in Middlewest broke, but they received some emergency assistance from the IMC. They do not like the Middlewest Labor Camp because the single men there drink and fight; it bothers Eva that nobody controls their behavior.

The Vásquez family received food stamps but still were not able to save much money for the winter. They barely have enough money to return to Texas. They think that the labor camp manager is unfair because he will not return their rental deposit of fifty dollars because of some problems with the apartment. They claim that the apartment had the problems when they moved in, and the deposit certainly represents a large amount of money to them. Romero said the following about race relations: "We hardly ever go out to dinner. When we go back to Texas we drive straight through. We only stop to nap and to buy groceries. We decided to go out to dinner. Everyone in the restaurant was looking at us. We felt so uncomfortable we left."

Romero holds a confusing set of beliefs about his circumstances. He wants to attend vocational school to become a mechanic, but he does not have any money to finance his education. He doubts if he can gain acceptance because he does not have a high school diploma and he has to work to support his family. Yet he has not given up on the American dream: that you can get ahead in America if you try hard enough. Romero vacillates between his pessimism and the hope that someday his family will prosper.

Carlos Cortez lives with his parents in the Hop Town Labor Camp. He has migrated from Texas with his parents for as far back as he can remember. He speaks fluent English; his parents understand English but lack the confidence to speak it. Carlos serves as interpreter when his parents need to talk to Anglos.

His parents grew up in Mexico, and Carlos said that they prefer to live like traditional Mexicans. They generally remain in the camp to avoid interacting with Anglos; they listen to the Spanish radio station and attend Spanish mass. They always eat Mexican food, mostly beans and tortillas, because they only earn $7,000 a summer. The family only leaves the camp on Sundays to attend church, purchase food, get gas for the car, and wash their clothes at the laundromat. When the family members are not working, they rest. They live a spartan life: their apartment furniture consisted of a kitchen table and chairs, an ancient television sitting on an empty crate in the living room, and their beds. These items constituted the entire furnishings of their apartment when I met them.

Carlos said that he worries about the lack of work and the low wages; he does not think that the family has saved enough money to get through the winter. He told me that he did not intend to marry, because he could not raise a family on his wages. The family refuses to apply for food stamps although they meet the eligibility requirements. Carlos concluded by claiming that the family can survive because they know how to get by with little money.

Juan Zapata, a twenty-four-year-old Mexican American, lives at the Hop Town Labor Camp. He grew up in Mexico. The INS deported his family several times before they received legal papers. Juan only attended school for three months before beginning life in the fields. He has traveled all over the United States as a migrant worker. He has relatives in Middlewest but he has only migrated to Idaho for the past two years.

Juan shared with me much of his knowledge about "getting to know the ropes" upon arriving in a new area. He had no money when he arrived at Middlewest. He stayed with relatives until he could rent his own apartment, and his relatives told him where he could receive emergency assistance. His next problem was gaining information about how to contact the crew bosses. From talking with other workers, he learned about the best jobs that are available to migrant workers. Fighting fires for the Bureau of Land Management pays the highest wages, and the BLM frequently hires large crews during the fire season.

Juan considered himself lucky to obtain the second best work, a job at the sugar factory, because they needed extra workers on the day he applied. Juan then spent the late fall and early winter working the four-month campaign at the sugar factory. During 1991 Juan had five different jobs.

In the winter, however, Juan could not find work. He met the eligibility requirements for food stamps and unemployment insurance. The insurance can be manipulated to a slight extent, since the recipient can choose when to have the payments begin, allowing the worker to receive the highest benefits. Juan listens to the Spanish-language radio station because he likes the music and also because he obtains information pertinent to Mexican Americans, such as information about work availability and the schedules of performances of the good Mexican bands.

Juan said that when migrants have car trouble it helps to know the local Mexican American mechanics, who generally live in the camps, because they're the only ones migrants can afford. He told me that he generally buys cars from private parties; most migrant workers do not trust used-car salesmen. Juan learned that license plates cost significantly less in Idaho than they do in Texas. He said that few migrant workers have checking accounts but they do have savings accounts. He also inquires about the location of the best low-income medical clinic. I asked Juan if racism is a problem for Mexican American migrant workers. He replied: "Most migrant workers do not have much interaction with Anglos. When we go to the stores and businesses, some Anglos will look at you. By the way they look, you can tell that they don't think you belong here. Just by how they look they tell you your presence is offensive. I have had to face this all my life, so it is not that much of a problem because I expect it."

Amelia Morales is a grandmother. I arrived at her apartment in the Middlewest Labor Camp just as she returned from the fields where she had been topping onions. As I explained my research project, she kept rubbing an arthritic knee and moaning because of her aching back. Her three grandchildren sat quietly watching cartoons on a snowy television screen. She has custody of the children because their mother has a drinking problem and is unable to provide care for them.

Amelia's husband of thirty-seven years left her because, as he said, "We raised our kids and we're not raising any more." She told her husband she didn't have a choice. She receives assistance, but the money doesn't go far enough; therefore, this sixty-year-old grandmother has to top onions, which is the most physically demanding field work. An unrelated middle-aged Mexican American woman was also living in the apartment. I learned that Mrs. Morales had taken her in because she had no money and her boyfriend had left her stranded at the labor camp.

I interviewed two Mexican American migrant women whose responses to my interview were incoherent. They seemed very confused and I could not make sense of many of their responses. They could not clearly present to me an account of their recent experiences. However, I was able to obtain some information from these interviews by listening to the tapes several times. Their confused mental state is quite possibly the product of their chaotic lives. Their lives had lacked any permanence for several years and the extreme instability had left them exhausted. They moved often; they had lived with two or three different men; they drank excessively; and they had held many jobs, but only for short periods of time. Seeing the fear and pain exhibited in the appearance and the demeanor of these women, who were living on the edge, just barely hanging on to a human life, was a sobering experience for me.

When I interviewed Deli Gonzáles, she had just moved into the Budget Motel. She had money for one week of rent because of the rental assistance she received from the IMC. Tony, a man with whom she has lived for three years, had not been able to find work. They had started back to the state of Washington when their car broke down. With only enough money for food, they had to live in the car for a week.

Deli had a crying baby on the bed beside her. Flies in the room took turns investigating the baby and the spoiled, half-eaten cans of food left on the table. There was no refrigerator, so it was necessary for them to buy their groceries daily.

Deli said that her husband, from whom she has not obtained

a divorce, has her three other children. The courts awarded custody of them to her husband because she had left the children with their grandparents. She wants her children back, but she acknowledged that the courts will not assist her because she and Tony drink excessively. Deli fears that Tony is going to leave her, because he threatens to do so when he drinks. With her shabby clothes, tangled hair, and desperate eyes, Deli appeared wilted, as though she had just finished running a marathon. Her soft, defeated voice echoed her state of depression. I could not help but feel that she was losing her race for survival.

The leisure time of many Mexican American migrant workers is used to go into town for gas, shopping, and to use the laundromats. They also go to church and watch television. Migrant families do not have the financial resources to participate in the consumer-oriented lifestyle of the Anglo middle class. They live separate lives from the Anglos. Their dream is for their children to become educated and better able to participate in elements of the life that is denied them.

Many Mexican American migrants resemble the Sanchez family. They work hard, go to church, love their children, and never cause any trouble. They live lives preoccupied with day-to-day survival. Unfortunately, the Anglos of Middlewest and Farm County often do not see the quiet dignity of these Mexican American migrant families.

Housing

Much of the housing for Mexican American migrant workers was initially provided by the farmers. Older Mexican Americans in Farm County described as primitive the housing provided by the farm associations. The units consisted of one small room with a wood stove and no insulation. Sanitary conditions were substandard because of the lack of running water in the units and the communal toilets and showers. Most of the units did not have window or door screens.

A report, *A Roof Over Our Heads* (1980), by the Idaho

Advisory Committee to the U.S. Commission on Civil Rights stated that nine farm labor housing entities served migrant workers in southwestern Idaho. It also reported that much of the housing available to migrant workers was deplorable. Today, only three farm housing operations remain in Farm County. Farm County farmers said they closed down the units they operated because of "unnecessary government regulations." The condition of farm housing today varies widely.

In 1991 the State Economic Opportunity Office (SEOO) evaluated the housing units at the Middlewest Labor Camp. Its report states that a serious housing problem exists because of the lack of affordable housing for migrant laborers. The report also states that overcrowding exists in the available housing units and that local communities appear reluctant to rent to migrant workers. The SEOO report records the fact that the 112 apartments at the Middlewest Labor Camp have a 60 percent occupation rate year around. Since they do not have sufficient insulation or adequate heating units, these units do not meet the year-round requirements for housing.

In a 1991 letter to SEOO, the director of the Western Idaho Community Action Program reported that in serving large numbers of low-income Mexican Americans they found inadequate housing to be their most serious problem. The program claims to have assisted forty Mexican American families in one week at the Middlewest Labor Camp. These Mexican Americans had no choice but to sleep outdoors or in their vehicles.

The situation for migrant, H2A worker, and undocumented Mexican American worker housing has to be horrendous for Farm County. The local television station in 1991 carried a story reporting that single males from Mexico were sleeping in abandoned buildings and garages.

The housing expert for the Idaho Migrant Council shared his frustration over the housing problems facing migrant workers. The IMC field administrators find many labor housing operations to be grossly inadequate, but the IMC is reluctant to lodge complaints with government agencies because the farmers' associations have said they then will simply tear down the facilities.

If the frugal farmers were willing to tear down these housing units, it does not take much imagination to appreciate what their quality is.

From my observations in interviewing Mexican American migrant workers in their apartments, trailers, and labor camps I found the majority, but not all, of the migrant housing to be substandard. The Hop Town Labor Camp has decent housing for Mexican American migrant workers but this camp is the exception. The majority of Mexican American migrant families live in apartments that are overcrowded and inadequately maintained. Few of the housing units have washers and dryers; the kitchen appliances and heating units are antiquated. Most housing units for migrants are not properly maintained, which means that most are in need of extensive repairs.

Middlewest Labor Camp

The Middlewest Labor Camp is technically part of the town of Middlewest but there is a two-mile gap between the labor camp and the town. The Middlewest Labor Camp is a rural ghetto. The housing could only be described as wretched. If the camp existed in town and had greater visibility, there would most likely be an outcry to either eliminate or improve this housing. My Mexican American informants assured me that many such labor camps exist across southern Idaho. The Middlewest Labor Camp has a housing capacity of 900, but a member of the Middlewest Housing Authority said that he believes the camp has approximately 1,400 residents. Many Mexican American families residing in the camp exceed the prescribed limit of five persons per apartment. One migrant family I interviewed consisted of ten family members living in an apartment.

The Middlewest Labor Camp has two sections. One section has forty-six wood houses built during World War II. These houses look to be in an advanced state of dilapidation. The exterior wood cries out for a coat of paint; the yards have more weeds than grass. The walls of some buildings are covered with graffiti. Empty bottles, cans, and other litter cause the camp to resemble a trash dump. The interiors of the homes and apartments match the abysmal appearance of the exteriors. Most units need numerous repairs to appliances and bathroom fixtures. The interior walls have holes and need paint; the floors do not have protective coverings of any kind.

The summer daytime temperature in Farm County can remain in the nineties for six to eight weeks. After a day of hard labor in the hot fields, the farm worker must return home to a small apartment that can feel like an oven. Some Mexican Americans live in the uninsulated apartments in the winter. Frost collects on the interior walls and the residents may turn on all the gas burners on the kitchen stove in an attempt to stave off the cold. Even then, they must wear winter coats or other extra clothing in order to stay warm. Many Mexican American subjects reported that their children frequently have colds or pneumonia.

A typical apartment at the Middlewest Labor Camp is sparsely furnished with items that have little or no monetary value. The units consist of four rooms, including two small bedrooms. The kitchen floor space measures approximately eight by ten feet. The table and chairs could hardly be given away. Most families have to eat in shifts because of the small size of the room and its table. The bathrooms commonly feature leaky faucets and noisy toilets needing repairs. Water problems have ruined the floors of many apartments. The apartments look, feel, and smell uninhabitable due to an accumulation of dirt, stains, and crumbling cinder blocks. The inmates at the Idaho State Penitentiary have better housing. What happens to the psyche of those living in poverty conditions, when they know that a sentence to the state prison would improve their housing, food, and medical care?

Cars, pickups, and vans are an integral part of the labor camp scene. Occasionally, one sees a recent model car or truck but, for the most part, the typical Mexican American migrant worker (no Anglos lived in the camp during the research period) drives an older model car that has seen better days. Mexican Americans appear to like big American cars, but part of their popularity lies in the affordability of these cars. Many of the vehicles have mechanical problems, and with many of these cars in various states of repair, the camp can bear a striking resemblance to an auto-wrecking yard.

One can frequently observe Mexican American men working on the cars. Migrants do their own auto repairs because they cannot afford commercial garages. If the mechanical problem exceeds the men's technical knowledge, they then use the informal network of both migrant and permanent resident Mexican Americans who have training in auto mechanics and will repair the migrants' cars at an affordable price. This sharing of expertise exemplifies the sharing nature of Mexican American culture and its solidarity, although some sociological writers see this cooperation mainly as a response to poverty conditions (Connor 1985).

Some labor camp residents complain about the noise, drinking, and car traffic at night. They maintain that the family people do not cause any trouble—it's mostly the single, young males who drink and fight. Liz Jarvez, a camp resident, said, "When it comes right down to it, all the problems in the labor camp come down to one thing: alcohol; it causes all the problems."

Because of the devastating poverty in their own country (Davis 1990), Mexican nationals—mostly young, single males—migrate from Mexico for the summer farm season. Typically, they attempt to save half their earnings to take back to Mexico. Some of these men live in large groups, in housing that at best would be called shacks; some Mexican nationals also live in the Middlewest Labor Camp.

During the period of my field research, some crimes (mostly misdemeanors) occurred in the labor camps, and one murder did occur at the Middlewest Labor Camp. Newspaper accounts of the crime and interviews with camp residents indicate that the murder resulted from a fight between two young men over a woman. A young observer of the fight was accidently shot and killed.

If it were society's intent to create criminals, the living conditions of the typical farm worker would be a perfect spawning ground. Most Mexican nationals and some migrants are young males with a limited education and frequent periods of unemployment. Add to this the fact that most Anglos hold racist views toward Mexican American migrants and avoid contact with them. Stir into this mix a group of single men who remain on the fringes of the local Mexican American community. Conflicts inevitably arise, and these conflicts often are aggravated by the police, who are anxious to separate out the "unfit."

Virtually every aspect of the Middlewest Labor Camp provides evidence to support the radical exploitive sociological model. A colonial arrangement develops because the elected government officials create and maintain the labor camps. Politically, the labor camp is part of Middlewest; the city government has authority for the camp, but the camp does not receive city services such as street and park maintenance. No one on the city council campaigned at the labor camp for election. The county does not provide regular police service to the camp. The state of Idaho, manifests good intentions by assisting in writing grants for new housing, but this will simply extend the life of this ghetto. The camp is unofficially but effectively considered to be "out there" somewhere and that allows all levels of government to shirk responsibility for the housing conditions.

The Farmers Home Administration (FHA), a division of the U.S. Department of Agriculture, provides the capital necessary to build migrant farm housing. The arrangement is ironic because few yell louder about government taxation and welfare than farmers, and yet these same farmers have their workers' housing costs assumed by the government. Furthermore, almost all migrant workers meet the eligibility requirements for food stamps, a program of the Department of Agriculture, and one which would not be so greatly used if migrant workers could earn better wages. Yet in both cases Anglos interpret governmental assistance programs as evidence of the inferior status of Mexican American migrant workers. The situation could be termed a Catch-22, because migrant workers are oppressed and yet are blamed for the results of such oppression.

Housing Authorities

The Farmers Home Administration has the ultimate authority regarding the farm labor camps, and it establishes the rules and regulations for these facilities. The FHA requires that each camp be governed by a housing authority. The mayor of the town in which the labor camp is located appoints a governing board. The boards in Farm County are primarily made up of local farmers, which leads to some interesting analyses concerning their governance. It is almost like the old company towns where the company governs the town and not only controls people's work but also their houses. One wonders why farmers are considered the best governors of these camps and why the tenants have no representation on the boards.

I interviewed five housing authority board members in Farm County. These people did not perceive any problems with the governance or the maintenance of the labor camps. The ideas that the labor camps might be governed non-democratically or that the managers might abuse their authority were ones they had not seriously addressed. The board members believe that the labor camps are run fairly and that the migrant workers should be thankful such inexpensive housing is available.

The living conditions at the Middlewest Labor Camp have many similarities to urban barrios, yet the board members do not perceive such an arrangement as a problem. The board generally ignores or is indifferent to the complaints of the tenants. The oppressive conditions are exacerbated by having Anglo managers who do not speak Spanish in charge of camps where all of the tenants are Spanish-speaking Mexican Americans.

Camp managers have far more power than do the managers of most rental complexes, because there is practically no other low-income housing that will be rented to Mexican American migrants. Having a captive set of tenants creates a situation where camp managers have less accountability and a wide latitude in their management of the camps; they know that most complaints will not be considered legitimate. The tenants also know that the housing board will not often respond to their complaints, even when they have sought out the support of the Idaho Migrant Council or the Idaho Legal Aid office. The managers are basically unchallenged when they retain the deposits of tenants, regulate visitor privileges, evict tenants, and rent to whom they choose.

Camp managers have numerous complaints about the tenants. They claim that the tenants do not properly maintain their housing units, and they feel that the Mexican American migrants do not share the values of cleanliness or the need to care for property. Each manager I interviewed listed a series of complaints: the need to constantly repair appliances and paint the facilities; the children destroying the playground equipment; parents allowing their children to destroy mattresses; and the accumulation of junk and clutter in the yards, which makes the whole place an eye-sore. The conclusion is that Mexican American migrant families are considered incapable of living as "normal human beings." The Middlewest Labor Camp manager summed up the sentiment: "Look, they [Mexican American tenants] do not follow the rules and they tear things up. They can't get housing in Middlewest because of their poor reputation. They deserve discrimination. Their culture is mostly bad. They have a tendency to fight, they only live day to day, and they have no initiative."

The managers justify their control of the labor camps because of the character of Mexican American migrants. The managers and the board believe that migrants regularly get into trouble and are involved in "all kinds of shenanigans." Migrants are seen as being abnormally involved in criminal behavior, especially that which involves violence and drugs. A number of migrant tenants told me that the Hop Town Labor Camp "is run like a prison." A key informant who attended a board meeting of the Middlewest Housing Authority said that a board member, who had previously been the manager at the camp for twenty-two years, opposed placing washers and dryers in the new housing units because the tenants lack the ability to operate such equipment. One labor camp has required that tenants surrender their driver's licenses as security when they cannot afford the rental deposit.

Hop Town Labor Camp Dispute

The most compelling experience of my field research involved observing a series of meetings which addressed issues regarding the labor camp at Hop Town. The situation at this labor camp provides a clear example of the treatment of Mexican

American migrant workers. An informant suggested that I might be interested in attending a meeting of tenants of the Hop Town Labor Camp (HTLC). Seven Mexican American tenants had gathered for an evening meeting with the Idaho Migrant Council's field manager and a Legal Aid lawyer.

The tenants had several grievances, including unfair resident evictions, unfair court action against residents, evictions of tenants because of the manager's decision that they did not earn their income from farm work, harassment of tenants, and firing of people for speaking Spanish. The manager was portrayed as having no respect for the tenants, who he demeaned with his abrasive manner and rhetoric.

The most serious complaint related to a Farmers Home Administration policy that allows forty-five units to receive a rental subsidy. The other two area labor camps use all of their rental subsidies, but at the Hop Town Labor Camp, thirty-three subsidies remain unused. The tenants accused the manager of intentionally neglecting to inform them of the availability of assistance and of incorrectly disqualifying them for the rental assistance.

The IMC representative confirmed that the camp manager had a history of mistreating the tenants. Tenants complained of inadequate communications with the manager because he does not speak or understand Spanish. The manager does have an Mexican American office worker who can translate for him, so the housing authority believes this situation does not create a serious problem. The manager has been accused of spying on the residents. Some tenants believe that he does not respect their privacy, and they say he has entered their apartments when they are not at home.

Another complaint involved the guest policy. The housing authority has concerns about overcrowding and has set limits on how long guests can stay. The tenants must notify the office when they have guests. Some tenants believe that the manager unnecessarily harasses them when they have guests. They also believe that he does not follow housing authority rules in renting to people, claiming that he acts capriciously when deciding who meets the eligibility requirements for residency. The group accused the manager of telling people that there are no vacancies when, in fact, vacancies do exist.

Another complaint involved the rule of no pets being allowed to the tenants in the labor camp, while the manager regularly brings his dog to the office. One tenant reported that the manager threatened to evict him because his spouse was absent. To prevent their eviction, the tenant had to have his wife call the manager from Texas to inform him that she would be back by the end of the week.

Alfredo Ramirez was the principal leader of the tenant group at the Hop Town Labor Camp. He said that his family had been migrating illegally to California for several years. Alfredo finally received a green card (legal status) to work in the United States. He told me, "I love Mexico but the economy is so bad I cannot make a living." I asked why he was organizing the tenants. He replied: "No one I talk to likes this manager; he mistreats everybody. He is just a bad guy. He kicked my son and his family out of the camp. It was unfair. Somebody had to do something; we are people too."

I interviewed two of the farmers on the board of the Hop Town Housing Authority. The members of the housing authority believed that the manager does a good job. They acknowledged that he was not good with people but said that he "keeps good records and financial reports." The farmers also said that renters always complain about managers—it goes with the job.

I had the opportunity to observe one meeting of the Hop Town Housing Authority at noon in the Hop Town Cafe, at which they were to discuss tenants' complaints. The housing authority members kept the tenant committee and the Legal Aid lawyer waiting one hour after the scheduled meeting time. The Mexican American farm workers became nervous and finally returned to work in the fields. They worked for the son of the chair of the housing authority. The Legal Aid lawyer, by himself, presented the grievances of the tenants. The lawyer only presented four problems; he thought this was the best strategy because too many complaints might overwhelm the board:

(1) The tenants wanted to establish a grievance committee that complies with the policy of the Farmers Home Administration.

(2)   The court illegally evicted one Mexican American woman and ordered her to sell her car to pay the back rent.

(3)   The tenants desired to apply for the rent subsidy provided by the Farmers Home Administration.

(4)   Tenants needed to know how much of their income has to be earned from farm work to be eligible to reside in the HTLC.

The board's non-verbal and verbal responses sent a clear message that they did not consider the complaints to be legitimate grievances. The board chair and the manager dominated the discussion. They did not believe it necessary to establish a grievance committee, and they felt that the tenants should come to the board if they have any problems. The Legal Aid lawyer finally convinced the board that the tenants have the right under the policy of the Farmers Home Administration to establish a grievance committee consisting of two tenants and two members of the housing authority.

The manager, who functions as an ex-officio member of the housing authority, informed the lawyer that the tenants must be elected to serve on the committee. This was an interesting requirement since neither he or the board members face elections. The chairman of the board then appointed the manager to the grievance committee, although most of the grievances concern his own behavior.

After the Legal Aid lawyer departed, the housing authority continued its meeting. The members proceeded to discuss their options and how to respond to the grievances. Some of the discussion was obviously for my benefit. The manager said, "These tenants are just a few malcontents who don't represent anybody. Boy, this lawyer is a pain in the ass; he doesn't work, he only feeds at the public trough."

A Mexican American utility man for the labor camp also spoke for my benefit. In his monologue, he attacked the general credibility of the tenants and mentioned several instances of damage to mattresses and appliances. He also talked about the criminal, drinking, and drug problems of the tenants. All these negative comments occasioned a great many non-verbal expressions of consternation by the board. The message from the board, manager, and utility man was that the tenants were incapable of caring for the facilities. The board views migrant tenants as generally lacking the ability to live decently.

The attitudes of the housing authority members and the manager emerge from how they responded to the accusation that they had taken a Mexican American female tenant to court for not paying rent that she in fact had paid. Her Legal Aid lawyer had documents verifying that the woman had paid her rent. However, she failed to appear in court, and in such a situation the judge must find in favor of the plaintiff. The woman had to sell her car to pay the court fine.

The manager still insisted that this woman be kept from returning to her apartment because she had criminal relatives who visited her there. The manager also accused her of operating a business from her apartment, which is against the rules. She sold Tupperware to the other women in the camp. The housing authority recognized they would have to allow her to return but decided to threaten her with another eviction.

The housing authority has been known to bully and threaten with eviction certain tenants who share their housing with relatives or otherwise break the housing rules. To the housing authority, this behavior provides proof of the cheating character of Mexican American migrant workers. The rules of the Farmers Home Administration forbid more than one family living in a unit. Although there are good safety and health reasons behind this rule, the housing authority does not seem sensitive to the fact that relatives share housing because they have no money and no other place to live.

The most frightening aspect of this meeting was my knowledge that the housing authority knew I came to the meeting with the Legal Aid lawyer and the migrant tenants. One would assume that, at least for my benefit, the board and manager would attempt to present themselves as fair and reasonable men, and I have no doubt that several comments were made for my benefit. The housing authority members and the manager did not say Mexican American migrant workers are inferior to Anglos nor were any racial epithets heard; but that seemed to be the best they could do. I can only wonder how these people regularly act since they lack any accountability.

A year later, Mike Jones, the same Legal Aid lawyer, requested that I attend an evening meeting at the Hop Town elementary school. A new tenant group had called this meeting in an attempt to organize the camp because of the continued abusive behavior of the camp manager. Fourteen tenants, representing seven families, spent the evening attempting to develop a strategy to remove the manager. This current HTLC tenant group had related complaints to those expressed the previous year.

A week later, this group of tenants met with the director of the IMC. They met in the city park on a cold and windy day, for fear that a manager's spy might see them if they met in the labor camp. The committee told the director of their difficulties organizing tenants because the manager had intimidated them. They feared losing both their housing and their jobs. The director told the tenants that he would arrange a meeting with the state director of the Farmers Home Administration.

According to the director of the IMC, the meeting with the director of Idaho's Farmers Home Administration accomplished little; the committee received a full measure of standard bureaucratic procedural discourse, which essentially resulted in no action, because the tenants did not follow the prescribed grievance policy.

Conclusions

This chapter attempts to build a strong empirical case for the radical exploitive sociological model as best explaining the circumstances of Mexican American migrant workers. Ideology can lead to indifference and a denial of any race problems. The Anglo farmers did not perceive their actions as the exploitation of migrant workers. A common response was, "Nobody is forcing them to work here." If a society does not perceive a problem or ignores it, then it follows that such a society will be unable to solve that problem.

Another feature of the exploitive model is the perceived significance of race. America is a country of immigrants. The Mexican American migrant represents one chapter in that history. These people left their homes to escape poverty, and came to America with the hope that their children could live the American dream. Many migrants are not American citizens, though they have green cards that allow them to work in the U.S.; and this too is a common thread in America's immigrant history and social fabric.

The inability of the Anglo community of Middlewest and the Anglo farmers of the county to respond sympathetically to the poverty of Mexican American migrant workers appears to relate to their perception of Mexican Americans as being a separate race. One minister commented on his congregation's sponsorship of Russian refugees in Middlewest: Anglos offered their homes, cars, and assistance in finding an apartment, buying groceries, and obtaining services from government agencies. The minister reported that many Romanians also had come to Middlewest and received far greater assistance than have Mexican Americans. He said that the Anglos of Middlewest would never provide these services to the Mexican Americans.

The European refugees and immigrants to Farm County have church sponsors; they have ready access to resources and programs; Middlewest civic organizations raise funds to help provide them with the opportunity to take advantage of educational and training programs; and the community finds adequate housing for them. European immigrants are not found working in fields surrounding Middlewest. Though many of them, like the Mexican Americans, do not speak English and have a limited education, they are not stigmatized by the Anglos in the way that Mexican Americans are.

The oppression of Mexican American migrant workers is most disturbing when it results in the failure to provide a decent opportunity for migrant youth to be educated. Traveling with their parents, they miss a significant amount of school. Many must work in the fields to help support their families. Even though a low-income health clinic exists in Farm County, many migrants cannot regularly afford its services. The housing conditions of

most migrant workers is further evidence of their living under oppressive conditions. The social problems arising from
conditions of poverty coupled with the large number of single
males living away from their homes and families exacerbates
their common plight.

Observations in this chapter support one of the most important factors in the radical exploitive model, the economic
exploitation of migrants, who work in a secondary job market
that generally pays only the minimum wage and involves many
periods of unemployment. Their family wages generally remain
far below the poverty level.

The most important aspect of the exploitive model is its ideological factor. Most Anglos are unable to see or recognize
the oppressive poverty and abuse of Mexican American migrant
workers because they hold a belief that poverty is the consequence of one's individual failure. Most Anglos ignore or are
indifferent to Mexican American poverty because their lives focus on their own self-interest. Some Anglos in Farm County
enclose themselves in an Anglo world—they have no interaction
with nor any observations of Mexican American migrant workers. Their consequent lack of attention unintentionally enables
a colonialism to go unchecked.

The final feature of oppression portrayed in this chapter is the
lack of a political voice for Mexican American migrant workers.
They are not eligible to vote. The resident Mexican Americans,
the Idaho Migrant Council, and Mexican American leaders have
had little success in addressing the many needs of migrant workers. The operation of the farm labor camps serve to maintain
undemocratic and oppressive conditions for Mexican American
migrant workers who live there. The situation of many Mexican
American migrant workers in Idaho can be seen to violate both
our democratic and religious principles.

Chapter 8

INSTITUTIONALIZED RACISM AS PART OF THE EXPLOITIVE MODEL

I tell you, God could care less about the poor. Tell me, why must we live here like this? You're so good and yet you have to suffer so much. . . . Each step that he took toward the house resounded with the question, why? About halfway to the house he began to get furious. Then he started crying out of rage. . . . And without even realizing it, he said what he had been wanting to say for a long time. He cursed God. Upon doing this he felt that fear instilled in him by the years and by his parents. For a second he saw the earth opening up to devour him. . . . He thought of telling his mother, but he decided to keep it secret. All he told her was that the earth did not devour anyone. . . . Not yet, you can't swallow me up yet.

–Thomas Rivera

Introduction

This chapter will focus on the social institutions of Middlewest and how they function to exclude Mexican Americans from full participation in local society, thereby maintaining them in a colonial status. More than a decade ago sociologists developed the concept of *institutionalized racism*—a situation where a social institution operates, intentionally or unintentionally, to deny opportunities to minority groups. Such a situation assists in the maintaining of minorities in a subordinate position (Feagin 1989).

193

The radical exploitive theorists contend that the structure of the economy in a society is crucial in determining the social status of a person in the society. One's *social class* is determined by his/her position in the local economic structure. The owners (capitalists) have immense *power* to determine the quality of life of other people in the society.

Primary questions to be answered are: what insights can be gained by using the radical exploitive model? and what aspects of the theory are misleading and erroneous? Throughout the writing of this book, my attention kept returning to these questions. From the examination of the race relations in Middlewest I have come to the conclusion that the insights provided by the radical exploitive model outweigh its limitations. It will be necessary here to examine the contribution of each social institution to the maintaining of the racial minority in a semi-colonial status.

I have modified the radical exploitive model to emphasize its ideological component. The ideology of the Anglo community explains its indifference to the social conditions of Mexican Americans and its lack of concern about existing race relations. The ideology facilitates negative attitudes about the Mexican American population on the one hand while it maintains that all Americans have an equal opportunity to succeed.

Some Mexican Americans in Middlewest become assimilated and some succeed economically while retaining their ethnicity— a situation predicted by those supporting the pluralistic model. However, I believe that the structural barriers to economic advancement for the Mexican Americans of Middlewest and Farm County are extensive enough to warrant my use of the exploitive model. Only the radical exploitive model adequately portrays the essential nature of the subordinate position of the Mexican American people of this study.

Marilyn Frye (1983), in her essay on oppression, provides an important insight into the nature of institutionalized racism:

> Cages. Consider a bird cage. If you look very closely at just one wire in the cage, you cannot see the other wires. . . . You will be unable to see why a bird would not just fly around the wire any time it wanted to go somewhere.

Furthermore, even if, one day at a time, you myopically inspected each wire, you could not see why a bird would have trouble going past the wires to get anywhere. It is only when you step back, stop looking at the wires one by one. And take a macroscopic view of the whole cage.... It is perfectly obvious that the bird is surrounded by a network of systematically related barriers, no one of which would be the least hindrance to its flight, but which by their relations to each other, are as confining as the solid walls of a dungeon.

The Local Newspaper

My analysis of the newspaper utilizes the work of Spector and Kitsuse (1987) and that of Best (1989), all of whom use a constructionist perspective for understanding social problems. This perspective recognizes the complex nature of social problems, and these authors reject the idea that only objective conditions define social problems. From their perspective, social problems have a subjective nature; in other words, they must be constructed by "claims makers." The constructionists examine the process of how certain social conditions come to be recognized as social problems.

In *Images of Issues* (Best 1989), a book of readings from the constructionist perspective, many of the researchers found that newspaper and television accounts and claims about a putative social condition were crucial in transforming that phenomenon into a social problem. The claims makers not only make assertions about some social behaviors as being problematic but they also make observations regarding the causes of the problem, which lead to a set of solutions for the designated problem.

Reinarman and Levine (Best 1989) examine the construction of the crack (drug) problem in the inner cities, and they have drawn a particularly relevant set of conclusions from their analysis of the local newspaper. They believe that the media influences politicians and other moral entrepreneurs to join a group of crusaders in vilifying the deviant behavior of minority groups and calling for a crime control approach to the perceived problem. American society is manipulated into making scapegoats of the victims instead of examining the social and economic problems that underlie their deviant behavior.

As part of my field research, for six months I conducted a content analysis of the local daily newspaper to assess the amount and type of coverage of the Mexican American population in comparison to the coverage of the Anglo population. The analysis of the *Daily News* reveals that the Mexican American community is correct in believing that the paper has an anti-Mexican American orientation. One example is found in the weekly coverage of the arrests and sentencing of criminals. Many papers do not print this type of list. The *Daily News* accurately lists Mexican American names, but the list includes a disproportional number of Mexican American offenders. Also, the printing of the list continuously reinforces a negative image of the Mexican American community. This practice is unusual because the data seems to be of little intrinsic interest; it would be comparable to list the number of houses sold each week. The *Daily News* also repeats or continues the stories relating to Mexican American offenders much more than is typical for newspapers.

Herein lies an example of modern racism. The paper accurately reports the crimes in Middlewest and Farm County; but why does it select those government statistics? The paper does not question the actions of law enforcement and the courts, which could be seen as selectively enforcing laws against Mexican American offenders.

A feature that clearly illustrates the negative orientation of the *Daily News* toward Mexican Americans is the paper's coverage of criminal arrests in other states. The paper frequently presents crime stories with pictures that involve a Mexican American offender. Why would the Middlewest subscriber be interested in run-of-the-mill crimes by Mexican American offenders in other states? The Boise daily newspaper did not carry any of these stories. I doubt that this practice occurs unintentionally.

The primary method by which the *Daily News* presents and creates a criminal image of Mexican Americans is by printing a higher proportion of negative columns and stories than positive stories. Approximately 15 percent of the articles about Anglos in Middlewest report on their criminal activities, whereas 85 percent of the paper's stories report on positive or neutral accounts of the Anglos in Middlewest. The paper's treatment of Mexican Americans is just the reverse: 75 percent of the stories examine criminal activities of Mexican Americans in Middlewest while only 25 percent of the stories carry a positive or neutral image.

Institutionalized racism is not often challenged, because few people understand that a newspaper not only reports on but also creates social realities. It would be possible to be a reporter for this paper and not have any prejudicial attitudes toward Mexican Americans and yet still be participating in these racist practices. The inaccurate image presented by the crime reports in the newspaper is magnified because most Anglos are not aware that Middlewest has more Mexican Americans among its population than is generally believed. In the summer, the number of Mexican Americans may approach 35 percent of the county's population.

The *Daily News* faithfully reports the crime but not all the positive activities within the Mexican American community. For example, I attended a dinner sponsored by Mexican American Catholics to honor the migrant workers. The paper did not cover the dinner and entertainment, but the arrest of a Mexican American received front-page coverage. The unbalanced coverage of the violent, drug-related, and criminal acts by Mexican Americans is exacerbated because law enforcement officers also arrest Mexican Americans for crimes of poverty such as not having car insurance.

Criminologists (Quinney 1977) recognize that people from minority and lower-class backgrounds generally have higher arrest rates. A poverty environment reduces legitimate opportunities and enhances deviant opportunities (Cloward and Ohlin 1960). The creation of minority criminals also occurs because of the tendency of police to apprehend members of racial minorities (Haskell and Yablonsky 1974). Criminologists have developed a large body of research indicating that racial minorities receive biased treatment at every stage of the criminal justice system

(Platt and Cooper 1974). Adding to this class bias in Middlewest is the view of the *Daily News* that the wedding of a local banker's daughter has social interest whereas that of a migrant couple lacks reader appeal. The negative image created by the *Daily News* may be partially unintentional, but it contributes significantly to the negative perceptions most Anglos in Middlewest have of the Mexican Americans in their community.

During the period in which my content analysis of the newspaper was conducted, four editorials criticized the local Mexican American community. One called bilingual education a "stupid idea." Another concluded that the Mexican American Caucus's plan for redistricting "is absurd." The paper did not print a single editorial supporting a Mexican American issue.

Of those Middlewesterners who subscribe to the local paper, approximately 85 percent of the Mexican Americans and a majority of middle-class Anglos I interviewed believe that the *Daily News* focuses on the negative—especially on criminal activities of Mexican Americans in Middlewest. Does the mass media shape or does it reflect social sentiments? Many Anglo subjects specifically said that the paper narrowly presents the Mexican Americans as criminals, but later they too affirmed the criminal nature of Mexican Americans. Can people be influenced even when they know the media is attempting to influence them? Certainly the advertisers think so.

The following comments by a Middlewest businessman reflect the Anglo view on Mexican American crime.

I am probably going to be called prejudiced for this. It's because of the Mexicans. The crime is, regardless of what people say, when you read it in the paper, that is who is committing these crimes. The bulk of them; yes, a few Anglo kids. From what I read, know about, 80 percent of the crimes are by those people. I am not saying all Mexicans are bad. I know some nice Mexicans. The migrants come in and out, then they have those gangs, and I am sure a lot of drugs are involved. . . . I don't know why the Mexicans—they go to same schools as my kids. They have jobs.

Several major stories in the *Daily News* during the time of the content analysis examined the programs established to reduce gangs, drug trafficking, and vandalism in Middlewest. Following a rash of burglaries and acts of vandalism for which the police had arrested Mexican American suspects, the newspaper reported on the Chamber of Commerce's establishment of a crime-prevention program. The paper ran a story on the Department of Health and Welfare when it received a grant with which it hired a Mexican American to work with at-risk and gang youth. This article followed months of other reports on Mexican American gangs. The reports in the newspaper left little doubt that these problems existed because of the Mexican American population of Middlewest. The community's institutions appear to be concerned about Mexican American crime, yet nobody knows, understands, or cares to learn why the Mexican Americans have a higher proportion of criminal activity.

There is a circular nature to institutionalized racism. The chief of police of Middlewest told me in an interview in the fall of 1990 that the newspaper had created the Mexican American gang problem. A year later, in an interview with a *Daily News* reporter, he said that Middlewest did have a Mexican American gang problem. This chapter will describe how various institutions participate in and reinforce the deviant image of Mexican Americans.

A racially sensitive newspaper operating in a community that has a significant Mexican American minority very likely would reverse the proportion of positive to negative articles on the Mexican American population. This could be accomplished by having a Mexican American section of the newspaper with a majority of the articles portraying Mexican Americans in a positive light. It would hire Mexican American reporters and present the Mexican American perspective on community issues. Some articles might be printed in both Spanish and English. A sensitive paper would attempt to educate the Anglo community about Mexican American culture and issues.

The Mexican American community in Middlewest has the responsibility of informing the newspaper concerning upcoming social, political, and cultural events and to request coverage of these events. A crucial way to modify this situation would be for the *Daily News* reporters to be required to seek out Mexican American leaders whenever they plan to write an article that in some way reflects negatively on the Mexican American community. When the *Daily News* begins to question why Mexican Americans participate in deviant behavior, instead of just reprinting police reports, it could sensitize the community regarding the causes of minority crime. This approach might lead to investigative reporting on the housing problem, discrimination, unemployment, and lack of medical assistance to impoverished Mexican Americans.

The Economic Institution

A key component of the radical exploitive perspective of race relations is the inequity in employment where Anglos are systematically employed in higher paying and higher status positions. One's social class and race play a role in determining what type of employment that person can secure. In a capitalistic industrial economy it would be expected that first-generation Mexican American immigrants would be primarily employed in low-paying jobs that do not require education, training, or fluency in the English language. The fact that immigrants can only earn a poverty wage says something about how capitalism functions in general and affects all workers.

The radical exploitive model holds to the position that a capitalistic economy will take advantage of any group of workers that society perceives as being subordinate to the dominant group. In America, women and racial minorities regularly fill the necessary requirements because a tradition and ideology exist to legitimize the payment of lower wages to them.

The economic position of the Mexican American population in Farm County reveals that they are exploited. More Mexican Americans work in the fields as migrant or seasonal workers than work at any other type of employment in Farm County. The majority, even second- and third-generation Mexican Americans, do farm labor and factory work. This is the secondary job market, and it includes many part-time jobs as well as lengthy periods of unemployment. Mexican Americans for the most part do not have access to the better paying blue-collar and white (Anglo)-collar jobs that require only a minimum education. Idaho government statistics (Department of Commerce 1992, Department of Employment 1991a) show that Mexican American unemployment is double that of the Anglo population. Their poverty rate of 33 percent is three times that of the Anglo community.

During the period of my field research I toured and interviewed managers and workers of the local area factories. Several companies have factories located in Middlewest or in communities close to Middlewest. They include food processing plants, trailer factories, seed companies, and companies that cater to the needs of a farm economy. Large numbers of Mexican American men and women work in these factories. In the two area potato-processing plants, a sugar beet factory, and the seed companies, almost 30 percent of the work force is Mexican American.

Most Mexican American factory workers earned $6.00 an hour or less at the time of this study. The women, as a group, earned the lowest wages. At all of these factories, even at the trailer factories, the work is seasonal. The workers face layoffs for a significant period during the year. For example, the sugar factory has a fall processing period called a "campaign" that lasts for approximately five months, and during this period the company hires several hundred additional workers. This means that most Mexican American workers there fall below the government guidelines for poverty although they work what would be considered full-time for this company. Of course, many Anglo factory workers also experience poverty as a result of the structure of the capitalist economy. A tour of the sugar factory revealed that Mexican Americans primarily are employed in the packaging section of the plant, which requires the hardest manual labor and pays the lowest wages. Throughout the rest of the plant Anglos predominate. The manager leading the tour openly acknowledged that there existed a "Mexican Section" of the plant.

The management, white-collar, clerical, and professional workers in these plants generally are not Mexican American.

Some Mexican Americans have reached a supervisory level, but not in proportion to their numbers in those workplaces. In one potato processing plant, only one Mexican American holds the advanced position of supervisor, manager, or lead worker although there are fifty such positions. The local dairy has more than 100 employees and most of the positions do not require university training; however, only two of the dairy's employees are Mexican American. Another example of the racial division of jobs is found in a large corporation that operates several businesses. Approximately 500 Mexican Americans work in the company's food processing plant, but the other divisions have no Mexican American workers. Mexican Americans are seldom employed at the higher-paying blue-collar jobs such as driving a truck or rebuilding railroad cars. The local hospital has 600 employees but only four percent have Mexican American surnames; most of them work at housekeeping, records, and clerical tasks.

I also interviewed people in many smaller businesses in Middlewest—banks, clothing stores, furniture stores, drug stores, department stores, grocery stores, restaurants, auto dealerships, and smaller specialized businesses. These businesses had few Mexican American employees; those few were found in entry-level positions. For example, the largest store in town has approximately fifty employees, only two of which are Mexican Americans. One of these two holds the position of custodian.

Some businesses and governmental agencies do have several Mexican American employees, especially those entities that have many female employees in traditional secretarial and clerical positions. One telephone marketing business employs women as sales personnel; several Mexican Americans work there for a wage slightly above the legal minimum. Some departments within the local criminal justice system have less of an imbalance of Mexican American workers although the pattern of having few Mexican American employees also occurs in governmental offices located in Middlewest. Affirmative action policies have not transformed Middlewest, but it is extremely difficult to prove a racist policy held by a business. The city, county, and state governmental agencies all had few Mexican American employees. The 1990 census reports that Mexican

Americans represent 20 percent of Middlewest's population, and demographers believe that minority populations are generally undercounted. Mexican Americans account for three percent or less of the work force in most Middlewest government offices, and most of these hold the lowest paying positions. The city government has two Mexican American employees out of 125 workers.

Many jobs in these local businesses and governmental agencies do not require a college degree. The Middlewest Post Office has fifty-one employees, none of whom is Mexican American. According to the postmaster, the qualifying examination can be passed without a high school diploma. Few Mexican Americans living in Middlewest have a college education, which means that few work in the professional sector of the economy. Less than two percent of public school teachers are Mexican American.

This data depicts a pattern similar to that faced by Mexican Americans throughout the United States. Feagin (1991) examines census data that illustrates that Mexican Americans have significantly higher unemployment, higher concentration in low-income jobs, and a median income that is approximately 70 percent that of Anglos.

Middlewest has several firms that employ ten to forty workers. Many of these businesses exist because of the farm economy; they involve constructing or repairing farm machinery and farm equipment. Again, not many Mexican Americans work in these blue-collar positions except at a horse-trailer factory. I interviewed two owners of businesses who said that they would not hire Mexican Americans. The owners claimed that they are not good workers. For example, the owner of a farm equipment manufacturing company that employs forty-five workers said: "I will tell you this, though, they are not a reliable people. The ones that come in and out, even the young ones. They are not reliable; come good to work for a week or two, pretty soon they do not come to work.... No, I don't know why they stop coming to work. I just don't hire them anymore."

The average annual income in Farm County is significantly below the state average. The county also has the highest crime rate per capita. Farm County has by far the most Mexican Americans of any county in the state of Idaho. Sixty percent of the Mexican Americans work in three categories: agricultural work, production work, and general labor (Idaho Department of Employment 1991a). This is a grim set of statistics for the Mexican American population of Middlewest and Farm County. However, these numbers provide empirical support for the radical exploitive model of race relations. The fact that Mexican Americans face more periods of unemployment and significantly lower wages than the average worker supports the view that Mexican Americans are an economic underclass in Middlewest and in Farm County.

It is useful to examine the process of recruitment and selection of employees. It was not uncommon from my interviews to find that a worker had been informed of an opening by relatives and friends who work at that business. It certainly helps if that person has friends who will vouch for his character to the boss or supervisor. Friends and relatives also can help prepare a prospective worker for the job skills required and the attitudes expected by the personnel department. If no Mexican Americans are employed in a business, the "good old boy" tradition often excludes potential Mexican American workers. Some Anglos confirmed that this network helped them obtain their job. Conducting the field research, I discovered that some Mexican American families had as many as six to ten relatives working in the same factory. These people acknowledged that their relatives assisted them in obtaining their positions.

The fact that two separate communities exist in Middlewest means that many Mexican Americans do not apply for positions because "Mexican Americans do not work" in that particular business. They assume that the company or business will not hire Mexican Americans. Additionally, potential Mexican American workers usually will not have the information and inside knowledge necessary to acquire the position.

Farmers are the recipients of many support programs from the government. To alleviate the poverty and oppressive conditions of Mexican American farm laborers will require increasing the minimum wage, supplementing the income of part-time workers, and providing health insurance to all workers. Currently neither public sentiment nor the political will exists to establish government programs to diminish poverty in America. Idaho farmers cannot solve this problem because they are in competition with other farmers. However, you might think that because the farmers have observed the poverty of their workers they might be leading a political movement on behalf of farm workers. But such is not the case. It will take a national program to assist farm labor. Sociologists and others including Robert Bellah et al. (1985) have warned the American public about their lack of social responsibility and their undue focus on their own self-interest.

The Oppression of Female Mexican American Factory Workers

I listened to seven Mexican American women who work for a food processing plant present their grievances to lawyers of a prestigious Boise law firm. The factory employs 350 workers, approximately fifty of whom are Mexican American. The women felt that they did not receive promotions because of their ethnicity. They presented several examples of Anglo women who had less education, work experience, and seniority receiving promotions instead of them. They claimed that Mexican American women are not considered for supervisory positions, and said they face constant harassment by their supervisors, who force them to work during their lunch and coffee breaks. They said that they had to do jobs without proper training and that they face the constant threat of suspension.

These Mexican American women felt that their supervisors think that Mexican Americans are not good workers. They claimed that the supervisors yell and scream at them and said that they feel left out and unwanted. The Mexican Americans work in the three lowest-paying positions in the plant. Helen Flores has worked for the company for sixteen years and earns $12,500 a year. She said she has applied for seven better-paying positions in the company and has yet to be promoted.

Maria Torres works part-time on Sundays doing cleanup work, a job she has been doing for several years. An opening for full-time cleanup occurred and she applied for it; however, the company hired an Anglo woman with no experience with the company.

The women complained that the company doctor forces Mexican Americans to work while injured yet allows Anglos to collect workmen's compensation. The women told of Mexican Americans continuing to work with serious injuries for fear of losing their jobs if they did not. Valencia Salinas said, "The Anglo workers and management all stick together. They make us feel like we're not wanted there." The women feel that their problems increased six years ago when the company hired a new plant manager, who they believe hires and promotes Anglos. If they go to the personnel department about it, they not only receive no assistance but they get labeled as troublemakers. The women said that many other Mexican Americans have similar problems but fear doing anything because they think they will be fired.

A most serious complaint came from Jane Carranza, who recently went to the company credit union to withdraw the $5,000 she had saved through the company's payroll deduction plan. She was told that she had no money and no account. The women believe the company will cheat them in every way that is possible.

The comments above do not represent a full review of these women's work circumstances. Still, their lawyers wonder if they should sue the company, because of the risk of losing the case and the company firing the women. The many complications that could make it difficult for the women to win their case include the following: industrial workers frequently have conflicts with management that do not have merit; other workers often will not testify on their behalf; the women claimed that two other Mexican American women will testify against them in order to ingratiate themselves with the bosses; some of the incidents occurred years ago, so they would be hard to substantiate; several of the women do not write or speak English, which fact could be used against them; and the women might not be able to articulate their grievance when testifying in a court setting.

The case of these Mexican American women is significant because it illustrates how racism continues in America. Their lawyers doubt they could win this case. Whose word has the most influence in our society: the manager of a company or uneducated minority women? The problem arises out of the dehumanization created by our capitalistic economy. Capitalists often exploit workers because it is profitable to do so. We allow poverty to exist because minorities have little power. Political institutions, the media, and the corporate world have not placed Mexican American poverty and underemployment on the agenda. This climate creates an atmosphere of indifference to and invisibility of the exploitation of Mexican American workers. Many people in Farm County and Middlewest see the employment status of Mexican Americans as a consequence of their deficiencies and culture. Few Anglos appear to have an understanding of the role played by the structure of the economy in creating and sustaining the economic inequality of the Mexican American community.

Political Institutions

Farm County has the reputation of being the most Republican district in the state. The conservative Republican rhetoric in Farm County calls for a reduction in the size of government, lower taxes, and fewer regulations on business. However, the Mexican American community needs just the opposite in order to overcome their disadvantaged economic, political, and social position. The political barrier between the Anglos and Mexican Americans is large and difficult to breach.

Farm County elects few Democrats. In 1990 the Democrats fielded a full slate of candidates for the first time in years, but the political rhetoric of most Democrats who ran for office had considerable similarity to that of the Republicans. The Democratic candidates ran a much stronger race than usual—the five Anglo Democratic candidates, running against strong Republican incumbents, nearly got elected. Although all lost their bid for election, four of the five received from 45 percent to 47 percent of the vote.

Two Mexican Americans ran for the state legislature as Democrats. They received 33 percent of the vote in Farm County. An interesting race was the contest between Juan Celedón, the director of the Idaho Migrant Council who ran against John Carter, a non-incumbent Republican. Carter resides in Middlewest, where he is a practicing attorney; the IMC has its headquarters in Middlewest although Celedón lives in a nearby town.

Celedón had a large group of volunteers who worked on his campaign, yet he only received 27 percent of the Middlewest vote. Carter spent $10,000 on the primary election, because the winner of the Republican primary generally wins a seat in the legislature. When I interviewed Carter in the fall, he was serene and confident; he had no doubts about winning the election. He had raised $5,000 for the general election but only spent $3,000 of those campaign contributions.

Celedón should have been a strong candidate because he heads a large organization and a staff of one hundred. Nearly all the Mexican American leaders in southwestern Idaho supported his candidacy. He has considerable experience as a public speaker, having been a Mexican American leader for many years. Yet Celedón's vote total was approximately eighteen percentage points below those of Anglo Democratic candidates who ran against incumbents. The eighteen percent deficit probably reflects an anti-Mexican American vote.

The Celedón campaign strategies and tactics did not significantly differ from those of the other Democratic candidates. I believe that the governor's office, the state Democratic party, and the Idaho Education Association did not support the Celedón campaign with endorsements, campaign workers, or finances as much as they did the campaigns of the Anglo Democrats in Farm County. Few Anglos in Middlewest ever attended any of Celedón's campaign activities, especially fund raisers.

Celedón waged a comprehensive campaign that matched that of any candidate in Farm County. He attended all the political forums and his presentations did not differ in quality from those of the other Democrats. He knew that most Mexican Americans in Farm County either do not or cannot vote. He did have a few Anglos on his campaign committee, but the fact that there is a gap between the Anglo community and Mexican American community in Middlewest meant that Celedón did not have a network of relationships within the Anglo power structure and the Anglo middle class.

The Anglo power structure of Middlewest, which includes the corporate owners, the plant management, businessmen, and large farmers, pledged its money and support to Celedón's Republican opponent. However, an Anglo Democrat who ran for the state legislature from Middlewest knew many members of the Anglo power structure socially and some of these people supported his campaign.

Carter's candidacy benefitted because his law firm represents many in the local power structure. He also belongs to several legal organizations that assisted his campaign. Carter belongs to the Kiwanis Club and has served as president of that organization. This provided him with a set of influential supporters, each with a network of politically active friends. His father had a long and distinguished medical career in Middlewest. His wife serves as a local judge, creating another set of supporters. The Carter family belongs to a church that has a high status congregation, thus enabling Carter to build additional influential friendships.

Carter had many built-in advantages because of his social and professional network. These relationships and contacts did not develop as part of a political strategy on Carter's part but were merely the result of his social position in the community. At times Carter looked out of his element—he did not seem to enjoy the political process and he did not seek out the limelight. He did not campaign with the intense ideological conservatism of most Republican candidates. He ran a low-key campaign and he was hardly visible in the hoopla of election campaigning.

The landslide political victory of Carter was not a conspiracy; on the contrary, it is how American politics works. It relates to who you know and how much money you can raise. Celedón obviously was deficient on both counts. The result was inevitable—Carter received 73 percent of the vote in Middlewest. Carter undoubtedly would have won if his opponent had been an Anglo Democrat; however, the victory probably would have been of a lesser magnitude. Most of the Anglo business and civic leaders I interviewed accurately predicted that it was impossible for Celedón to win. Their confidence came from knowing that Celedón did not know the Anglo business/civic leaders and did not belong to any of their community organizations. The gap between the Mexican American and Anglo communities must be of considerable proportions if we consider that Celedón has led the most influential Mexican American organization in the state for twenty years. How is it that the Anglo power structure does not know him?

Most Mexican Americans in Farm County cannot vote because they either are migrant workers, lack citizenship, or have not registered to vote. Most who can vote do not participate in the political process even when Mexican Americans are on the ballot. Mexican Americans do not have sufficient numbers by themselves to win an election even if they all voted. Their minimal participation in the electoral process may be because they have a separate community, or they may be intimidated by the process, or they may see political elections as an Anglo domain. Mexican American culture itself may inhibit political participation. Many Mexican American subjects I talked with perceived all politicians as corrupt and as not addressing the concerns of the Mexican American population. This attitude might derive from experiences with the undemocratic politics of Mexico.

Armando Aguirre, the deputy director of the IMC, created a Mexican American political organization in an attempt to politicize the Mexican Americans of Farm County. However, the organization only has a dozen active members. The organization did recruit several volunteers to assist in a Mexican American voter registration drive that was undertaken with little success prior to the elections in the fall of 1990. The Mexican American leaders are a determined bunch, however; they just keep trying no matter the odds or the past failures.

The limited role of Mexican Americans in Middlewest politics appears to reflect the role of social class in elections. My field research confirmed that both lower- and working-class Anglos and Mexican Americans do not vote to the extent that do middle-class people. The limited education of the working class is a significant factor in their absence from political participation; many lower-class Anglos and Mexican Americans said they did not understand the political process.

The implication of the fact of having no Democrats and no Mexican Americans in local and county governments is that political officials and governmental entities may ignore the needs of the Mexican American population. The treatment of Mexican American children in the schools and the establishment's often harsh response to Mexican American gangs may not be regularly questioned because no Mexican American politician is in office who can come to their defense. If the Mexican American community had political power they could more effectively challenge the institutional racism in Middlewest and Farm County. Additionally, the Mexican American community also then could benefit from an expansion of social services and programs to expand employment and other opportunities.

An example of the consequences of the political powerlessness of the Mexican American community can be seen by examining the state legislature's creation of a reapportionment plan. The Mexican American leaders of Idaho created the Mexican American Caucus because they could find no legislative support for their reapportionment plan. They requested that the legislature establish three minority electoral districts. Both political parties ignored the plan. A federal civil rights law has made it illegal to gerrymander minority districts, and since the largest concentration of Mexican Americans in Idaho is in Farm County, the Mexican American Caucus has now filed suit in federal court requesting that minority districts be established in Idaho.

A prime example of the political subordination of Mexican Americans was found in a recent political campaign in Middlewest. In the late 1980s the Anglo business and civic leaders wanted to elect a new city council because of the turmoil created by the current office holders. The continued media coverage of the petty attacks of one set of city officials against another was becoming an embarrassment. Community leaders decided to run three of their candidates in order to return decorum to the city council. One of their candidates was a Mexican American businessman who had lived in Middlewest less than a year. The community leaders did not consult with the local Mexican American leaders, revealing their paternalistic attitude toward Mexican Americans. They believed they had done the Mexican Americans a favor but, in fact, this action was seen as an insult to local Mexican Americans since the candidate had no ties to the local Mexican American community.

The colonial status of Mexican Americans and their powerlessness can be appreciated by looking at the small-town politics of Farm County. Hop Town has a population of 1,500. Sixty-five percent of the population is Mexican American, yet not one Mexican American has been elected to the city council. In the election of 1990, the Anglo election officials refused to allow Mexican American voters to use a write-in sticker. Later in the day, the state attorney general's office issued a statement allowing voters to use stickers for write-in candidates, but the ruling came too late to assist the Mexican American candidate.

Since most the citizens of Hop Town are Mexican American, why are not at least some of the public officials Mexican American? The Mexican Americans of Hop Town feel intimidated and are afraid of offending the Anglos of the community because they work for Anglos in the nearby fields and factories. The absence of political power means that although 75 percent of the school children have a Mexican American heritage, the school operates with Anglo teachers and administrators. The curriculum is designed for white middle-class children. The mayor of Hop Town informed me that not a word of Spanish should be spoken in the local schools. The political control of Hop Town by Anglos also affects how the police operate in the community. The mayor appoints the board of directors to the Hop Town Labor Camp. Only Mexican Americans live in this part of Hop Town, but the Anglo board and manager function in the interest of the area's farmers.

Politics is more than elections; it involves the policies, programs, and administrative decisions of governmental entities. For example, the farmers, according to several sources, have influence with the Farmers Home Administration that allows them to maintain control of the migrant labor camps. The implication of this arrangement is that Mexican American tenants will have an unsympathetic hearing for their complaints. Lawyers for Idaho Legal Aid informed me that Idaho farmers belong to the Farm Bureau, an organization of political influence which attempts to eliminate Legal Aid because of the assistance it provides to Mexican American farm workers.

A related issue to one-party control is how that control enables the dominant party to define social problems and the response to those problems. For example, the public school administrators do not define the Mexican American dropout rate as a problem but many Mexican Americans do. The politicians do not call for the creation of culturally diverse school programs.

Most political figures concentrate their attention on supporting and assisting economic growth. The Middlewest civic and business leaders also devote much their of their energy toward this goal. In American politics special-interest groups support candidates who will protect their interests. Middlewest is no different; why should the community be concerned about ethnic issues and problems when Mexican Americans only constitute a minority of the population? Anglo candidates can be elected while ignoring the Mexican American constituency.

While I was conducting my research, the mayor did not mention one word about Mexican Americans in his yearly report on the state of the city, and the superintendent of schools had not read the task force report on problems of Mexican American education. One state legislator from Middlewest wanted to make English the official language of Idaho, though almost all of his Mexican American constituents oppose such a bill. Another legislator from Farm County fell asleep at a Mexican American meeting. The Anglo leaders of Middlewest do not adequately know the Mexican American people or their culture and they appear to have little desire to change this situation.

I asked the Mexican American leaders which Anglo leaders—business, civic, or political—they could turn to when problems arise that affect the Mexican American community. They responded that when the chips are down, when they challenge the Anglo establishment, no Anglo politician will come to their assistance. For Mexican Americans to achieve parity, an interconnected colonial system of beliefs and institutions would have to be dismantled. Realistically, social justice for Mexican Americans in Middlewest and Farm County is in the distant future.

Religion

A community study would be incomplete if it failed to examine the role of religion. Middlewest has approximately fifty churches. I interviewed five Mexican American and five Anglo clergymen. Few in Middlewest question the integrity of the clergy, whose position enables them to have more intimate knowledge concerning their congregations. Three of the Anglo ministers had fathers who were pastors in the same church. The Anglo ministers believe that Middlewest rates high on its religious commitment compared to urban communities.

The Anglo ministers recognize that the politically conservative nature of their congregations is in part a consequence of its many elderly members. One Anglo minister depicted the political orientation of Middlewest as a quasi-McCarthyism. The local churches have taken a strong stance on public decency; they helped to close down an X-rated movie house and an adult bookstore. In the schools, the sex-education class instructors must limit their discussion to abstinence as the only acceptable method of birth control.

Three of the Anglo ministers and three of the Mexican American ministers described their churches as having a pentecostal philosophy. These churches practice a religious fundamentalism that contends humans have lost their way. Their congregations are required to read the Bible and live their lives according to their denomination's interpretation of it. The congregations publicly confess and repent, and the churches demand that their members abstain from dancing, movies, and alcohol.

Four of the Anglo clergymen ministered in churches that had few or no Mexican Americans in the congregations. Three of these ministers said that race relations in Middlewest are a serious problem and that many of their members have prejudiced views about Mexican Americans. One Anglo minister believed that the solution to the community's race problem will be solved by the assimilation of Mexican Americans.

One Anglo minister of a church with 400 members said:

> Race relations are not good and I am not sure they are going to get any better. The churches are concerned, we try to move on it, but we are not having much success. The gang culture is such, makes it hard to crack. A lot of prejudice against the Spanish. I don't know what it will take to correct it. You hear a lot of things said like what you would hear in the South in reference to the blacks. People resent that a Spanish person would buy a house in their neighborhood or even rent to them. This fellow across the street, he is Spanish, he keeps his place immaculate.... It is clean, people comment about that, that he is unusual because he is a clean Mexican.

Another religion represents ten percent of the church-going population and has several congregations. One hundred Mexican Americans belong to this faith but have their own church and separate services. The few Anglo subjects I interviewed from this faith had particularly negative views toward Mexican Americans. Some members of this church's leadership adamantly support the English language law although their church has separate Spanish-language services for the Mexican Americans. One of this church's officials views Mexican Americans as troublemakers and he tells his children to avoid the Mexican children. The leader of the Mexican American services is Spanish and has extremely negative opinions about his Mexican American congregation. He considers Mexican Americans to be less intelligent than Europeans.

Another Anglo minister's experience provides insight into how Anglos view Mexican Americans. He said:

> I was on a grand jury; this is probably something I am probably not supposed to tell. Last summer sixteen of us were on a grand jury. One lady was Mexican American.

We had a crime committed on the boulevard, a crime by a Mexican American man. The Mexican American stole six tapes from a pickup. He was in the pickup when the owner came out. He grabbed the six tapes and ran. The owner caught him and said, "Give me the tapes back." The Mexican American did not speak English. Another Anglo guy came up. He said, "Are you going to let him get away with this?" The other guy said, "I am going to leave this alone." The other guy had been drinking, he also knew karate. He took a kick at the Mexican American, hit him in the head. Knocked him out. He fell on a rock and he died. The testimony was that the Anglo guy was using racial slurs, you Mexican so-and-so. The grand jury did not indict, only minimal charges. Only me and the Mexican American woman voted for anything stronger. . . . That is something that will always stand in my mind; I consider myself a good persuader, first time I ran up against racism and could not sway the argument. This guy was a murderer, that is what he was. Things were said like, who committed the original crime. Stupid; no, misguided. I was a very disturbed human being. I met it face to face. This it what it would be like, to live in the South. The man should have been locked up. He didn't even call 911. . . . It was plea bargained down to probation, no jail time.

I interviewed two Mexican American Catholic priests, one from Middlewest and the other from a small town near Middlewest. Both Catholic churches have large parishes with Spanish language services for Mexican Americans. Both priests said that the majority of their Anglo parishioners are prejudiced against Mexican Americans. The priests remarked that the Anglo parishioners complain about the Mexicans, such as: "Father, why are they dirty, why are they speaking Spanish, and why don't they go back to Mexico?"

Both priests have attempted to integrate the services but the tensions became such that the integrated services were canceled. The priests both said that they feel remorse because of the unwillingness of Anglos to assist Mexican Americans living in poverty. Father Acuna shared with me many examples of racial intolerance in his community. He believes that Anglos sometimes act to undermine Mexican American culture. The businesses, police, schools, and churches attempt to subordinate Mexican Americans. Father Acuna believes that the Catholic church in Idaho has less concern for its Mexican American members, and he thinks that Anglo priests do not appreciate Mexican American culture. The Mexican American churches do not receive a proportional share of the church's resources.

Father Acuna was born and educated in Mexico. He said that the Anglo priests do not appreciate that Mexican Americans come from an Aztec heritage where "religion is in the bones" of the people. He thinks many Anglo priests see their Mexican American members as uneducated and unchurched. The Anglo priests push the English language instead of learning Spanish themselves. Mirande (1985) confirms Father Acuna's view of the negative role of the Catholic church in supporting the dominant class at the expense of Chicanos.

Most Mexican Americans in Middlewest belong to the Catholic faith; however, I found there were also several small Mexican American churches. I interviewed three Pentecostal ministers: Jose Delgado, the Assembly of God minister with a congregation of eighty; John Flores, a Pentecostal minister with seventy members in his church; and Jesús Pérez, also a Pentecostal minister, with a congregation of fifteen members. The Assembly of God's pastor works full time as a minister, whereas the two Pentecostal ministers have factory jobs. Each of the three has a limited education.

I discovered that Mexican American Catholics are more likely to be stable, working-class people. The Mexican American fundamentalist churches have more members who are in a lower-class position because of the unstable nature of their employment. As I interviewed several members of these fundamentalist churches, it became apparent that many of them had in the past, or were currently coping with, personal problems.

Mexican Americans who find themselves unable to deal with poverty, unemployment, divorce, family violence, alcohol, or drug abuse have neither the financial nor the cultural inclination to seek professional psychological assistance. For many, their way of coping with their problems is to join a fundamentalist church that will assist them in bringing order to their lives. The ministers of these churches understand this and focus their preaching on human weaknesses such as womanizing, drinking, and family violence. They visit the jails and the homes and the bars to assist the members of their churches.

Alcohol abuse is the most common problem. The fundamentalist ministers function by having the sinners admit their shortcomings and the need for a power beyond themselves. The practice is not dissimilar to the "twelve steps" program used by Alcoholics Anonymous. The practice includes attending church services several times a week in a small, intimate, familylike congregation. The minister recognizes the weaknesses of the flesh and has time to address each person's problem.

Many Mexican Americans perceive God as part of their daily lives. They referred to God in the interviews more than did the Anglo subjects. The churches play a significant role in maintaining Mexican American culture in Middlewest. The Catholic church fosters Mexican American culture through ceremonies such as weddings, baptisms, funerals, and the Virgin of Guadalupe Mass.

The Criminal Justice Institution

Many Mexican Americans in Middlewest believe that the criminal justice system discriminates against them. I conducted twenty interviews with criminal justice personnel and spent a month observing various aspects of the criminal justice system in Middlewest. My field research involved personnel from both the city and county; I conducted interviews with policemen, probation officers, lawyers, an assistant prosecuting attorney, judges, a court interpreter, and a public defender.

The state of Idaho report *Crime in Idaho* (Bureau of Criminal Identification 1990) shows that Mexican American youth and adults account for approximately 40 percent of the arrests in Farm County. If we recall that for much of the year the Mexican American population for Farm County may approach 30 percent, then the Mexican American crime ratio is not nearly as disproportional as most Anglos believe. My field research and interviews suggest that some of the problem of crimes by Mexican Americans is the result of the perception of some in the justice system that Mexican Americans have a criminal nature. Some of the problem is also a consequence of the severe poverty facing many Mexican Americans in Farm County.

According to the chief of police, city leaders, business leaders, and the mass media, crime in Middlewest is "out of control." Yet these same community leaders also state that the community is quiet and peaceful. This seeming contradiction is not as strange if the reader understands that Anglos do not really accept Mexican Americans as part of Middlewest. The image of Mexican Americans as criminals has done more to separate the Mexican American and Anglo communities of Middlewest than has any other factor.

One reason for the concern among Anglos about Mexican American crime is that the number of Mexican Americans has increased dramatically in Middlewest. Mexican American crime that used to be confined to the labor camps has moved into Middlewest and become more visible. In the summer of 1991 the cumulative frustrations of Mexican Americans erupted in acts of crime. A series of murders, assaults, robberies, burglaries, drive-by shootings, and incidents of Mexican American gang violence has convinced Middlewest that it has a serious crime problem.

The initial response of the Anglo leaders and the criminal justice system was to build a new jail and establish a crime commission. The chief of police announced a "get tough" policy: "If they [Mexican Americans] spit on the sidewalk, we will arrest them." The Anglo community leaders also supported the chief's creation of a special team of officers to target Mexican American gangs.

Criminal justice personnel from the local to the state level focus on Mexican American drug trafficking in Idaho. Law enforcement personnel often publicize drug busts of Mexican Americans and show videos of drug paraphernalia and the armed raids. However, certain criminal justice personnel informed me of the biased nature of drug enforcement. An

Anglo public defender and an Anglo district judge each told me that a priority of drug enforcement was to apprehend Mexican Americans. The judge said that law enforcement goes after Mexican Americans because "the Mexicans are the only ones dumb enough to sell drugs to a narc."

The Anglo police officers I interviewed claimed that their department does not target Mexican American offenders, although three of the five Mexican American officers I talked with believed that their departments do practice selective enforcement. All of the Mexican American officers felt that racist jokes have become part of their work environment and are used by Anglo officers to keep them in their place. One Mexican American officer said, "The patrol officers do pick on Mexican Americans. They do look for them. The Mexican Americans get stopped for not having a valid driver's license and for not having insurance. I've done it a few times myself."

Three of the Mexican American officers believe that some of their fellow officers and supervisors dislike Mexican Americans. They believe that certain judges render harsher sentences on Mexican American offenders. The chief public defender made the following comments: "Look, this is a redneck county and the court reflects that attitude. The judges give harsher sentences. An Anglo and a Mexican American committing the same offense, say a felony—the Anglo guy will get probation while the Mexican American gets from three to ten years. The racism is in all aspects of the system, from bail to sentencing. . . . If a group of Mexican American males get together, they believe that they are going to start fighting or get into some kind of trouble."

During the year of my field research there was a steady escalation of concern on the part of Middlewest's social institutions about Mexican American juvenile delinquency. Initially many Anglos and Mexican Americans thought the *Daily News* was exaggerating the seriousness of the gang problem. In the fall of 1990 several Mexican American youths were expelled from school for fighting. The news media decided to do a series of reports on Mexican American gangs in Middlewest. The mayor appointed a crime commission and it conducted a series of town meetings denouncing the crime problem, but without linking it with any particular race. The police department received a grant from the federal government to help solve the gang problem. The chief of police transferred a Mexican American officer, who had a high school education and no special training, to work with the youths to solve the problem. The Mexican American leaders predicted that the project would fail because of its lack of a plan and resources to assist the many Mexican American youths who needed assistance. The city council passed a curfew law—its penalty was to jail parents if their children were on the streets late at night. Again, it appears to me that the unnamed target of the program is the Mexican American community.

Many Mexican American youths spend most of their time on the streets because they do not have jobs. They soon begin to be arrested for vandalism, burglaries, assaults, knifings, and shooting incidents. The Department of Health and Welfare established a position working with youths and hired an untrained Mexican American. The only area in which Middlewest approaches being an equal opportunity employer is in the social control agencies.

The mayor created a gang task force of Anglo and Mexican American civic leaders, and they solicited advice from the Boy Scouts and a young female high school graduate. This committee had good intentions but little expertise and no resources. Their initial programs were somewhat superficial but nonetheless positive. They opened two school gyms in the evening and have established a Mexican American boxing club. But these programs and the committee's good intentions do not address the institutional source of the problem.

Data released in 1992 from the juvenile detention center in Middlewest reveals that nearly 50 percent of those detained are Mexican American youth. One reason for the higher rate of detention is probably that many Mexican American parents do not vigorously come to the defense of their children. Recently, at a junior high school in Boise, several youths were expelled from school for wearing certain clothing and possibly being members of a gang. Their Anglo middle-class families rallied to challenge the school's authority. As a result, the school administration reconsidered its position. Mexican American parents often are not familiar with or even aware of the strategies that could be used to prevent the negative labeling of their youth.

Most citizens in Middlewest believe that the community has a gang problem. One sociological theory (Eisner 1969) of juvenile delinquency is called "labeling theory." It sees adolescence as a process during which youth develop their identities and experiment with various persona. Labeling theory contends that despite their basically good intentions, schools and police sometimes negatively label youths as delinquent and that this may be the key ingredient in creating the very behavior they hope to contain. This can occur because the definition of self depends to a considerable extent on how significant others see us. During 1991 the establishment institutions, the newspaper, the schools, the police, and the city council of Middlewest perhaps helped to create Mexican American delinquents by their systematic negative labeling of the youths.

Sociological research on juvenile gangs for the past fifty years indicates that youths turn to gangs for status, support, friendship, and loyalty. The problem is particularly acute for second- and third-generation minority groups. A recent very good account of Mexican American gangs is James Vigil's book *Barrio Gangs* (1988). He uses the term "multiple marginality" to help explain Mexican American gangs. Mexican American youths have few opportunities because they live in poverty. The consequences of poverty can include family instability, family violence, alcohol abuse, and divorce. The young males have generally been unsuccessful in school and have had negative interactions with the police. They elicit discriminatory behavior. They have few or no successful role models and sometimes feel ashamed of their parents because they lack education and are considered unsuccessful by modern American standards.

Vigil examines the need of these youths for respect and acceptance. With their comrades, they share society's rejection; they respond by banding together to create a subculture in which they dress, talk, and act alike. These under-class Mexican American kids want to be recognized and respected; when they cannot find that in their family and schools then the socialization process moves to the streets. Proving their masculinity and challenging authority become a strategy by which young males search for respect. The more they fail, the more anti-social their behavior becomes.

All of Vigil's "multiple marginality" factors are at work for the two Mexican American gangs in Middlewest. The War Lords and the Crips together include from fifty to seventy-five Mexican American youth. Two of the Mexican American gang members I interviewed were attending night school—the Middlewest high school had expelled them. Their mothers, who spoke little English, had values and a life-style closer to that of traditional Mexican culture. These mothers have little ability either to assist or control their sons, who exist within two cultures, succeeding in neither.

Only two of the Anglo subjects I interviewed seemed to understand the predicament of young Mexican American males in Middlewest. One older Anglo policeman aptly observed, "Kids are like dogs. If you kick them enough they are going to bite you." A teacher at the vocational school remarked, "If you treat these Mexican American boys with respect and let them know you think they are intelligent, you find out that they can be darn good students." This Anglo teacher used to be in the public schools where he observed that, although it was unintentional, it was unbelievable how most teachers failed to work with the Mexican American young people because they believed they could not do the work.

It is not just a few but the majority of Mexican American youth who remain in the barrio under-class. The school administrators, teachers, mayor, city council, and chief of police all insist that they want to assist the Mexican American community and that they are not racist. However, they seem to be unable and unwilling to recognize that the Anglo social institutions of Middlewest have to change. The educational and employment needs of Mexican American youth are not met, yet Middlewest keeps blaming the victim.

The farm economy brought Mexican Americans to Farm County; however, instead of fulfilling its responsibility to educate, train, and pay living wages to Mexican American families, the Anglo establishment maintains them in a colonial status. The Mexican American under-class position either is viewed as normal or it is ignored by Anglos. The dominant ideology says that all Americans have equal opportunities while it also maintains that "they" have a criminally oriented culture. The process of the criminalization of the Mexican American community thus works to justify their economic subordination.

I did not meet any Anglo villains in Middlewest. The Anglo community leaders sincerely want to solve the crime problem, but they fail to recognize that they have helped to create the crime problem by excluding Mexican Americans from equal participation in the social institutions of Middlewest. The solution to the juvenile gang problem is not a recreation room and a social worker but employment at a living wage for the parents and an education for their children.

Two particular shooting deaths occurred in the area during the summer of 1991. As mentioned earlier, a Mexican American youth was shot and killed at the labor camp during an altercation between two young Mexican American males over a woman. The boy who was shot was a bystander, one of several people who had gathered to observe the fight. The police arrested the assailant and charged him with murder. The other death occurred when a retired sheriff shot and killed a man. The circumstances involved a separated couple. The ex-sheriff was protecting the former wife of the man he killed. The prosecuting attorney declared the killing an act of self-defense. The altercation with the ex-husband prior to the shooting by the sheriff had occurred over several days. Mexican Americans asked, "Why were these deaths treated so differently by the criminal justice system?"

Mexican American leaders believe that the greatest systematic injustice to Mexican Americans comes from their arrests for traffic offenses. These include not having a valid driving license, driving with a suspended license, not having automobile liability insurance, and driving while intoxicated. The state's 1991 annual crime report statistics on arrests in Farm County reveal that Mexican Americans account for approximately 50 percent of these offenses.

During the month I spent observing misdemeanor arraignments, I recognized that a disproportional number of Mexican Americans faced charges of no driver's license and no insurance, and that this was the extent of the charges against these offenders. A policemen cannot know that a person does not have insurance or a valid license until he has stopped a driver. A legal question arises because the officers lack probable cause to stop a vehicle on these charges. Why, then, do the police consistently arrest Mexican American drivers on these charges? Why don't the judges ask this question? An Anglo district judge for Farm County, who earlier had been the county's prosecuting attorney, when asked about selective enforcement against Mexican Americans replied, "Yes, for driving violations the probable cause is being a poor Mexican."

The lack of justice for Mexican American offenders also occurs in court. Neither the prosecuting attorney's office nor the public defender's office have any full-time staff who are Mexican American or who speak Spanish. The court does have available two Mexican American interpreters but these women have absolutely no training in the law. A not uncommon scenario is a Mexican American offender who speaks little or no English pleading guilty to a charge without understanding how the court system functions and without knowing his legal rights.

I witnessed a forty-six-year-old Mexican American man, with his wife in court, who pled guilty to shoplifting. He had taken a pair of coveralls and some underwear, and he said he needed work clothes. Although the man had no prior criminal record, he received a substantial fine and three days in jail. A degradation process began as the judge asked him to explain the cause of his criminal behavior. The middle-class judge had no problem pontificating that one's economic circumstances are no excuse for breaking the law.

Another Mexican American male was charged with not having auto insurance and failure to appear on the date of his hearing. The man attempted to explain to the judge that he had no money and that he had gone to California to visit his sick mother. The judge rejected this account and kept telling the offender to plead "guilty" or "not guilty." With a sense of resignation, the man pled guilty. He was fined $565 and sentenced to three days in jail. He told the judge that he did not have the money but did have a job, and the judge arranged for him to pay $50 a month and to serve the jail time on the weekend.

I interviewed this offender following his appearance in court. I asked about his reaction to the court proceedings. He did not know how he could make the $50-a-month payment to the court; he said that at times he has no work and that when he does work the family still has no extra money. I asked the man how much he earned the previous year. The judge had fined the man five percent of his gross income; for a person making $30,000 per year this would amount to a fine of $1,500.

I asked an Anglo district judge about the high fines for such low-income people. His response was that poor people frequently do not pay the full amount of their fines, and that this makes it necessary to increase the fine, in order to obtain what was wanted in the first place. Yet the informal policy almost forces the poor to be delinquent on their fines. I asked both the chief public defender and a district judge how the conservative views of Farm County affects the courts. The public defender said that the effect is essentially to overcharge the Mexican American offenders, who face larger fines and longer sentences. The judge told me that he tries to consider the community sentiment when preparing his sentencing remarks. This Anglo judge said that he places higher bail and sentences on poor Mexican Americans because they are more likely to be recidivist, whereas the Anglo middle-class person usually has a good job, which means to the judge that he or she is unlikely to be back in court.

My view of selective enforcement of the laws by the police received corroboration from many Mexican Americans who provided me testimony of how the police treated them. Many Mexican American teenagers reported that the police not only watch them whenever they are in a group but on occasion even make them leave the park although they have committed no offense. Others presented examples of what they thought to be unfair treatment by the police. Two Mexican American ministers and a Mexican American priest offered other examples of the police mistreatment. They have observed inter-racial disturbances in which the police only arrest the Mexican Americans.

A Mexican American leader shared with me the circumstances surrounding the arrest of a young Mexican American male. The man had quarreled late at night with his wife; he left, but after talking with his sister returned to apologize and make up with his wife. An Anglo neighbor came out and fired five shots at the brother and sister. When the police arrived on the scene they arrested the Mexican American husband. He received a $300 fine and a suspended sentence but the Anglo man was not arrested.

Roberto Campa, a Mexican American lawyer, has for ten years defended many of the local Mexican American offenders who can afford a private attorney. Campa claimed that the entire criminal justice system is racist. From his experience, he believes juries have less sympathy for Mexican American offenders and that Anglo judges have no appreciation for the poverty and cultural conflicts facing the Mexican American community. He painted with words a portrait of the type of offender who receives the harshest penalty. The most important characteristic is the person's race (Mexican American), but the darker-skinned, uneducated Mexican American who is not fluent in English receives the worst treatment in the criminal justice system. Roberto Campa recognizes that lower-class Mexican American males live in a social environment where an appearance in criminal court almost becomes inevitable. He says that it is just a matter of time after the police see a Mexican American male with the wrong crowd.

An Anglo district judge I interviewed freely shared insider information about the court system. He saw himself as sympathetic toward Mexican Americans and as non-racist, yet his words revealed that much of his decision making is race and class oriented. The judge shared the following view of Mexican culture: "The fact is adult males get drunk out of their minds every weekend. The boys start getting drunk when they are ten years old. Excessive drinking is just part of Mexican culture. This explains why they are involved in criminal behavior."

The findings of my research do not stand alone. Alfredo Mirande (1985) reviews the history of the criminalization of Mexican Americans in the Southwest. Leo Romero and Luis Stelzner (1992) find that not enough contemporary research has been done on the relationship between Mexican Americans and the criminal justice system. However, what is available also tends to confirm the findings of my research. Contemporary social science research reveals that Mexican Americans generally mistrust the criminal justice personnel and that the statistical data available confirms the discriminatory treatment of Mexican American offenders.

The following recommendations, if enacted, could reduce the amount of crime involving Mexican Americans in Middlewest. The criminal justice system should seek out and hire Mexican Americans in all professional categories. Court proceedings against a Mexican American should not proceed unless the offender is represented by a lawyer—preferably a Mexican American who speaks Spanish. The police should be instructed to cease arresting Mexican Americans without probable cause. The state should provide, at reduced cost, auto liability insurance for all low-income drivers. The courts should provide outreach educational programs to educate Mexican Americans about automobile laws and penalties. The fines for low-income people should be reduced, recognizing that unrealistic fines only induce nonpayment violations. Even then, most of these recommendations would be limited in their results, because only by providing decent wages can Mexican American crime in Middlewest be significantly reduced.

Social Services

The studies of Blea (1980) and Horowitz (1986) report that the Chicano communities in Pueblo and Chicago did not have adequate access to the social service programs in those cities, and the programs were found to be severely underfunded. Since most of the Mexican American population in Farm County live in poverty, I wanted to find out about the quality and the accessibility of social services for the Mexican American community in Middlewest. I interviewed nine staff members and five administrators of social service agencies that have programs in Middlewest or in Farm County. The consensus of these people was that social services cannot provide adequate food, housing, and health care to local poor Mexican Americans and Anglos.

The O'Neill Health Clinic for low-income families is located in a town seven miles from Middlewest. Its founders established this medical facility to assist Mexican Americans; low-income Mexican Americans from all over Farm County and Middlewest patronize it. Half of the clinic's personnel speak Spanish; patients pay on a sliding scale, but many Mexican Americans informed me that they could not even afford the reduced fee.

Dr. Jones of the clinic recognizes the plight of Mexican Americans in Farm County. He said that the county board of health treats Mexican Americans in a condescending and paternalistic manner. He also said that county authorities sometimes deny payments for the care of indigent Mexican Americans. He thinks Middlewest would be a natural location for a low-income health clinic but the Anglo leaders of Middlewest will not support such services. Some of Dr. Jones's Mexican American patients have told him that they cannot obtain services from physicians or from the hospital in Middlewest. Dr. Jones said, "If you are a Mexican American living in Middlewest you have less access to medical care, there's no doubt about it."

Melissa Scheffer, a nurse at the O'Neill Clinic, has had hundreds of Mexican American women as patients for prenatal care. Scheffer has had first-hand information from countless Mexican American patients who have been denied services. She vociferously denounced area physicians, hospitals, and the county's health and welfare program for denying services to low-income Mexican Americans. I asked Melissa what additional medical services are necessary to serve low-income Mexican Americans. She said that the first priority should be to reduce the cost of services. She then said that Mexican Americans need the following services: an increased number of Spanish-speaking medical personnel, transportation to clinics, education regarding birth control, a reduction in the cost of prescriptions, and an increase in preventive health services.

The Salvation Army major in Middlewest reported that most of their services go to low-income Mexican Americans. The Army has a long list of programs: winter heat assistance, provision of food baskets and Christmas baskets; summer camps; and emergency assistance for rent, food, and gas. The major told me that the problems have intensified because of the number of unemployed and working poor in the Mexican American community. He said: "Things are getting so bad, I don't know how they make it. At the end of the month they have absolutely nothing.... Even though the United Way budgeted this program $100,000 and we raise good money, it is just not enough. Almost 50 percent of those we serve are becoming permanently indigent."

Arlene Jones, the director of the local community action program, had a similar story. Her program provides emergency assistance and food commodities. She said that it is the largest such program in the state but that the resources still do not meet the needs of the clients. She said: "You may think the state is having a booming economy but you wouldn't believe the extent of poverty in Middlewest.... Yes, we serve a disproportional number of Mexican American families.... The housing situation is acute.... We just help them to survive.... It is the economy, not the people, that keeps them in poverty."

I interviewed the director of the Department of Health and Welfare, Rubén García, who presented a bleak assessment of services to Mexican Americans. García confirmed that Farm County has the highest poverty rate in the state and that his department serves many Mexican Americans. When asked about the characteristics of the Mexican American clients, he said that they do not use many of the programs provided by the department. He emphasized that Mexican Americans basically do not use the counseling and mental health programs because in their culture a person should not discuss personal problems. He felt that the department needs more Mexican American social workers and also needs to recruit Mexican Americans from outside the state. The department has improved the number of its Mexican American support staff.

I talked to staff at the Idaho Migrant Council and at the Catholic church concerning their assistance programs for local Mexican Americans. These organizations provide emergency assistance for rent, gas, and food, but they said the demands for assistance exceed their resources. Francisco Garcia of the IMC captured the essence of the process: "These people just go around in circles trying to obtain assistance. We never have enough funds so we send them on to another agency. After awhile you can see the hopelessness and resentment."

I interviewed four staff members, including the director, of the Southwest District Health Department, located in Middlewest. Its programs include nutrition education; distribution of food commodities; and the Women, Infants, Children (WIC) program. The WIC program places its emphasis on improved prenatal assistance and also provides for the immunization of children and for family planning. Its health center has a grant to assist pregnant teenagers and to provide adolescent mothers with parenting classes—a program that already has enrolled 105 teenage girls.

Farm County has the highest teenage pregnancy rate in the state. To make matters worse, the state of Idaho has the lowest number of physicians per capita in the nation. The director of the Southwest District Health Department said, "We are in the dark ages! Many low-income people, especially the Mexican Americans, go without medical treatment. We have a growing clientele and nowhere near enough funding."

Lupe Esquivel, a Mexican American nurse, has worked for the district for seventeen years because she wanted to help her people. Approximately 40 percent of her patients come from poor Mexican American families. Lupe treats pregnant patients; she can recall many stories of low-income women being denied treatment by the private health system. She said that knowledge of the health district travels by word of mouth—many pregnant Mexican American migrant workers do not know that these services exist. She also said that many of her patients have little knowledge of the human reproductive system; the district office spends much of its resources educating clients.

The director of the district's teenage pregnancy program provided me with a recent report from the national Coalition of
Hispanic Health and Human Services Organizations (1990). This
report examines the root causes of Mexican American teenage
pregnancies: low self-esteem; academic underachievement; a
perceived lack of a good future; a sense of powerlessness; and
parents who have a limited education and a low income. To
reduce Mexican American teenage pregnancies would require a
dramatic change in the social and economic relations between
Mexican Americans and Anglos in Farm County. It was the same
old song, spinning on and on, only the groove gets deeper. The
recording was the same at each social service agency. How can
this record be broken?

As part of my social services research, I also interviewed two
establishment health administrators: one worked for the Middlewest Hospital and the other for the largest group medical
practice in Middlewest. These men praised the quality of health
care in Middlewest and did not believe that anyone is denied
access to health care in Middlewest. They insisted that Mexican
Americans received the same quality of medical care as Anglos.
These people sing their own song; they do not listen to Spanish
music. They do not hear the song of the poor, a melancholy
tune filled with pain.

I interviewed Helen Kirkham, who works for a Boise consumer advocate organization. She informed me that Middlewest
has no such agency. She has had a steady stream of Mexican Americans seeking her assistance. According to Helen, the
auto dealers on the Middlewest boulevard are the worst offenders. She said that many Mexican Americans buy vehicles that
become inoperative shortly after the purchase. She also discussed other problems Mexican Americans face, such as their
vehicles being illegally repossessed or them unknowingly being
charged excessive interest. One tactic used by car dealers involves selling the buyer a life insurance policy that will pay for
the auto if the owner dies. Helen believes that Mexican American consumers face systematic abuse, and she said that they
receive little or no assistance from the Better Business Bureau
or the legal system. She also said that the bankers only care

about getting their money; they do not care if the consumer gets cheated.

I then interviewed Kay Simmons and Alberto Sánchez, who work as licensed DUI evaluators. In separate interviews they both agreed that Mexican Americans often do not receive fair sentencing, because there are not enough Mexican American evaluators. They both said that Mexican Americans do not receive adequate counseling due to the lack of Mexican American lawyers. Mexican Americans receive court sentences to attend an alcohol counseling school; however, these schools conduct their sessions in English. The Mexican Americans never participate in any of the class discussions. Kay Simmons concluded that Mexican American alcohol offenders receive unfair treatment by the criminal justice system. From her experience, she believes that the judges give Mexican American alcohol offenders longer sentences and that the jailers treat Anglo offenders better.

Conclusions

The Anglos of Middlewest generally are good people but their treatment of Mexican Americans is not adequate. Yes, Mexican Americans commit more misdemeanor crimes and some types of felonies, but nobody tries to understand why. America has developed an "invisible oppression." Mexican Americans are not denied the vote, though few exercise this right. A powerful ideology extolling freedom and equality hides the reality of inequality. Indifference, denial, and ideological blinders work to impair the ability of Anglos to see racial injustice. Anglos in Middlewest honestly cannot understand the relationship between their behavior, the orientation of their social institutions, and the oppressive poverty of Mexican Americans. No one distorted this social reality any better than the U.S. Senator from Idaho who said at a Republican rally in Middlewest, "Essentially, the government is in the business of taking money from hard-working people and giving it to people who do not want to work."

The majority of Mexican Americans live in or near the poverty level. They consistently face part-time jobs and periodic unemployment. The extraordinary degree to which Mexican Americans are denied participation in the politics, religion, and economy of the dominant group provides strong support for the radical exploitive explanation of race relations in Middlewest and Farm County.

Most Mexican Americans in Farm County are second-generation Americans, but they are treated as outsiders. Neighboring Boise has had a greater in-migration in the last five years than has Middlewest, and the Boise Chamber of Commerce welcomes each new resident. Most of these newcomers are Anglo, but I believe the comparison still has merit because it reveals that Middlewest and Farm County, as a consequence of their conservative ideology, create a narrow definition of what makes a person a "real" American. For most Anglos in Middlewest, being Mexican American equates with being a foreigner.

Mexican Americans are disproportionally represented as offenders in the criminal justice system and as recipients of social services. In both cases, Mexican Americans are victimized by the unfair and inadequate treatment of these two institutions. The result is that Mexican Americans fail to receive adequate assistance when the inevitable financial problems arise, while the criminal justice system seems to operate to ensnare, degrade, and construct a criminal image of Mexican Americans whose only crime is living in poverty.

The first step toward solving racial inequality would be to recognize that a problem exists. The second step would be to evaluate the ethical and moral responsibilities of the dominant society toward those less fortunate than themselves. A third step would be to appreciate the humanity of the Mexican American people.

Chapter 9

THE EDUCATION INSTITUTION

The Culturally Democratic Learning Environment model is a new approach to education that takes as its starting point a newly emerging philosophy in education known as cultural democracy. The advocates of this new philosophy propose that it is the institutions, not the students, that must change. They want the institutions to take into account each student's cultural background, language, learning ability, and personality. In other words, the educational institution must be altered to provide a culturally democratic learning environment that is consonant with the past learning experiences of the students it serves.

–Luis Leal and Pepe Barrón

Introduction

When contemplating field research one never knows which social relationships will be the most important for the study. In this study, research on the schools produced my greatest insight into Mexican American–Anglo relations in Middlewest. Both the quantity and quality of data collected on the schools was the result of my greater opportunity to observe the social interactions between Mexican Americans and Anglos functioning within this social institution. More educational data was recorded because Mexican American teachers and students function inside the school and they observed first-hand certain derogatory attitudes and behavior of Anglo students and Anglo teachers toward Mexican American students. For example, Professor John Smith, a teacher-placement coordinator at the local private college, stated that he frequently heard Middlewest teachers make prejudicial comments about their Mexican American students.

On one level, the Middlewest High School appears to have a normal school atmosphere. During intervals between classes, the halls fill with noisy, talkative, and energetic students. Raucous sounds from the gym classes can be heard as one enters the high school. There is no indication of any mistreatment of Mexican American students on a casual tour of the facilities; in fact, the opposite is true. While I was conducting interviews at the school, a Mexican American male had just led his school to the state tennis championship. A plaque in the main hallway recognizes the accomplishments of a deceased Mexican American coach. However, one sees very few Mexican American youths in the accelerated classes, while there are many in the remedial and vocational classes.

Walking the halls and sitting in the classrooms, I found students and teachers actively engaged in the learning process. The teachers appeared to know not only their subjects but also the contemporary methods of engaging students in the pursuit of knowledge. Some teachers have received awards, honors, and fellowships for their academic excellence. I overheard a teacher reprimanding a student for not working up to his capabilities; the teacher appeared to have a genuine concern for the student.

Judy Markel, an English teacher, during an interview in the coffee lounge, shared with me both the philosophy and teaching techniques used by her department. She radiates a professional enthusiasm and she impressed me with her keen knowledge of instructional techniques. Judy teaches accelerated classes for the top students and she has little patience or empathy for the below-average student. She does not work with deficient students nor has she much pedagogical interest in those students. It is not her job to work with deficient students; it appeared to me that few teachers in the Middlewest school district see it as their responsibility.

Most Anglo students and teachers are both unable to see and would deny that Mexican American students have a subordinate status in the schools. They do not miss the Mexican American dropouts and they are not aware that Mexican American students fill the classrooms of the alternative schools. The alternative school program serves those students outside the mainstream.

The students who fail the "regular" school attend the alternative school, which has far less status and fewer resources than the regular high school.

Almost all permanent resident Mexican American families have at least one child who has received a GED (graduate equivalency diploma) in place of a regular high school diploma. The school administrators dislike the fact that some of their resources are being used by the alternative school, and they do not willingly accept responsibility for the failure of approximately 50 percent of the Mexican American students.

Field Research Techniques

I interviewed forty Anglo and Mexican American subjects who were involved in educational institutions in five southwestern Idaho communities. The focus of my educational field research was the Middlewest High School. I interviewed students, teachers, counselors, administrators, members of the school board, college professors, and state school administrators. Additionally, a student research assistant interviewed ten Anglo and ten Mexican American students.

While conducting the field research I attended several meetings, including those of the school board, and observed many school activities. I attended dances, athletic contests, and assemblies. I interviewed students at the regular Middlewest High School and at two alternative schools. I even had the unusual research experience of interviewing a class of twenty Mexican American students.

The Mexican American community and Mexican American teachers uniformly agree that the needs of Mexican American students are not being met. No one has accurate statistics on the Mexican American dropout rate, but two reports—*Report of the Task Force on Hispanic Education* (Idaho State Board of Education 1991) and *Hispanic Youth Dropout Prevention Report* (Task Force on the Participation of Hispanic Students 1990)—estimate that between 40 and 60 percent of Mexican American youths do not complete high school. The Mexican American teachers believe that most Mexican American children leave school in junior high because of their deficiencies in academic skills caused by inadequate bilingual training.

The View of Anglo School Personnel

The Anglo teachers and administrators in Middlewest believe that Mexican American parents are responsible for the dropout problem because the parents are not educated, the family speaks Spanish in the home, and Mexican American parents do not join the PTO (Parent Teacher Organizations). Additionally, Anglo school personnel think that parents voluntarily withdraw their children from school to work in the fields to help support the family.

Several Anglo administrators and teachers I interviewed appeared defensive and resentful. Their refrain was basically "come to the school, come to our classrooms, we are doing a good job. We want to educate all kids. Students' skin color does not matter to us." The superintendent of the Middlewest schools kept insisting that "the schools have made tremendous progress, just tremendous progress." The professional educators do not think that the school is responsible for the problem of dropouts; they maintain that Mexican American parents and children have to change their behavior. These well-intentioned school personnel in some ways perceive the Mexican American community as the enemy because it critiques their expertise. These educators appear to have not been exposed to the methodologies of teaching in a multicultural environment. They appear narrow-minded because of their inability to adapt and be flexible to the needs of a multicultural student body.

The school superintendent described in a public meeting the progress being made with Mexican American students. He did not believe that a 40 percent dropout rate for Mexican American students in grades 10 through 12 is a serious problem, and he failed to discuss the fact that the largest dropout of Mexican Americans occurs during the junior high school years. He selectively used school statistics to claim that 12 percent of the school personnel are Mexican American, whereas less than 2 percent of the teachers are Mexican American. He appeared to believe that since half of the cheerleaders and school radio announcers are Mexican American, all Mexican Americans are receiving a quality education.

The administrators and educators believe that good teaching, curriculum, and counseling are the same for all students. They seem to think that if they add a few Mexican American cultural activities, this should suffice. Little empathy or understanding exists for most Mexican American youths, who face a multitude of problems including poverty and a different set of cultural values, and who speak English as a second language. The area schools include 20 to 30 percent Mexican American students, who are taught as though they were middle-class Anglos.

A year after the field research was conducted, Mexican American leaders of Middlewest told me about the most recent crisis in the Middlewest Junior High School. The school had recently expelled several Mexican American youths, and school administrators have ruled that these students will not be reinstated. The Mexican American leaders feel frustrated because they believe the school administrators have no respect for Mexican American students and parents. They feel that the vice-principal dislikes Mexican American children. The Mexican American leaders believe that they must sue the school on behalf of the students.

Another aspect of the educational problem involved the Mexican American community's concern that at one elementary school students are placed in a three-by-eight-foot box for disciplinary reasons. School administrators claimed that the box was a necessary educational device for behavioral management and that it was not misused; however, a Mexican American social worker publicly stated that the box was primarily used against Mexican American students and that the children were not monitored. Some Mexican American children have spent more than a week of cumulative time in this box. The social worker had counseled Mexican American children who were afraid to return to school for fear of being placed in the box. After months of pressure, the school finally removed the box from the school.

The problem facing the Mexican American community results from the society's inability to see institutionalized racism.

Everyone in Middlewest knows that Mexican American youth have a high dropout rate but few understand the role of the schools in causing the problem. They think that since Mexican American youth sit in the same classrooms and receive the same instruction, it must be their fault.

An essential component of the conflict between Mexican American leaders and Anglo school administrators can be easily overlooked, yet it applies in all of Middlewest social institutions: the Anglo school administrators consider themselves to be the experts and they dislike anyone criticizing or challenging their authority. They hold positions of power and, therefore, are able to rebuff those groups demanding change. Outsiders, in this case Mexican Americans, are just not viewed as having legitimate complaints. The Anglo school administrators vacillate between paternalism and colonialism. They say, "Our doors are always open; come and talk to us.... Look at what we are doing for you." Yet, when they continue to receive criticism, they dismiss or invalidate it and deny that a problem exists.

The Middlewest junior high school principal had a guest editorial in the *Daily News* on January 30, 1992. In this editorial he criticized local Mexican American leaders for wanting to weaken academic programs and have special favors for Mexican American students. He even used the movie *Stand and Deliver* to promote his view that the schools should have higher expectations of Mexican American students if they are to succeed. No matter how well-meaning this principal may be, he conflated high expectations with adherence to a curriculum designed for Anglo middle-class students. This principal did not offer one change that school administrators or teachers could make to assist Mexican American students. Judging from the editorial, it is easy to understand why a Mexican American leader said, "We thought we were still speaking in Spanish because he didn't hear a word we said. He just kept blaming us and our kids for the problem."

The high school counselor did not perceive that Mexican American students had any special needs or problems. The high school principal, an ex-coach, said that his teachers feel offended by the thought that they needed sensitivity training with regard to Mexican American students, because they believe that they treat all students the same. Neither he nor the teachers recognize that treating all students alike may well be inappropriate for a culturally diverse student body.

Mexican American leaders and parents do not want favoritism or a watered-down education for their children. They do want to have more teachers who speak Spanish and who can teach a curriculum relevant to the experiences of Mexican American youth. The curriculum should become flexible enough to offer courses or to modify existing courses in which Mexican American culture, literature, history, and music support the identity of the Mexican American student. Mexican American students need to have additional years of bilingual education. Most of all, Mexican American students need teachers who respect them and who will provide the extra assistance needed by students who come from a non-Anglo culture.

Anglo teachers recognize that many Mexican American students have a hostile attitude toward them, but they fail to grant legitimacy to the views of the Mexican American students. Some teachers said the Mexican Americans' claim of being disliked by teachers is a rationalization for their own failure. This response possibly relates to the fact that Mexican Americans are in a subordinate position in the community. They could not be so easily dismissed if they had political and economic power in the community.

The following remarks came from my interview with Bill Coleman, a Middlewest High School teacher who teaches a class in which 50 percent of the students are Mexican American.

Well, there is a tremendous amount of stress among Mexican Americans. Now think back of watching the news in the last month. You hear about any stabbings and knifings? This is what Middlewest is famous for. I am definitely not trying to put Mexican Americans down, it's just their lifestyle; there is stress. Why can't a Mexican American clean up their yard and not have cars parked on the lawn? ... Why can't they straighten up and act like Americans? Yes, there is stress; Middlewest has to have security guards and that sort of thing and it costs us money. They just have different values. There are not everyday hostilities, we get along OK. But they have a different upbringing, you know. Take a person like yourself, if you were given a new house, no problem, you would keep it up, but not the Mexicans. Sounds like I am running them down, but I am just trying to explain the difference. If you give a Mexican American a house, it would be a dump. In Middlewest you can go down the street—nice house, nice house, then a beat-up Mexican house, it's just a different world. Look, how many Mexican Americans do you think went to the sports and RV convention? Well, it was only a few; they are not into sports like I am.

I interviewed several Middlewest High School teachers who believe that many Mexican American kids have deficient academic skills by the time they get to high school. However, the school does not provide any systematic program to assist these youths to attain those skills. One teacher said that the high school has special programs to assist the most advanced students but not to assist those at the bottom. Another teacher claimed that most of her remedial students cannot pass the class. She agrees that Mexican American kids have very low academic skills, but she does not know why.

Awards Assembly

Near the end of the school year, I attended an awards assembly. It provided a crucial empirical documentation of the social and academic positions of Mexican American students in the Middlewest High School. In the lengthy ceremony, school officials presented 175 awards to students. The awards recognized academic and athletic achievements, as well as clubs and class officers. The Mexican American students accounted for 28 percent of the student body for the academic 1990–91 year; however, they received less than 2 percent of the awards. Most of their awards were for their participation in athletics. One Mexican American boy received awards for being an honor student, class president, and an athlete. When I asked Mexican American students about this boy, they said that he was not one of them because he does not speak Spanish and has only Anglo friends.

The school presents awards to the students showing the "best effort." The awards went to a Mexican American boy and girl. I thought that the symbolic message was obvious: "You Mexican Americans are not as intelligent as Anglos, but isn't it nice that we can give you an award." Later, when I interviewed the class of Mexican American students, they were quite aware of both the implications and consequences of this awards assembly. The Mexican American students said they knew the Anglos would get all the awards.

My research assistant examined the last five years of the high school annual. She found that for those five years few Mexican American students belonged to the school clubs and organizations, with the exception of the journalism club. The Mexican American girls accounted for an average of 7 percent of the cheerleaders, queens, and athletes; Mexican American boys comprised 10 percent of the student athletes. Only a few Mexican American students participated in band and singing groups. A school annual usually primarily contains pictures of the students. A notable feature of the Middlewest annual is the absence of pictures of Mexican American students. They represent nearly 30 percent of the student body, but only five percent of the pictures in the annual are of Mexican American students.

A progressive school administration could implement many programs to integrate Mexican American students more fully into the school. The music programs could capitalize on the Mexican American community's rich cultural traditions of singing, dance, and music. Teacher advisors to clubs and organizations could actively recruit Mexican American students. The athletic programs perhaps could be extended to include boxing since many Mexican American boys are involved in and attracted to this sport. Administrators could establish goals to increase the participation of Mexican American students and assist them to achieve success in all academic and extracurricular activities.

Teachers could be evaluated on their efforts to enhance the success of Mexican American students.

School Officials

The Anglos of Middlewest pride themselves on the high quality of their schools, some of which have been the recipients of national awards for excellence in the 1980s. They believe that they have the best school system in the state. The Anglo community and local school administrators are proud of the fact that the community has never turned down a bond issue, but they downplay the additional fact that the Middlewest schools have one of the lowest per pupil expenditures in the state. And some educators might question the quality of a school that has a Mexican American dropout rate of 50 percent.

My field research included interviews with two school board members. They seemed to have little appreciation of the problems facing minority students. They believe that the schools are doing an excellent job and they do not see the need for any significant changes in the schools' programs. The board members believe that Mexican American students drop out of school because the parents and children do not value education. The concerns of the Mexican American community about the education of their children have not reached the school board. It would take a heroic effort to convince the school board to make changes and provide additional resources to attempt to reduce the number of Mexican American dropouts.

During my interviews with them, school administrators avoided a dialogue concerning the fact that the local schools have a significant minority population. They did not accept the need to expand the quality and number of years of bilingual education for Mexican American students. They support the traditional role for American schools, which is fostering the assimilation of minority groups. In 1990 and 1991 the two Idaho task force reports referred to in the introduction of this chapter presented a lengthy list of recommendations to improve the education of Mexican American students; the Anglo school administrators had not read these reports at the time I talked with them.

Research projects have both supported and rejected the effectiveness of bilingual programs (Cafferty 1992). Cafferty concludes that bilingual programs implemented with adequate resources and committed teachers can be effective. The students involved in such projects gain in both intelligence and self-esteem. But she also admits that historically the retention of ethnic languages has been politically controversial in the United States.

Many Anglo school personnel perhaps could be deemed as parochial, since they acquired their advanced education in Idaho and have lived most of their lives in Middlewest. They have little or no experience with minority groups or alternative cultures, and they do not seem to recognize the positive aspects of cultural diversity in America. The local superintendent of schools received all his academic training at the local college and has never lived or taught anywhere but Middlewest. He also has close ties with many conservative political figures in the community. This is most likely not the academic background that will provide innovative leadership to create an effective educational environment for minority students.

The Pursuit of Unity

A clear example of the school administration's disinterest in Mexican American education emerged from a series of meetings established by the superintendent of the Middlewest schools to address the Mexican American educational "problem." The superintendent gave the meetings the title, "In Pursuit of Unity." This interracial committee consisted of Anglo school administrators and Mexican American leaders. I interviewed many of the participants to obtain their reactions to this project.

The committee divided into four subcommittees: High Expectations, Attendance and Discipline, Home/School Communications, and Welcome/First Impressions. These subcommittees met for several months and developed fifty-three recommendations. Such a lengthy and extensive list appeared unrealistic since this was the school district's first attempt to implement procedures to assist Mexican American students. The recommendations created by the committees have merit, but I believe that the underlying intent remains that Mexican American students and parents must do most of the changing. The four subcommittees did not make any recommendations for curriculum changes or bilingual classes to assist Mexican American students.

The Mexican American leaders began the meetings in a positive frame of mind because it was the first time the school district had bothered to talk to them. The principal of the high school said that the idea to create a committee came in response to the existence of Mexican American gangs in the high school. The junior high school principal, meeting with Mexican American leaders in another setting, said that it would be impossible to add courses to provide assistance to Mexican American students because the academic day has no time for additional courses. This principal had listened to explicit concerns of the Mexican American community and responded by saying there was just nothing that could be done. He served on the Pursuit of Unity committee.

Prior to the meetings, the two statewide task forces had published reports of their in-depth studies of the Mexican American dropout problem. The school administrators had not read these reports. The unity committee's recommendations did not create a time-line for implementing the recommendations or an estimate of funds and personnel required. No teachers had served on the committees. I interviewed teachers, including the president of the Middlewest Education Association, who said that the teachers did not even know such a committee existed. Some teachers I interviewed said that this was a typical administrative ploy. They claimed that Middlewest school administrators establish committees whose real purpose is to "cool out" those concerned, but that they have no intention of changing anything.

The following fall, the Mexican American leaders of Middlewest questioned the sincerity of the school administrators. A year after the Pursuit of Unity meetings the schools had not implemented the recommendations. The Mexican American leaders are frustrated because of all the time and work spent with nothing to show for it. My field research developed a schizophrenic aspect because, on the one hand, the school administrators had little to say in their interviews about the issue of Mexican American education in their schools; on the other hand, they were involved in a major project, The Pursuit of Unity, to address this very problem.

It would take courageous leadership by the school administrators to implement programs to meet the special needs of Mexican American students such as expanding the bilingual program; teaching Mexican American culture, literature, and history; and initiating an aggressive program to hire Mexican American teachers. These programs would cost the schools a significant amount of money. That the school administrators opted for the status quo is understandable. Middlewest is a politically conservative town; most Anglos in Middlewest support the English Language Bill and oppose bilingual education. Some Anglo school administrators have testified in front of the state legislature in support of the English Language Bill. Robert Bahruth, a professor of education at Boise State University, made statements worth quoting on the plight of Mexican American public education in Idaho: "It is ironic, but not surprising that in our materialistic society a person is punished for robbing hubcaps, yet no law appears on the books to hold persons accountable for the academic assassination occurring when minority children are denied an equal educational opportunity. These children, victims of the rigid educational system, are condemned to a life of hard labor and economic hardship and our society does not even perceive this as a crime."

Anglo Students

Anglo students, having busy adolescent agendas of their own, generally ignore Mexican American students. The teachers at Middlewest High School agree that the students do not focus on academics but on their jobs, cars, dates, and athletic activities. The teachers say that the primary student social groups at the school are athletes, stoners, skateboarders, Mexican Americans, preppies, and nerds. Anglo students typically see Mexican Americans as troublemakers because they fight and they get expelled. Anglo students do not perceive academically and socially successful Mexican American students as "Mexican American"—they are seen differently because of their success. This selective perception reinforces the negative image of the less successful Mexican American students.

Most of the Anglo students I interviewed believe that most of their peers have engaged in premarital sex, yet they express surprise that many girls get pregnant. The Anglo students interviewed believe that approximately 75 percent of the students drink and smoke tobacco on the weekends; they also think that 30 to 40 percent of the students have tried hard drugs. Whereas their parents like Middlewest as a place to live, they generally have a negative attitude toward Middlewest. They say they have nothing to do and that they are bored. One student said, "Middlewest is an average-nothing town."

Anglo students have views toward Mexican American students that reflect their parents' perspective. They do not perceive themselves to be prejudiced although the following quotes would suggest otherwise. One seventeen-year-old athlete, Dick Lance, said, "I don't like the Mexicans, they're punks. There was a bunch of little short Mexican guys popping off to me and my friends. We went after them and it made me feel good." Jack, a farmer's son, commented, "The Mexican American contribution to Middlewest is nothing; they're just a lot of trouble." He believes Mexican Americans receive adequate pay because, "If they drop out of school then that's all they deserve." He believes there is a high degree of racism in the school and community but maintains "How can you not be prejudiced? They deserve it, the way they act and you can see how they live."

My research assistant asked Jack if Mexican American students should receive assistance to improve their academic success. His response was negative. Ironically, later in the interview, Jack discussed the special programs of assistance for his own dyslexia.

A sixteen-year-old Anglo student, Jane Smith, whose parents own a local furniture store, wants to be a teacher. The following quotation represents her views toward Mexican Americans: "We try to close our eyes and ignore them, but people always say, don't go to Middlewest. Everyone knows we have the Mexicans.... The Mexicans work in the fields; they don't try to improve themselves; they don't apply themselves.... They have as much or more opportunities than we do. A lot of them don't care; they give up and live on welfare."

Mexican American Students and Parents

As previously mentioned, one myth accepted by the school personnel and the community contends that Mexican American parents do not value education for their children. They accept the idea that Mexican Americans prefer to work in the fields and lack motivation to achieve an education. My research showed that nothing could be further from the truth. The aspiration of most Mexican American parents is that their children obtain an education that will enable them to escape farm labor. Many Mexican American parents intentionally take their children to work in the fields to demonstrate how demanding the work is, hoping that this experience will motivate the children to study.

Another myth contends that only Mexican American migrant children drop out of school. From my interviews with resident Mexican American families, the data shows that most of them have children who have dropped out of school. Approximately half of these Mexican American youths matriculate at an alternative school where they complete their GED.

I began to wonder why Mexican American youths often have more success in the alternative school settings. School personnel at the county's alternative schools believe their success with Mexican American students comes from respecting the young people, building the self-esteem of the students, having an attitude that Mexican American youth have intelligence and can learn the material, and instructing the youth at their level of competence.

Bill Jones, an Anglo teacher at an alternative school who had taught for twenty years in a small town near Middlewest, said that the regular school's teachers unintentionally reject many Mexican American kids. As Bill saw it, the mainstream teachers spend too much time blaming and demeaning Mexican

American children and, eventually, this becomes a self-fulfilling situation. He believes that most teachers refuse to recognize that Mexican American kids come from a different cultural background. He also believes that teachers should teach Mexican American culture instead of rejecting it. Bill introduced me to two Mexican American gang members. He liked those boys and he felt that because of his attitude they will pass their classes. Bill said that most of the Mexican American kids can make it through high school. He thinks the Middlewest schools have done more to create Mexican American gangs than have the kids themselves, because the schools kicked most of them out.

Helen Krepel, a principal at one alternative school, spent ten years as a teacher and administrator in a school near Middlewest. She claimed that the regular schools systematically fail Mexican Americans, and she said that most Anglo teachers have no understanding or appreciation of the problems facing Mexican American kids. She believes that skin color plays a crucial role in the failure of Mexican American students. She said that Mexican American youths cannot learn from teachers who dislike them and think they have little academic capability. Helen claimed that a new group of immigrants from Romania have received much better treatment in the school than Mexican American kids. She thinks that the Anglo community and schools need to accept a "cultural democracy" where one respects cultures other than European.

Most Mexican American parents and Mexican American youth believe that the schools of Middlewest discriminate against them, although some Mexican American families have become economically successful. Their children generally have a higher level of assimilation and are less likely to be fluent in Spanish. They also are likely to be successful in school. These Mexican American students often have more Anglo friends than Mexican American friends. Most successful Mexican American students speak fluent English without an accent. Many of these parents and children believe Middlewest has a low level of racism. Still, fewer successful Mexican American students attend college than do their Anglo counterparts.

The generalization that the academically successful Mexican American student will have a high degree of assimilation should be viewed as an oversimplification. The social world is far more complex: some Anglo teachers work hard to assist Mexican American students; some Mexican American students become bicultural; some Mexican American boys deserve to be expelled. Nonetheless, the fundamental problem with the Middlewest schools is that they do not meet the academic needs of most Mexican American students. Mexican American students do not drop out as much as they are "pushed out" of the Middlewest school system.

The average Mexican American parents and their children have a lower- or working-class economic status. Most parents claim that their children are not treated as well as Anglo students. A number said their light-skinned children were accepted more in school than were their dark-skinned children. A recent high school graduate told me the story of her school counselor who went around telling the other teachers, "Hey, look here, this is a smart Mexican." She says she felt both sick and embarrassed.

Many Mexican American parents shared accounts of the inappropriate punishment of their children. One Mexican American parent claimed that the teacher did not let her child go to bathroom; another parent said that her child told her the teacher made fun of him. Some Mexican American parents became emotionally upset and angry at how their child's self-confidence and self-esteem had been undermined. One woman said that her son's junior high school teacher told him and his friends that they would never graduate from high school. Dolores García reported that her daughter had straight As and the school still placed her in remedial classes. Her son had even more problems. She said that the school administrators think all the Mexican boys are in gangs. Another woman lamented: "It is so hard for Mexican boys in school. They fight back. My boys were treated bad. They were told they were dumb. They all got expelled. We came to Idaho so our children would have a better life, but they're working in the fields."

Young Mexican Americans shared with me some of their school experiences. Julio, who graduated with an A average, said, "Even though I was a good student the teachers were not friendly to me. They told me to stop asking so many questions. They would generally ignore me. The Anglo students would call us 'Spics.' I did have some Anglo friends but they would ask me why I talked to the Mexicans." Frederico summed up his school experience, "I always felt left out, that I was not accepted. My parents couldn't afford the clothes. I never knew I could be somebody."

Gloria Pedraza, a young Mexican American woman, recently graduated from Middlewest High School. She received straight As in her first year at a state university. Gloria said, "I went through high school denying my ethnicity because the teachers did not like Mexicans, but what could I do?" The advisor for Gabriela Delgado, another Mexican American university student who had an A average in high school, told her that she could not do college work. The counselor told her to consider attending a vocational program.

Rosalinda Martínez said that when she started school in Middlewest she did not speak English. The school kept her in a separate ESL (English as a Second Language) class for eight years. She said that she felt retarded because they didn't teach her anything. She continued: "If you grow up in Idaho you can't see the racism, because it becomes normal. I had a relative come from Mexico; he said he could not believe how badly we are treated. He said he would not go to school with me again."

Many of the Mexican American students I interviewed said that the teachers did not like them and always blamed them for any trouble at school. Another Mexican American student, Leticia Cortez, worked in the Middlewest school office, where she overheard countless negative comments about Mexican American students. Leticia claimed that the school personnel would frequently make negative remarks after a Mexican American student left the office. Other Mexican American students interviewed said that Anglo students and teachers did not make direct racist remarks to them but that they sensed through the nonverbal communications (especially facial expressions) and indirect remarks that those people do not respect Mexican Americans.

The Mexican American students claimed that they can "just sense" when the Anglos don't like them.

Mexican American students turn to one another for support because of this negative treatment and their own poor academic records. They begin to see Anglo teachers and administrators as "the enemy." The interaction between Mexican American students and school personnel becomes a predictable relationship that deteriorates over time. Each side becomes locked into hostile attitudes regarding the other; however, the teachers and administrators should know better.

The conflict between Mexican American students and school personnel takes many forms. Mexican American boys generally react more aggressively in rejecting teachers, and they represent the highest category of youths expelled from school. Another mechanism Mexican American youths use to maintain solidarity in a hostile environment is to reject those Mexican American students who obtain good grades. The Mexican American students with good grades get labeled "wanabes."

Mexican American Teachers

Susan López teaches English as a Second Language classes to Mexican American high school students. She has fifteen students in her class, the parents of whom have recently immigrated from Mexico. Susan said that her students do not have a chance to succeed. She thinks that for these students to be educated, the school would have to provide additional bilingual teachers and resources. She also believes that these children should be mainstreamed into some regular classes. Susan said, "They want the Mexican Americans for cheap labor but they don't want to educate their kids."

Ernesto Castillo is the only full-time Mexican American teacher in the Middlewest High School. He said that because he has taught at the school for years the Anglo teachers express their racism in front of him. He estimated that 85 percent of the teachers make prejudicial comments about the Mexican American students. Castillo told me that the teachers do not like Mexican American students and they do not think Mexican

Americans have the academic ability of Anglos. He said that the Anglo teachers complain about how much of a discipline problem the Mexican American students are, but he recognizes that the negative attitude toward Mexican Americans is associated with the fact that many Mexican American students do not do well academically.

Castillo has taught at the school for more than ten years, yet he has no friends among his fellow teachers and he is not invited to their social gatherings. He is married to a Anglo teacher and when they attend her school socials he is treated like an outcast. Ernesto said that of the many states he has lived in, Idaho has the worst racism.

Jesús Chávez teaches elementary school in Middlewest. Most of his teaching experience is in the federally funded migrant program. He does not think that his fellow elementary teachers are racist, but he believes that the schools do not meet the needs of Mexican American students. Jesus has experience about the needs and problems facing minority students whose first language is not English. He said that the existing migrant education program does not work. He thinks that the Mexican American children do not have enough time to learn English during the school day. The language program only lasts three years, but research on bilingual education indicates that grade-school students need seven years of language training to become fluent in English. The bilingual programs in the Middlewest schools produce Mexican American students who can speak English, but they have a limited vocabulary. According to Chávez, their language skills are not adequate to understand the teachers' vocabulary of instruction. Each year, the average Mexican American student falls further behind. By the time the students reach junior high school they are deficient in basic skills. And it is here that the conflict begins between Mexican American students and Anglo teachers. Many of the Mexican American youngsters fail their courses and the teachers begin to perceive Mexican American students as being academically deficient. The Mexican American youth recognize that they are seen as failures. This perception damages their self-esteem which, in turn, leads to hostility against the school. Many drop out of school. Negative feelings accumulate in both the teachers and the Mexican American students.

Chávez says that the bilingual and minority educational training programs recommend that in order to solve the dropout problem the Middlewest schools will need more Mexican American teachers, an expansion of the bilingual program, and a curriculum that makes use of Mexican American culture. The critical ingredient is more bilingual instruction. Chávez doubts that the community and the current school administration will ever initiate a comprehensive bilingual program. He said that one of his most disappointing experiences came from listening to an associate superintendent from Middlewest testify to the state legislature on behalf of the English Language Bill.

Positive Programs and Recommendations

Some of Idaho's educators appear to know how to improve the success of Mexican American students and how to reduce their dropout rate. If the public schools of Middlewest would adopt the recommendations of the two task force reports (1990, 1991) and introduce programs modelled after the School of Education programs at Boise State University, they could dramatically reduce the incidence of failure of Mexican American students.

If a physical education instructor has a student in a wheelchair in class, the teacher knows that a different program and approach will be necessary in order for this person to become physically fit. The rest of the class is not held back, and may in fact gain some appreciation for human abilities. Hopefully, the other students will learn that their wheelchair-bound classmate is not as handicapped as they thought. Our society has learned that physically handicapped people can be productive and successful. The Middlewest school system needs to learn this lesson in reference to its Mexican American students.

Anglo educators need to become more culturally sensitive. Anglo teachers need to appreciate that Mexican American students behave differently in part because they live or have roots in a culture that has a different set of norms and values. These different ways of behaving affect how Mexican American students learn and how they respond to their teachers.   The multicultural education experts explain that teachers need to know that the Mexican culture requires children to be quiet. Mexican American students will be less likely to participate in class and will not be comfortable if required to recite a lesson. Mexican American students learn that it is polite to avoid eye contact when spoken to by an adult because this shows respect for them. The Mexican culture places a lesser value on individualism and competitiveness, and it is less future-oriented. In the classroom, this means that Mexican American students will be more likely to sit in the back of the room and be less verbal. Each of the above traits can easily be misinterpreted as a sign of the Mexican American student's lack of interest in school.

The Idaho task force reports insist that the schools' curriculum must change to reflect the multicultural nature of their students. This means that the Middlewest schools should examine Mexican American literature, history, culture, and traditions. This change is necessary in order to enlist the Mexican American students' interest and to reflect their life experiences. Mexican American students' self-esteem will be increased by learning about the poetry of Sandra Cisneros and the novels of Rudolfo Anaya, for example. Anglo students can also benefit from being exposed to the literature of another culture.

Freddy Santos, a Mexican American elementary school teacher, wants to write a book on the history of Mexican Americans in Idaho. He has many Mexican American students and dislikes the fact that none of the grade school history books on Idaho mention Idaho's Mexican Americans. He wants to apply for a grant that would enable him to research and write that history.

I asked Santos what factors contributed to his becoming a teacher. He said that he had one Anglo teacher who liked him and encouraged him. This teacher kept assuring him that he could do the work and provided additional instructional assistance whenever it was needed. Santos said that some Anglo teachers go out of their way to help Mexican American students.

Most of the Mexican American teachers I interviewed have had many negative racial experiences in their careers. Toni and Sharon Díaz represent a minority success story. They started their careers in the 1970s as teacher's aides in a small town in Farm County. They wanted to assist Mexican American youth. This led them to enroll in and graduate from the Boise State University bilingual program in education. A few years later they became the first students to be awarded master's degrees in bilingual education in Idaho. Today, both are teaching in the same small town where they began as teacher's aides.

Toni and Sharon have faced many trials in their educational careers. Sharon reported that at the beginning of one fall term she had some Anglo students who transferred out of her classroom. She learned that the parents of these children did not want their children being taught by a Mexican. Both Toni and Sharon claimed that their school administrators have mistreated them because of their race. Later, they did not receive the standard pay increases upon completion of their master's degrees. They said that school personnel have openly made racist remarks to them. They feel that their school has not made a significant attempt to improve education for its Mexican American students. The Diaz's dedication to the education of Mexican American youth has earned them the respect of the Mexican American people of Farm County.

Kate Cruz, an Anglo teacher married to a Mexican American, teaches at the high school in Hop Town, where the majority of the students are Mexican American. She says that on the surface the administration appears to be sensitive to Mexican American students; however, she thinks that the educational system, including the Anglo administration and teachers, maintain a program that is designed for Anglo students. Kate says that the majority of teachers have taught for years and have no training and few skills in working with minority students. Her greatest frustration comes from knowing that the majority of these teachers have no desire to change their teaching methods. She believes it would take a dynamic administrator and some new teachers at the Hop Town High School to make any significant improvement in the education of its Mexican American students.

Kate Cruz remarked that it can be "difficult and frustrating" to teach Mexican American adolescents who do not have the skills of the Anglo students because they have not had the opportunity to adequately learn English. The Mexican American students often also feel frustrated and soon begin to behave negatively and become noncooperative. Not long into the semester they typically will stop trying and will cease doing their homework. The marginal Mexican American students start getting into trouble and cause discipline problems. Cruz admitted that it is difficult to refrain from disliking them; she can understand why many Anglo teachers give up on the Mexican American students.

In one interview, I clearly witnessed a Mexican American student's defiance. Carmalita Peña's dislike of school and her hostility toward teachers seemed akin to an animal that resents an intruder in her domain. She said that school was okay and that she planned on becoming a lawyer, but I knew that she despised school. I had the feeling that at any moment she might strike out at me. Her demeanor and facial expressions were clearly signaling a boiling rage: she glared, sneered, stared, and feigned indifference to her school experiences. I could only wonder about the school experiences that could have created such bitterness.

The Middlewest school district does have some positive accomplishments to its credit in assisting Mexican American students. The recent appointment of a Mexican American elementary school principal allows a Mexican American advocate to be in a position to affect school policy and to present the Mexican American point of view to his fellow administrators. A most important advancement for Mexican American education will occur because of the redistricting of the elementary schools. The plan went into effect in the fall of 1991 and requires that the area's elementary schools have ethnic and social class balance. Prior to this, all the Mexican American grade school children had attended one school. The redistricting required community acceptance and passage by the school board. The school administration devised this project and skillfully orchestrated a citizen group to mollify community resistance. This group of community volunteers artfully presented the statistics, maps, and logic of redrawing the boundaries for the five elementary schools.

The Mexican American leaders shared with me the information that Warren Vinz, the Migrant Education Director within the state Office of Education, has always supported and helped to organize the Mexican American youth conferences. However, Mexican American leaders regret that he is the only person in the state Department of Education who actively supports improving the quality of Mexican American education in Idaho. Mexican American leaders dislike the fact that not one Mexican American is employed in the Department of Education. Some Mexican American leaders believe that the state superintendent of schools has done little to improve Mexican American education in Idaho. Some of the members of the task forces on Mexican American education told me that the Department of Education either did not respond to or gave no more than lip service to their recommendations. They believe that instead of providing leadership, the Department of Education represents an obstacle to improving Mexican American education in Idaho.

One of the positive programs for assisting Mexican American education in Middlewest and Farm County comes from the School of Education at Boise State University. The university has initiated several important programs to assist Mexican Americans to achieve both a high school and a college education. I interviewed three professors of education who are responsible for expanding the educational opportunities for Mexican American students at Boise State University. BSU has significantly increased its number of Mexican American students. Most of these students major in bilingual education. Two education faculty members have written and received grants in excess of ten million dollars to assist in educating high school dropouts and college students from migrant backgrounds.

This success story is documented by the graduation of sixty-seven bilingual teachers, most of whom teach in Idaho. The College Assistance Migrant Program (CAMP) which provides a one-year scholarship for youth from migrant worker families, has had an 80 percent success rate since its inception. These federally funded programs provide extensive additional services to the disadvantaged Mexican American students. The philosophy behind this is that many minority students will need classes in study skills and strategies as well as tutors, counselors, and mentors in order to achieve academic success.

A missed opportunity has resulted from the lack of attention given to Mexican American education by the local private college in Middlewest, which has only a token scholarship program for Mexican American students. Few Mexican American students have ever enrolled in this college.

It is not necessary for me to construct a set of recommendations to improve the education of Mexican American youth in Middlewest, because the task forces have already completed this project. They identified specific problems in public education in relation to Mexican American students and then provided a detailed set of recommendations to resolve these problems. Some of the most important steps the schools are advised to take follow. (1) Work to enhance Mexican American students' self-esteem. (2) Curricula must include Mexican American history, culture, and traditions in the United States. (3) Hire more Mexican Americans as teachers, counselors, and administrators. (4) Schools with significant numbers of Mexican American students must create extensive bilingual education programs and hire teachers who have training in teaching bilingual education. (5) Increase and improve communications between Mexican American parents and the school. (6) Require all teachers and administrators to enroll in courses and workshops to increase their cultural sensitivity. (7) Create special remedial programs to assist minority students. (8) Provide for parental education, counseling, and parenting classes. (9) Provide information to parents in Spanish. (10) Provide Mexican American students the opportunity to learn about careers through Mexican American role models, mentors, and course work. (11) Work to eliminate prejudice and bigotry in the schools. (12) Establish preschool programs for all disadvantaged students. (13) Provide monies for the research, monitoring, and evaluation of the individual school's programs that are designed to increase the success of Mexican American students. (14) Provide the monies and leadership at the state Board of Education and the state Department of Education to ensure that these recommendations are enacted.

It would be unrealistic to think that these recommendations could be implemented in a year or two, but a five-year plan would allow enough time for significant changes to occur in the education of Mexican American youth in Idaho.

As a teacher of minority studies, I have read of a number of successful experimental programs that are educating minority children from disadvantaged backgrounds. The crucial ingredient of these programs seems to be finding teachers and administrators who fervently believe in the educability of minority students. The essence of American colonialism can be seen in the failure of the Middlewest schools to educate Mexican American students. The American ideology holds that everyone can achieve success through the public schools. The educational institution supposedly enables individuals, regardless of background, to apply themselves and thereby obtain status and economic rewards in American society. Yet the American dream does not work for the majority of Mexican American youth in Middlewest and Farm County; instead, they are destined for the secondary job market, their self-esteem shattered and their intelligence demeaned. I believe that with the proper commitment the schools in Idaho can dramatically reduce the Mexican American dropout rate.

Photo by Richard Baker

Mexican American children waiting for a school bus in Middlewest.

Photo by Richard Baker

Students in the "Mexican American Life" course at Boise State
University.

Chapter 10
CONCLUSIONS AND RECOMMENDATIONS

Sometimes it takes a lifetime to acquire understanding, because in the end understanding simply means having a sympathy for people.
—Rudolfo A. Anaya

Introduction

America's race problem is a stubborn and constant factor in American history. Thomas Jefferson, while owning 200 slaves, spoke eloquently in behalf of creating a society based on liberty and equality (Onuf 1992). This incongruity was well characterized in the classical sociological work of Myrdal in *An American Dilemma* (1975), in which he contrasted the treatment of America's African American population with the ideals and rhetoric of our democratic values. The history (Grebler, Moore, Gúzman 1970; Barrera 1979) of Mexican Americans in the Southwest reveals a saga of mistreatment and the denial of their civil rights.

The paradox of America is repeated in contemporary Middlewest. The ideology of freedom, equal opportunity, and individualism blinds the Anglo community from seeing the social injustice faced by the Mexican American population. Middlewest race relations could only be characterized as overwhelmingly racist, yet most Anglos in the community do not perceive race relations as a problem in their community.

The following list includes the most frequent observations by Mexican Americans in Middlewest about the way that the Anglo community treats them. (1) Anglo clerks assume most Mexican Americans are shoplifters and follow them throughout the store.

(2) Anglos use racial jokes to remind Mexican Americans of their place in the community. (3) Mexican Americans believe that the police intentionally focus on the Mexican American community. (4) Mexican American parents feel that the school administration and teachers abuse their children. (5) Mexican Americans think that the local newspaper presents a negative image of them. (6) Anglos do not like Mexican Americans to speak Spanish in public. (7) Mexican Americans sense by their non-verbal expressions that Anglos do not respect them.

The findings of my field research in Middlewest and Farm County confirm the theoretical approach I have designated as the radical exploitive perspective, an approach that has several central elements. From my interviews with Anglos, I conclude that the critical element in maintaining Mexican Americans in a subordinate position in the community is ideological colonialism. Anglo conservative values were such that they blamed the Mexican Americans for their poverty. The Anglo community denies that it or its social institutions are in need of any modification.

The most encompassing unit of analysis of a society is its culture. Most Anglos in Middlewest demand the assimilation of the Mexican American population. They believe that the culture and people of Mexico are inferior to their own. Though America is a country of immigrants, Middlewest Anglos seem to fear those who are different. The clash of cultures has centered on the issue of English as the official language of Idaho. The lack of knowledge of Mexican American culture fosters the creation of stereotypes and myths.

The intense patriotic conservatism of Anglo Middlewest plays a key role in Middlewest's lack of tolerance for the Mexican American community. One aspect of this ideology is an arrogant assumption that the Anglo race and conservative values represent the "true" or "real" America. This denies the multicultural and multiracial nature of the United States. Consequently, non-Anglos with a different culture are expected to feel privileged to be part of this society and reject their own cultural heritage. Never have I seen so many American flags flying as in Middlewest. Few Anglos in Middlewest deviate from the party line.

Those sociologists using the exploitive model appear to be accurate in stressing the importance of the social class position of ethnic groups to account for their position of inequality. Of course, the migrant workers have the weakest position in the Mexican American community; however, the vast majority of resident Mexican Americans also face limited employment opportunities that relegate them to inferior economic and social status.

The research unmasks the role of the public schools in sustaining the inequality faced by the Mexican Americans. The excessively high dropout rate of Mexican American students and the administrative reluctance to provide leadership to adapt the instructional program to meet the needs of the Mexican American students was astonishing. Most teachers lacked the knowledge and interest to educate a diverse student body. As Foley (1990) discovered in his study, the public schools of Middlewest operate in a way that sustains the class structure of the community.

The field research documents that institutionalized racism is a leading factor in maintaining local Mexican Americans in a subordinate position in Middlewest. The local mass media, politicians, and criminal justice system all function both to sustain a deviant image of Mexican Americans and also to contribute to the oppression of this ethnic group. The overall social organization of Anglo Middlewest features ideological colonialism, economic exploitation, racism, school push-out, and institutionalized racism. The result for the Mexican American community is one of extensive poverty and the social problems associated with poverty.

The views of Mirande (1985) and Blea (1988) are supported by my research in that the local Mexican Americans have retained a strong and vibrant culture in Middlewest and Farm County. Family, kinship ties, and friendships are the crucial elements in maintaining the ethnic community. The Mexican American community has a number of dedicated leaders who work to resist the oppressive conditions established by the Anglo community. These leaders have created four organizations to intercede on behalf of beleaguered Mexican Americans and to organize cultural events that assist in sustaining the culture.

The local Mexican American professionals are mostly found in human services positions where they can provide assistance to their fellow Mexican Americans. More importantly, there is an unwritten norm requiring Mexican Americans to share, support, and come to the assistance of their fellows. The Mexican American community did not have to be taught the importance of self-help as a strategy for improving its social circumstances.

A Bleak Outlook

When Anglos in Middlewest heard a presentation of my research findings, they reacted with a set of questions: "Aren't they racist too?" "Why don't they like us?" "Aren't these people better off than if they were in Mexico?" "Doesn't someone have to do this work?" These questions could be seen to indicate the Anglos' failure to recognize how they as a community treat Mexican Americans. Moreover, they could demonstrate the limited ability of the community members to visualize the possibility of changing their social relationships with the Mexican American community.

Educating the Anglos of Middlewest and Farm County to appreciate cultural differences and racial equality will not be a simple task. One's culture and society can and does, to a greater degree than even a veteran sociologist appreciated, create and sustain social realities.

Solutions

The local employment market could be monitored in an attempt to encourage employers to hire more Mexican Americans. The dairy, city government, hospital, and factories have many positions that do not require special education or training. The city council and employers could create an local affirmative action agency that would work toward increasing the number of Mexican American workers in better paying jobs. The same group of business and civic people who are working for economic justice could also assess local employers on their fairness in promoting Mexican American workers. A plan and a timetable could allow for a gradual transformation of the composition of the work force. It might take a decade for Mexican Americans to achieve economic parity in blue-collar jobs but eventually there would not be a need for an affirmative action program.

In both the vocational-technical and the professional areas requiring college degrees, local employers could provide scholarship monies to pay for the training of future workers. For example, the county hospitals and medical associations could provide financial assistance for Mexican Americans interested in nursing, technical fields, and medicine. These scholarships would require the recipient to work in the local medical facilities for a specified period. Such programs do not have to be race specific, they can be open to any candidate from a low-income family.

The key to economic parity for Mexican Americans is not a specific program but a recognition that the low number of Mexican Americans in higher paying jobs is in part the result of employers' hiring practices. If Mexican American workers are found to lack the necessary skills for a job, human rights-oriented employers could create an apprenticeship and training program for potential Mexican American employees. All levels of government could provide reduced taxation and other benefits to innovative employers.

The public school system is a critical social institution whose goal and mission is to provide the necessary skills to prepare a student for employment beyond the minimum wage positions or to prepare the student for college and eventual professional employment. A majority of local Mexican American students have been pushed out of the public schools because the schools have retained an inadequate curriculum as well as counselors, teachers, and administrators who are oblivious to the ideas, strategies, and resources needed for teaching students who have a different language and culture. In-service training or summer courses could provide the necessary training. Of course, the school administrators would have to convince an unwilling public to provide more resources for as many as eight years of bilingual education for Mexican American students. Such a program is not favoritism; it is a necessary educational tool for this student population. Two crucial programs recommended by the Task Force on the Participation of Hispanic Students in Vocational Educational Programs (1990) are the establishment of a proactive program to hire Mexican Americans teachers and a significant modification of the curriculum to include material from the Mexican American culture.

The criminal justice system in Farm County and Middlewest discriminates against Mexican Americans—the lack of Mexican American jurors, prosecuting attorneys, and public defenders results in harsher punishments for Mexican American offenders. The selective enforcement of the laws, especially in regard to Mexican American adolescents, helps to foster Mexican American antagonism toward the legal system and also helps to perpetuate the criminal image of Mexican Americans within the Anglo community.

It is not unusual for culturally sensitive criminal justice systems that include a large minority group within their jurisdiction to create citizen committees that have the authority to hear citizen complaints on police abuses and to participate with juvenile judges in deciding the disposition of these cases. Many creative alternatives could be introduced instead of fines and jail time to penalize offenders for crimes that are committed as a consequence of poverty. Programs could be developed to assist poor Mexican Americans in acquiring car insurance and driver's licenses. Treatment programs with Mexican American personnel could be instituted to assist those Mexican Americans having problems with alcohol abuse and family violence.

I do not mean to imply that Middlewest has not engaged in some of these activities. I recognize that the citizens of Middlewest might resent an outside "expert" telling them how to solve their problems. I am convinced, however, that once a community has a commitment to resolve its racial problems it can create the appropriate programs to move towards the goal.

To achieve social justice for the Mexican American community in Middlewest most probably will also require legislation and programs that can only be introduced at the national level. William Wilson (1987) wrote one of the most important books of the 1980s on race relations. Among his conclusions, he sets forth a set of recommendations that would allow America to become a racially just society. Wilson calls for universal programs of assistance for which all low-income people would be eligible. He thinks that job opportunities must be increased for minorities; health and dental clinics should be established to provide care for all low-income families. He supports a national health program. The minimum wage should be significantly increased. Decent and affordable low-income housing should be provided by the government. Job training and educational programs must be made available to all low-income people.

Another set of changes are necessary to reduce the exploitation of Mexican American migrant workers. During the transition period, the Middlewest Labor Camp will be needed. The manager should be a Mexican American who speaks Spanish, but the camp should move toward self-management. The labor camps could establish many programs to improve the quality of life for migrant workers. The residents have the right and the intelligence to help decide programs they would want.

The exploitation of migrant workers should be gradually eliminated. The first step would be to stop allowing legal migrant workers from Mexico to come to the United States. Farm workers should be organized into a union to increase their bargaining power with farmers. A serious problem for Mexican American workers is that their number is far greater than that necessary for the amount of work available. Efforts should be made to monitor this system and curtail the flow of migrants by registering migrant workers through a seniority system. With the help of current telecommunications and computer technology, Idaho officials could accurately assess how many agricultural workers are needed for a given time period. This would involve shifting workers among many farms. The goal would be to reduce the number of idle days for farm workers.

Human Rights Hearings

The Idaho Human Rights Commission held a hearing in Middlewest on November 12, 1992, because of rising ethnic tensions in Farm County. This three-hour meeting was held in the county courthouse. Anyone was allowed to speak for five minutes about their views and concerns regarding racial tensions. Most of the speakers were residents of Middlewest. The meeting was tense and emotional. The separation of the Mexican American and Anglo communities of Middlewest was the unspoken and underlying theme of the testimony. The hearings provided a good summation of my research and a powerful commentary on race relations in Middlewest.

The Anglo institutional administrators insisted that great strides have been made to reduce racial tensions, while the Mexican American leaders insisted that the problems have not been solved. At times the two opposing factions seemed to talk past one another. A considerable number of both Mexican American and Anglo speakers called for racial unity and harmony. These speakers focused on the need to change individual attitudes and interpersonal relations. Though their purpose was well intended, these speakers seemed not to be aware that changes in personal behavior will not remove racism from their social institutions nor will it affect the colonial nature of the situation.

The local Anglo school administrators and law enforcement officials stated that Middlewest did not have a serious problems in the treatment of the Mexican American population. Both school and law enforcement administrators said that their doors are open and they invited anyone in the community to come and visit them. However, a citizen concerned about racism in an establishment institution often will soon perceive such statements are somewhat hollow. Only when Mexican Americans acquire a meaningful number of administrators in these institutions will they be able to ensure fair treatment to the Mexican American population. In the meantime, senior administrators of these institutions could create boards with the mandate to observe and evaluate the treatment of Mexican Americans. These boards could be empowered to make recommendations, and they should be able to expect to receive a sympathetic hearing when they request changes.

The state of Idaho and its legislature could provide leadership in bringing about social changes. One step could be to expand the staff and budgets for the Human Rights Commission and the Idaho Commission on Hispanic Affairs. It would also be necessary to expand the authority to intervene in community affairs. A second step would be to direct the state board of education to provide leadership in creating programs to educate Idaho's minority students. The state could also increase the number of scholarships available for vocational and college education. The local private college in Middlewest could play a much larger role in assisting community change by establishing community programs to improve race relations.

The community of Middlewest appears to have a difficult time ahead of it. Bellah et al. (1985) and Daly and Cobb (1989) remorsefully report that the American people have lost their ability to be concerned with the "common good" and, therefore, are unable to deal seriously with poverty. Racial inequality persists because we live in a society where we are all too busy to take care of the health of our communities and ensure that justice is guaranteed for all our citizens.

Photo by Richard Baker

Dancers at a Mexican American voter registration drive in a local park.

Photo by Richard Baker

Sol de Acapulco, a local mariachi band.

BIBLIOGRAPHY

Achor, Shirley. 1982. "Life in a Dallas Barrio." In *Chicano Studies*, edited by Livie Duran and H. Russell Bernard. New York: Macmillan Publishing Co.

Acuña, Rodolfo. 1981. *Occupied America*. New York: Harper & Row, Publishers.

Aponte, Robert. 1991. "Urban Hispanic Poverty: Disaggreations and Explanations." *Social Problems* 38:516–528.

Ashabranner, Brent. 1985. *Dark Harvest*. New York: Dodd Mead.

Baca, Jimmy Santiago. 1992. *Working in the Dark*. Santa Fe: Red Crane Books.

Barrera, Mario. 1979. *Race and Class in the Southwest*. South Bend: University of Notre Dame Press.

Bean, Frank D., and Marta Tienda. 1987. *The Hispanic Population of the United States*. New York: Russell Sage Foundation.

Bellah, Robert N., Richard Madsen, William M. Sullivan, Ann Swidler, and Steven M. Tipton. 1985. *Habits of the Heart*. Berkeley: University of California Press.

Berger, Peter, and Thomas Luckmann. 1967. *The Social Construction of Reality*. Garden City: Anchor Books.

Berry, Tom. 1992. *Mexico*. Albuquerque: The Inter-Hemispheric Education Resource Center.

Best, Joel, Editor. 1989. *Images of Issues*. New York: Aldine De Gruyter.

Blauner, Robert. 1972. *Racial Oppression in America*. New York: Harper & Row, Publishers.

Blea, Irene I. 1980. "Bessemer: A Sociological Perspective of a Chicano Barrio." Ph.D. Dissertation, University of Colorado at Boulder.

———. 1988. *Toward A Chicano Social Science*. New York: Praeger.

Bonacich, Edna. 1972. "A Theory of Ethnic Antagonism: The Split Labor Market." *American Sociological Review* 37 (October):547–49.

———. 1976. "Advanced Capitalism and Black/White Relations: A Split Labor Market Interpretation." *American Sociological Review* 41:34–51.

————. 1989. "Inequality in America: The Failure of the American System for People of Color." In *Race, Class and Gender*, edited by Margaret L. Anderson and Patricia Hill Collins. Belmont: Wadsworth Publishing Co.

Borjas, George J., & Marta Tienda. 1985. *Hispanics in the U.S. Economy*. Orlando: Academic Press, Inc.

Braggs, Vernon, Jr., Walter Fogel, and Fred Schmidt. 1977. *The Chicano Worker*. Austin: University of Texas Press.

Boudrillard, John. 1975. *The Mirror of Production*. St. Louis: Telos Press.

Bureau of Criminal Identification. 1990. *Crime in Idaho*. Boise: Idaho Department of Law Enforcement.

Burma, John. 1970. *Mexican-Americans in the United States*. Cambridge: Schenkman Publishing Company.

Cafferty, Patora San Juan. 1992. *Chicanos in a Changing Society*. Cambridge: Harvard University Press.

Cain, Glen G. 1976. "The Challenge of Segmented Labor Market Theories to Orthodox Theory: A Survey." *Journal of Economic Literature* 14:1215–57.

Calarza, Ernesto, Herman Gallegos, and Julian Samora. 1969. *Mexican-Americans in the Southwest*. Goleta: Kimberly Press, Inc.

Camerillo, Alberto. 1979. *Chicanos in a Changing Society*. Cambridge: Harvard University Press.

Cloward, Richard A., and Lloyd E. Ohlin. 1960. *Delinquency and Opportunity*. New York: Free Press of Glencoe.

Coalition of Hispanic Health and Human Services Organization. 1990. *Establishing a National Adolescent Pregnancy Agenda for Hispanic Communities*. Washington D.C.: Coalition of Hispanic Health and Human Services Organization.

Cockroft, James D. 1986. *Outlaws in the Promised Land*. New York: Grove Press.

Connor, Walker. 1985. *Mexican-Americans*. New York: Arno Press.

Corcoran, Mary, Greg J. Duncan, Gerald Gurin, and Patricia Gurin. 1985. "Myth and Reality: The Causes and Persistence of Poverty." *Journal of Policy Analysis and Management* 4:516–36.

Cortes, Carlos E. 1974. *The Mexican American*. New York: Arno Press.

Cuciti, Peggy, and Franklin James. 1990. "A Comparison of Black and Hispanic Poverty in Large Cities of the Southwest." *Hispanic Journal of Behavioral Sciences* 12:50–75.

Cuzzort, R. P. 1989. *Using Social Thought*. Mountain View: Mayfield Publishing Co.

Daly, Herman E., and John B. Cobb, Jr. 1989. *For the Common Good*. Boston: Beacon Press.

Davis, Marilyn P. 1990. *Mexican Voices/American Dreams*. New York: Henry Holt and Company.

DeFreitas, Gregory. 1991. *Inequality at Work*. New York: Oxford University Press.

De La Garza, Rodolfo O., Frank D. Bean, Charles M. Bonjean, Ricardo Romo, and Rodolfo Alvarez. 1985. *The Mexican American Experience*. Austin: University of Texas Press.

Domhoff, William G. 1967. *Who Rules America*. Englewood Cliffs: Prentice Hall.

Douglas, Jack D. 1971. *The American Social Order*. New York: The Free Press.

Duran, Livie Isauro, and H. Russell Bernard. 1982. *Introduction to Chicano Studies*. New York: Macmillan Publishing Co.

Durkheim, Emile. 1938. *The Rules of the Sociological Method*. New York: The Free Press.

———. 1965. *The Elementary Forms of the Religious Life*. Translated by Joseph Swain. New York: The Free Press.

Dwyer, Carlota Cardenas de, Editor. 1975. *Chicano Voices*. Boston: Beacon Press.

Dye, Thomas R. 1990. *Who's Running America?* Englewood Cliffs: Prentice Hall.

Eisner, Victor. 1969. *The Delinquency Label*. New York: Random House.

Eitzen, D. Stanley, and Maxine Baca Zinn. 1989. *The Reshaping of America*. Englewood Cliffs: Prentice Hall.

Farley, John E. 1987. "Disproportionate Black and Hispanic Unemployment in U.S. Metropolitan Areas: The Roles of Racial Inequality, Segregation and Discrimination in Male Joblessness." *American Journal of Economics and Sociology* 46:129–50.

Farley, Reynolds, and Walter R. Allen. 1987. *The Color Line and the Quality of Life in America*. New York: Russell Sage.

Feagin, Joe R. 1989. *Racial and Ethnic Relations*. Englewood Cliffs: Prentice Hall.

———. 1991. "The Continuing Significance of Race: Antiblack Discrimination in Public Places." *American Sociological Review* 56:101–16.

Foley, Douglas. 1990. *Learning Capitalist Culture*. Philadelphia: University of Pennsylvania Press.

Franklin, Raymond, and Solomon Resnik. 1973. *The Political Economy of Racism*. New York: Holt, Rinehart & Winston, Inc.

Frye, Marilyn. 1983. *The Politics of Reality*. Freedom: Crossing Press.

Gamboa, Erasmus. 1990. *Mexican Labor and World War Two*. Austin: University of Texas Press.

Gans, Herbert J. 1982. *The Urban Villagers*. New York: The Free Press.

García, F. Chris. 1988. *Latinos and the Political System*. South Bend: University of Notre Dame Press.

García, F. Chris, and Rudolph O. de la Garza. 1977. *The Chicano Political Experience*. North Scituate: Duxbury Press.

Grebler, Leo, Joan W. Moore, and Ralph C. Guzman. 1970. *The Mexican-American People*. New York: The Free Press.

Greenstein, Robert, Kathy Porter, Isaac Shapiro, Paul Leonard, and Scott Barancik. 1988. *Shortchanged: Recent Developments in Hispanic Poverty, Income and Employment*. Washington, D.C.: Center on Budget and Policy Priorities.

Griswold del Castillo, Richard. 1984. *La Familia: Chicano Families in the Urban Southwest, 1984–the Present*. South Bend: University of Notre Dame Press.

Hammersley, Martin, and Paul Atkinson. 1983. *Ethnography*. New York: Travistock Publications.

Haskell, Martin R., and Lewis Yablonsky. 1974. *Criminology: Crime and Criminality*. Chicago: Rand McNally College Publishing Company.

Hayes-Bautista, David, Werner O. Schink, and Jorge Chapa. 1988. *The Burden of Support: Young Latinos in an Aging Society*. Stanford: Stanford University Press.

Hernández, José. 1983. *Puerto Rican Youth Unemployment*. Maplewood: Waterfront Press.

―――. 1990. "Latino Alternatives to the Underclass Concept." *Latino Studies* 1:95–104.

Hirschman, Charles, and Morrison G. Wong. 1984. "Socioeconomic Gains of Asian Americans, Blacks, and Hispanics: 1960–1976." *American Journal of Sociology* 90:584–607.

Horowitz, Ruth. 1986. *Honor and the American Dream*. New Brunswick: Rutgers University Press.

Hummon, David M. 1990. *Commonplaces*. Albany: State University of New York Press.

Hyer, Jannell. 1988. *Idaho Demographic Profile*. Boise: Idaho Department of Employment.

Idaho Advisory Committee to the U.S. Commission on Civil Rights. 1980. *A Roof Over Our Heads*. Washington D.C.: U.S. Commission on Civil Rights.

Idaho Department of Commerce. 1992. *Profile of Hispanic Population of Idaho*. Boise: Idaho Department of Commerce.

Idaho Department of Employment. 1991a. *Idaho Demographic Profile*. Boise: Idaho Department of Employment.

———. 1991b. *Migrant Seasonal Farm Worker Survey*. Boise: Idaho Department of Employment.

Idaho Migrant Council. 1990. *Community Needs Assessment*. Caldwell: Idaho Migrant Council.

Idaho State Board of Education. 1991. *Report of the Task Force on Hispanic Education*. Boise: Idaho State Board of Education.

Idaho State Economic Opportunity Office. 1991. *Marketability Study/ Caldwell Labor Camp*. Boise: Idaho Department of Health and Welfare.

Kasarda, John D. 1988. "Jobs, Migration, and Emerging Urban Mismatches." In *Urban Change and Poverty*, edited by Michael G. H. McGeary and Laurence E. Lynn, Jr. Washington, D.C.: National Academy Press.

———. 1989. "Urban Industrial Transition and the Underclass." *Annals of the American Academy of Political and Social Science* 501:26–47

———. 1990. "City Jobs And Residents on a Collision Course: The Urban Underclass Dilemma." *Economic Development Quarterly* 4:313–19.

Keefe, Susan E., and Amado M. Padilla. 1987. *Chicano Ethnicity*. Albuquerque: University of New Mexico Press.

Kilgrow, Julie M. 1989. *Canyon County Employment*. Boise: Department of Employment.

———. 1991. *Idaho Demographic Profile*. Boise: Department of Employment.

Kiser, George, and Martha Kiser, Editors. 1979. *Mexican Workers in the United States*. Albuquerque: University of New Mexico Press.

Kundera, Milan. 1990. *Immortality*. Translated by Peter Kussi. New York: Grove Weidenfeld.

Leal, Lewis, and Pepe Barron. 1982. "Chicano Literature, An Overview" In *Three American Literatures*, edited by Hustin A. Baker. New York: The Modern Language Association of America.

Lewis, Oscar. 1959. *Five Families: Mexican Case Studies in the Culture of Poverty*. New York: Basic Books.

———. 1966. *La Vida: A Puerto Rican Family in the Culture of Poverty—San Juan and New York*. New York: Random House.

Li, Peter S. 1988. *Ethnic Inequality in a Class Society*. Toronto: Wall and Thompson.

Livingston, John C. 1979. *Fair Game*. Sacramento: W. H. Freeman and Company.

Lofland, John. 1971. *Analyzing Social Settings: A Guide to Qualitative Observation and Analysis.* Belmont: Wadsworth Publishing Co.

López, Camillo and Terry López. 1989. "The Immigration Reform and Control Act of 1986—The Cure or Cause of Problems?" *Idaho Law Review* 25:329–74.

Lynd, Robert S., and Helen Merrel Lynd. 1929. *Middletown: A Study in Contemporary American Culture.* New York: Harcourt, Brace.

Lynd, Robert S., and Helen Merrel Lynd. 1937. *Middletown in Transition: A Study in Cultural Conflicts.* New York: Harcourt, Brace.

Mabbutt, Richard. 1990. *Hispanics in Idaho: Concerns and Challenges.* Boise: Idaho Human Rights Commission.

Madsen, William. 1964. *The Mexican Americans of South Texas.* New York: Holt, Rinehart and Winston.

Marble, Manning. 1992. *The Crisis of Color and Democracy.* Monroe: Common Courage Press.

Marden, Charles F., Gladys Meyer, and Madeline H. Engel. 1992. *Minorities in American Society.* New York: Harper Collins Publisher.

Marger, Martin N. 1985. *Race and Ethnic Relations.* Belmont: Wadsworth Publishing Company.

Massey, Douglas. 1981. "Dimensions of the New Immigration to the United States and the Prospects for Assimilation." *Annual Review of Sociology* 7:57–85

———. 1990. "American Apartheid: Residential Segregation and the Making of the Underclass." *American Journal of Sociology* 96:329–57.

Massey, Douglas, and Nancy A. Denton. 1987. "Trends in the Residential Segregation of Blacks, Hispanics, and Asians: 1970–1980." *American Sociological Review* 52:802–25

Massey, Douglas S., and Mitchell L. Eggers. 1990. "The Ecology of Inequality: Minorities and the Concentration of Poverty 1970–1980." *American Journal of Sociology* 95:1153–88

Mercier, Laurie, and Carole Simon-Smolinski. 1990. *Idaho's Ethnic Heritage/Historical Overviews.* Boise: The Idaho Ethnic Heritage Project.

Mirande, Alfredo. 1985. *The Chicano Experience.* South Bend: University of Notre Dame Press.

Moore, Joan, and Harry Pachon. 1985. *Hispanics in the United States.* Englewood Cliffs: Prentice Hall.

Moore, Joan W. 1970. "Colonialism: The Case of the Mexican Americans." *Social Problems* 17:468–69.

Muñoz, Carlos, Jr. 1972. *The Politics of Urban Unrest: A Model of Political Analysis.* Claremont: Graduate School of Government.

Murguia, Edward. 1975. *Assimilation, Colonialism, and the Mexican American People.* Austin: University of Texas Press.

Murray, Charles. 1984. *Losing Ground: American Social Policy, 1950–1980.* New York: Basic Books.

Myrdal, Gunnar. 1975. *Am American Dilemma.* New York: Pantheon Books.

Newman, Morris J. 1978. "A Profile of Hispanics in the U.S. Workforce." *Monthly Labor Review* 101:3–14.

Onuf, Peter S., Editor. 1992. *Jeffersonian Legacies.* Charlottesville: University Press of Virginia.

Omi, Michael, and Howard Winant. 1986. *Racial Formation in the United States.* New York: Routledge & Kegan Paul.

Ourada, Patricia K. 1979. *Migrant Workers in Idaho.* Boise: Boise State University.

Padilla, Flex M. 1985. "On the Nature of Latino Ethnicity." In *The Mexican American Experience,* edited by Rodolfo O. De La Garza, et al. Austin: University of Texas Press.

Parillo, Vincent N. 1993. *Strangers to These Shores.* New York: Macmillan Publishing Company.

Paz, Octavio. 1985. *The Labyrinth of Solitude.* New York: Grove Press.

Platt, Anthony, and Lynn Cooper. 1974. *Policing America.* Englewood Cliffs: Prentice Hall.

Portes, Alejandro, and Robert Bach. 1987. "Immigrant Earnings: Cuban and Mexican Immigrants in the United States." *International Migration Review* 14:315–41.

Portes, Alejandro, and Jozef Borocz. 1989. "Contemporary Immigration: Theoretical Perspectives on Its Determinants and Modes of Incorporation." *International Migration Review* 23:606–30.

Portes, Alejandro, and Ruben G. Rumbaut. 1990. *Immigrant America: A Portrait.* Berkeley: University of California Press.

Portes, Alejandro, and Cynthia Truelove. 1987. "Making Sense of Diversity: Recent Research on Hispanic Minorities." *Annual Review of Sociology* 13:359–85.

Quinney, Richard. 1977. *Class, State, and Crime.* New York: David McKay Company.

Reich, Michael. 1981. *Racial Inequality.* Princeton: Princeton University Press.

Reilly, Rosa Delgadillo. 1976. "An Analysis of Some of the Causes of the Drop Out Rate of Mexican-American Students in Nampa School District #131." M.A. Thesis, Boise State University.

Reimer, Cordelia W. 1985. "A Comparative Analysis of the Wages of Hispanics, Blacks, and Non-Hispanic Whites." In *Hispanics in the U.S. Economy*, edited by George J. Borjas and Marta Tienda. Orlando: Academic Press.

Romano, Octavio I. 1968. "The Anthropology and Sociology of the Mexican Americans," *El Grito* 2:13–19.

Romo, Ricardo. 1983. *East Los Angeles*. Austin: University of Texas Press.

Romero, Leo M., and Luis G. Stelzner. 1992. "Hispanics and the Criminal Justice System." In *Hispanics in the United States*, edited by Pastora San Juan Cafferty and William C. McCready. New Brunswick: Transaction Publications.

Rubel, Arthur J. 1966. *Across the Tracks: Mexican-Americans in a Texas City*. Austin: University of Texas Press.

Sánchez, Rosaura. 1983. *Chicano Discourse*. Rowley: Newbury House Publishers, Inc.

Schaefer, Richard T. 1991. *Racial and Ethnic Groups*. New York: Harper Collins College Publishers.

Simmons, Ozzie G. 1974. *The Mexican American*. New York: Arno Press.

Smith, James P. 1988. "Poverty and the Family." In *Divided Opportunities: Minorities, Poverty and Social Policy*, edited by Gary D. Sandefur and Marta Tienda. New York: Plenum Press.

Spector, Malcolm, and John I. Kitsuse. 1987. *Constructing Social Problems*. New York: Aldine De Gruyter.

Stack, Carol B. 1970. *All Our Kin*. New York: Harper & Row, Publishers.

Stolzenberg, Ross M. 1990. "Ethnicity, Geography, and Occupations of U.S. Hispanic Men." *American Sociological Review* 55:143–54.

Survey Research Center. 1988. *A Survey of the Extent of Racial and Religious Intolerance in Idaho*. Boise: Boise State University.

Szymanski, Albert. 1978. *The Capitalist State and the Politics of Class*. Cambridge: Winthrop Publishers, Inc.

Task Force on the Participation of Hispanic Students in Vocational Educational Programs. 1990. *Hispanic Youth Dropout Prevention Report*. Boise: State Division of Vocational Education.

Tienda, Marta, and Leif Jensen. 1988. "Poverty and Minorities: A Quarter-Century Profile of Color and Socioeconomic Disadvantage." In *Divided Opportunities: Minorities, Poverty and Social Policy*, edited by Gary D. Sandefur and Marta Tienda. New York: Plenum Press.

Tienda Marta, and Ding-Tzann Lii. 1987. "Minority Concentration and Earnings Inequality: Blacks, Hispanics and Asians Compared." *American Journal of Sociology* 93:141–65.

Tocqueville, Alexis de. 1956. *Democracy in America.* New York: New American Library.

Valentine, Charles. 1968. *Culture of Poverty: A Critique and Counter-Proposal.* Chicago: University of Chicago Press.

Verdugo, Naomi I., and Richard R. Verdugo. 1984. "Earnings Differentials among Mexican American, Black and White Male Workers." *Social Science Quarterly* 65:417–25.

Vidich, Arthur J., and Joseph Bensman. 1968. *Small Town in Mass Society: Class, Power and Religion in a Rural Community.* Princeton: Princeton University Press.

Vigil, James Diego. 1988. *Barrio Gangs.* Austin: University of Texas Press.

Wacquant, Loic J. D., and William J. Wilson. 1989. "The Cost of Racial and Class Exclusion in the Inner City." *The Annals of the American Academy of Political and Social Science* 501:8–25.

Waldinger, Roger. 1989. "Immigration and Urban Change." *Annual Review of Sociology* 15:359–85.

West, Stanley A., and June Macklin. 1979. *The Chicano Experience.* Boulder: Westview Press.

Wilson, William Julius. 1987. *The Truly Disadvantaged.* Chicago: University of Chicago Press.

INDEX

Boise, Idaho (*cont.*)
competing with, 51;
commuting to, 146; events in,
86, 87, 102; newspapers in, 1,
111, 163; political contacts in,
98; urban nature of, 36, 121;
welcomes new residents, 234
Boise State University, bilingual
program of, 257, 259; school
of education at, 255, 259
Boxing: Mexican Americans and,
89, 221
Boy Scouts: 120, 125
Bracero program: 58, 162
Bureau of Land Management
(BLM): 145, 148, 175
Businesses: competition, 40, 50,
51; development, 108, 121,
127; failure, 123

California: migrant circuit
through, 165, 173
Capitalism: and exploitation,
200, 207; Anglo support for,
42, 138; character and, 164;
power of, 194, 200
Castillo, Ana: 161
Catholic Church, activities of,
109, 197; Anglos and, 114;
compared to fundamentalists,
98; membership in, 151; needs
of, 116; practiced in
Middlewest, 77–80, 217;
priests in, 63, 113–15, 216;
welfare and, 231
Celebrations: Christmas, 31, 32;
Dieciseis de Septiembre, 75,
90, 102; Cinco de Mayo, 43,
52, 54, 75–77, 90, 110; Feast of
Our Lady of Guadalupe, 77;
fiesta, 43, 75–77, 90, 112;

Quinceañera, 79–80;
Statehood centennial, 86–87;
Weddings, 78–79
Center for Employment Training:
154
Chamber of Commerce: in Boise,
234; leadership program of,
107; projects of, 32, 34, 199
Chávez, César: 93
Chicago district: 82, 124, 156
Chicano paradigm: 116
Children: among Mexican
Americans, 60, 74–75; and
racist attitudes, 49, 128;
education of, 165;
employment opportunities of,
159; Mexican American goals
for, 150, 169; Middlewest as
place to raise, 124; migrant
work and raising, 143, 170; of
successful Mexican
Americans, 153, 154
Child support: 127, 170, 176–77,
178
Churches: and institutional
racism, 214–18; Anglo and
Chicano church socials
compared, 63; attendance, 27,
89
Cisneros, Sandra: 119, 143, 256
City Council: 32, 37, 183, 211,
212, 221
Claims makers: in defining social
problems, 195
Clubs: Coffee, 35; conservatism
of, 44; Elks, 30, 120;
Exchange, 30; Key, 35;
Kiwanis, 30, 209; Lion's, 30;
Moose, 120; Optimist, 30;
Rotary, 30, 45; separate for
women, 38; Shriners, 30

Cock fighting: 81
Code switching: 68
College Assistance Migrant
  Program (CAMP): 259–60
Comadre/compadre
  relationships: 61, 89
Community solidarity: 79, 80, 83,
  89, 101
Conformity in Middlewest: 53,
  71, 91
Conservative attitudes: and lack
  of toleration, 264; degree of,
  40; nature of, 43–45; of Anglo
  working class, 120, 121, 123;
  of church congregations, 214;
  of farmers, 131; of Republican
  politicians, 207, 209
Crew bosses: 138, 166, 167, 169
Crime: and alcohol, 149; and
  claims makers, 195; biased
  reporting of, 105, 196,
  197–200; causes of, 91, 182,
  224, 225; Mexican Americans
  blamed for, 46–48, 90, 124,
  126, 128, 139, 185; in schools,
  148; poverty and, 96, 97, 156,
  203, 233; rates of, 218, 219
Criminal justice system: and
  selective law enforcement, 92,
  100, 109, 145, 164, 215–16,
  233, 234, 268; and institutional
  racism, 218–28; creates
  deviant image of Mexican
  Americans, 86, 265; language
  and, 206, 227; Mexican
  American problems with, 99;
  Mexican Americans employed
  by, 202; racist nature of, 114,
  197, 227
Curanderismo: 81

Dance and music among
  Mexican Americans: 48,
  73–75, 78–80, 85, 90, 214
Democratic Party: 43, 99, 101,
  207, 208, 209, 211
Discrimination: Anglo denials of,
  54, 141; experienced by
  Mexican Americans, 12, 58,
  94, 114, 200; Idaho's
  reputation for, 58, 162; in
  employment, 100, 156; in
  courts, 152; in school, 150,
  157
Divorce: 120, 127, 157, 178
Drugs: among Anglo students,
  248; and church sermons, 97;
  and claims makers, 195;
  criminal justice system and,
  220; newspaper coverage of,
  197; prevention programs,
  108; traffic in Idaho, 2, 47, 48,
  219; use of, 96, 124, 126, 148,
  156, 185
Dubois, Idaho: racial incidents
  in, 2
Durkheim, Emile: theories of, 7,
  44, 52

Economic cycles: 33, 34, 47, 48,
  120, 121, 146, 194
Employment of Mexican
  Americans: 54, 104, 144, 146,
  159
English Language Bill: 70–72, 78,
  98, 124, 145, 213, 215, 217,
  247, 255, 264
Environmental Protection Agency
  (EPA): 44, 130
Equal Employment Opportunity
  Commission: 105
Ethnicity: and economic success,

Migrant Head Start program
(*cont.*)
102–3
Migrant labor camps: Anglo
attitudes towards, 136, 141;
child care in, 170, 176–77;
conditions in, 81, 135, 174,
178–90; controlled by farmers,
142, 212–13; evictions from,
100; Head Start programs in,
103; housing occupancy in,
64; lack of participation from,
94; management of, 184–86,
212, 269; remodeling of, 104,
106; seasonal workers living
in, 144, 148; Spanish spoken
in, 85
Migrant workers: Anglo attitudes
towards, 127; Catholics honor,
197; demographics of, 165;
exploitation of, 20, 141, 162,
163, 200, 269; farmers deny
responsibility for, 132; health
care of, 171–72, 191; housing
of, 178–90; life of, 165–71,
172–78; Mexican American
residents started as, 58, 110,
143; research expanded to
include, 3; weak social
position of, 265
Military Service: 120, 145
Montana: 103
Multiculturalism: 72, 129

Newspapers: and institutional
racism, 195–200; Anglo
perceptions from, 68; biased
reporting in, 74, 105, 147, 264;
coverage of Mexican
American athletes, 43, 88;
criticize Mexican American

leaders, 240; editorial
positions, 41–43; Mexican
American coverage in Boise,
111; report on murder in labor
camp, 182; report on youth
gangs, 220; role of, 199

Occupational Safety and Health
Administration (OSHA): 43,
44, 130, 131, 139
Oregon: Bracero program in, 58,
162; migrant circuit through,
165
Padrinos (co-parents): 61, 78, 89

Paternalism: 125, 137, 212, 229,
240
Pentecostal Church: 97, 214, 217
Pesticides: exposure to, 146
Pluralistic assimilation model: 13,
17, 157–58
Police: abusive treatment by,
108, 113, 168, 183, 211; arrests
by, 149, 152, 173, 197, 199;
bias against Mexican
Americans, 2, 217, 225–27;
Commission on Mexican
American Affairs meet with,
100; denials of bias, 270;
Mexican American
impressions of, 264; operate
in racist fashion, 114; raid
Mexican American dances, 48,
74; see Mexican Americans as
troublemakers, 147; selective
law enforcement by, 92, 152,
183, 196, 212, 219, 220, 226;
reports in newspapers, 200;
youth gangs and, 221, 222
Politicians: ignore Mexican
Americans, 213; influenced by

United Way (*cont.*)
  relief, 230

Victimization of Mexican
  Americans: and placing
  blame, 92, 127, 136, 164, 183,
  196, 223, 240, 249–50, 252,
  264
Volunteerism: among Mexican
  Americans, 76, 110; and Anglo
  leaders, 45, 46; in small town
  life, 37, 39
Voting: and Anglo working class,
  120; and Mexican American
  leaders, 110; for Mexican
  American candidates, 152,
  208, 212; migrant workers
  and, 164, 210; politics and,
  124; reasons Mexican
  Americans do not, 97, 233;
  registration for, 110, 115, 210

Wages: and resentment toward
  labor contractors, 167; of
  Anglo blue-collar workers,
  120; of fire fighters, 145; of
  large companies, 48; of
  migrant workers, 132, 136,
  138, 162; of youths
  relinquished to parents, 65; of
  seasonal workers, 148, 163; of
  women, 201, 205; work for
  low, 59, 92, 117, 122, 154,
  164, 170, 204; worry about
  low, 175
Washington: Bracero program in,
  58; migrant circuit through,
  165, 177
Weddings: as cultural events,

78–79; of upper classes
  reported on in newspaper,
  198; priests preside over, 113;
  religious nature of, 90
Welfare: Anglo lack of
  information about, 104;
  Anglos think Mexican
  Americans prefer, 49, 122,
  124, 126, 128, 132, 133, 138,
  139, 164; farmers' selective
  views of, 131; income and, 96
Women: access to health care,
  229; and IMC Head Start
  program, 103; and Mexican
  American family income, 149;
  Anglo working class, 119,
  123–26; chaotic lives of
  migrant, 177; effect of poverty
  on, 97; Mexican American
  leaders, 111; Mexican tradition
  of protecting, 65; oppression
  of, 205–7; self-esteem of
  Mexican American, 84; status
  of Anglo business, 38, 50;
  wages of, 201, 202; work of,
  150, 157
Wyoming: IMC Head Start
  program in, 103

Youth gangs: and Anglo
  perceptions of Mexican
  Americans, 47, 49, 67, 86, 124,
  126, 198, 219, 222, 251; crime
  and, 219; fear of, 156; in Idaho
  Falls, 2; Mexican American
  leaders and, 109; programs to
  reduce, 199, 221, 224; reasons
  for joining, 16, 222, 223;
  responses to, 246; schools
  and, 250; treatment of, 211